THE COMPLETE
ENCYCLOPEDIA OF
FLIGHT
1945-2006

THE COMPLETE
ENCYCLOPEDIA OF
FLIGHT
1945-2006

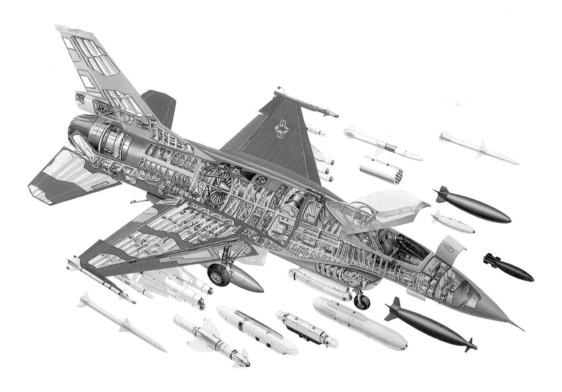

JOHN BATCHELOR & MALCOLM V. LOWE
with David Willis

CHARTWELL
BOOKS, INC.

Published by Rebo International b.v., Lisse, The Netherlands
in association with Publishing Solutions (www) Ltd., Great Britain

© 2005 Rebo International b.v., Lisse, The Netherlands and Publishing Solutions (www) Ltd., Great Britain

Text: Malcolm V. Lowe
Illustrations: John Batchelor
Production, layout and typesetting: The Minster Press, Dorset, Great Britain
Cover design: The Minster Press, Dorset, Great Britain

Proofreading: Jeffrey Rubinoff, Emily Sands

This edition published in 2006 by
CHARTWELL BOOKS, INC.
A division of BOOK SALES, INC.
114 Northfield Avenue
Edison, New Jersey 08837
USA

Printed in Slovenia.

ISBN 978 90 366 1717 8
ISBN 90 366 1717 0

Contents

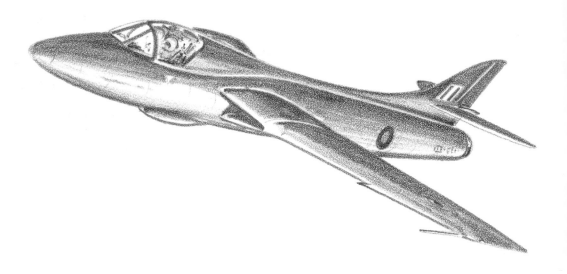

Introduction

Volume Three: From World War Two to the Present Day

The Second World War ended, after almost exactly six years of strife, in September 1945. It had been the largest, most widespread conflict that has ever taken place on earth. It touched the lives in some way or another – directly or indirectly – of almost every living person on Planet Earth. It not only involved combatants on the battlefield, but also directly affected whole civilian populations in their own homes. In addition, it was without doubt the most massive conflict in which aircraft have taken part – and it was arguably the most important conflict ever in which aircraft played a direct role in the execution and – perhaps most significantly of all – in the outcome. Aviation emerged from the war in a pre-eminent position, as the tool that had effectively won the war. Yet the conflict had changed aviation forever, and the post-war world was to see many significant developments in both civil and military aviation, and in the ever-advancing technology (and cost) that had become such an important part of the story of aviation.

This book deals with the era from the end of the Second World War up to the present day, and covers many of the important warplanes and civil transport aircraft of this continuing period in the history of aviation – and of the history of the world. It charts the significant progress that has been made in the development of aviation and aeronautics since the end of the war, not least the huge advances in aircraft propulsion, in the weapons that they carried and the use of composite materials in their construction. Many other important aspects are covered or touched upon, illustrated all the way by the world-famous artwork of John Batchelor. It has been possible to include many of the significant aircraft within the general period referred to by this book, but any work of this size that covers such a wide area necessarily pays more attention to some and less to others, no doubt to the exclusion of some people's favourites. There have been so many different military and civil aircraft, from a myriad (but sadly ever-dwindling number) of manufacturers, that to include every one from the post-World War Two period would be impossible without resorting to an almost infinite amount of writing, and so we have concentrated on a representative selection of the great and the lesser-known. This book is the final Volume of this Encyclopedia, and is an important companion to the first two Volumes of *The Complete Encyclopedia of Flight*.

Historical Background

From its limited and faltering beginnings in the late nineteenth century and early twentieth century, aviation had gradually taken hold following the successes of the Wright brothers in the United States during December 1903. The Wright brothers were the first men ever to successfully fly in controlled flight a man-carrying powered aircraft. This was most significant step forward in the history of aviation – the start of manned heavier-than-air flight. Those early days in the development of aircraft are described in Volume 1 of *The Complete Encyclopedia of Flight*. The successes of the Wright brothers began aviation as we know it today. As aviation gradually developed in the years after 1903, it was not long before aircraft began to be used for less than peaceful purposes. The first employment of aircraft in warlike activities took place in 1910 and 1911. The initial use of aircraft in conflict by an established military organisation seems to have been by Italy in 1911 against rebel forces in North Africa.

World War One began in August 1914. At that time a number of countries were developing military aviation organisations, or already had such structures in place. However, military aviation was in its infancy at the start of that war, and military aircraft were mostly low-performance, unarmed types more suited to simple visual reconnaissance than to more warlike activities. This reality changed very quickly. It was not long before aircraft started to be armed, and quite soon to take on an important status in the prosehcution of the war by all sides. By the end of the war, military aircraft were performing roles that are familiar to us today, because the potential of military aircraft was explored and developed during the conflict. Design,

construction and manufacturing techniques came on in leaps and bounds, and mass-production of aircraft, aerial weapons and aero engines was the norm at the end of the war in November 1918.

Just as importantly, the First World War not only showed how important aircraft could be in warfare, the conflict also saw the establishment of military organisations to properly manage and operate military aircraft. This process had commenced prior to the war, with most of the major countries attaching their fledgling air elements to newly-formed branches of their often long-established army organisations. In some cases naval aviation grew as an off-shoot of established naval structures. The subsequent enormous growth of military aviation led to the need to formalise these structures, and in some cases an independent air force was the result. In Britain, a separate naval air arm, the Royal Naval Air Service, was created in July 1914. The Royal Flying Corps, an offshoot of the army, had existed since May 1912. On 1 April 1918 these came together to form the Royal Air Force, an early example of the importance of

The Douglas Dakota gave sterling service during World War Two for the Allies. It continued in service well after the war and was involved in such Cold War events as the Berlin Airlift in the late 1940s.

military aviation elements being given their own autonomy within a leading country's military structures. A separate but related naval air arm, the Fleet Air Arm, existed in Britain during the inter-war period, and came fully under Royal Navy control in the late 1930s. Both the Royal Air Force and the Fleet Air Arm continue to exist today. In France, the Aéronautique Militaire (sometimes abbreviated to Aviation Militaire) was founded in 1910, with the Armée de l'Air being created in 1933/1934. In the United States, an aviation element of the Signal Corps was founded as early as 1907. This gave way to the U.S. Army Air Service in May 1918, and the U.S. Army Air Corps in July 1926. This service became the U.S. Army Air Force (technically called the U.S. Army Air Forces) just prior to the American entry into World War Two in 1941, while an independent air force did not arise in the United States until 1947. Again, in both France and the United States, a separate and important naval air arm also developed. The Luftwaffe of Nazi Germany was built up rapidly following the accession to power in Germany during 1933 of Hitler's National Socialists. This eventually large fighting force was totally defeated in 1945, and the partition of Germany after World War Two saw the eventual establishment of two separate German armed forces – until German Unification at the end of the 1980s and early 1990s finally brought these two separate threads back together again. In reality, virtually all countries around the world nowadays possess an armed forces structure that includes an air force of some kind. The post-Second World War period has also seen national armed services sometimes working together under such organisations as

NATO (the North Atlantic Treaty Organisation) and the United Nations, to intervene in conflicts elsewhere in the world, or to act as 'peace-keepers' between warring factions or to safeguard and protect a peace agreement.

The growing employment of aircraft in warfare without doubt changed the face of war forever. From those original small beginnings of military aviation prior to World War One, and thence through the huge build-up of military air arms in World War One, aircraft developed into fighter, bomber, reconnaissance, transport, training and a host of other military tasks that would have surprised (and probably shocked) the early aviation pioneers. Continuing development in the decades after World War One (nowadays this period is referred to as the inter-war years) witnessed ever-growing performance capabilities. These came about partly due to refinements in aircraft design and materials, and partly as a result of the growing performance capabilities of aero engines. The Second World War period witnessed further great strides in the development of aerodynamics and in propulsion – the greatest of these being the development and successful refinement of the jet engine. In more recent times, the use of composite materials in aircraft construction in place of metal has further developed the science of aviation. In related and no less significant technological advances, Mankind at last entered Space with the successful Space programs of the Soviet Union and the United States from the later 1950s onwards, culminating in the manned exploration of the Moon in the late 1960s and early 1970s. Similarly, the post-World War Two era has seen the widespread adoption of helicopters for military and civil use. It took many years for a successful helicopter layout to be developed, but in the latter stages of the Second World War helicopters began to appear in military service, and nowadays the helicopter is an accepted and very important part of aviation.

Arguably one of the greatest developments in aviation during the 1930s and into the 1940s was the creation, manufacture and successful testing of viable jet engines. The development of this form of propulsion is covered in the second Volume of *The Complete Encyclopedia of Flight* that refers to World War Two. In two countries in particular – Britain and Nazi Germany – jet engine development was successfully pursued by a number of individuals and aviation companies. Both of these countries were able to bring into front-line service jet-powered combat aircraft before the end of World War Two. At that stage, the United States and the Soviet Union significantly lagged behind the developments in both Britain and Nazi Germany. However, the defeat of Nazi Germany in 1945 resulted in much of the advanced technical information that had been generated by the highly advanced German aircraft industry falling into American hands. This, allied to Britain's rather misguided willingness to hand many of its jet propulsion and aerodynamics secrets to both the United States and the Soviet Union, led to the latter two powers eventually forging ahead in jet aircraft and jet engine design and manufacture.

The original rather primitive jet engines of the late 1930s and early 1940s were sometimes unreliable, and usually needed considerable amounts of fuel. At first, they offered power outputs that were hardly an improvement on the existing standard piston engines of the warplanes then in service. However, continuing development led at first to efficient and powerful axial-flow turbojet engines. Then the turbofan, a more developed and efficient jet

The English Electric/BAC Canberra was an important jet bomber of the 1950s onwards.

engine, was successfully put into production. The introduction of the afterburner, in which fuel is injected into the jet blast at the rear of the jet engine to augment its power for short periods, considerably increased the performance capabilities of military jet engines.

Developments in aerodynamics related to the higher speeds and capabilities promised by jet propulsion helped to push the performance capabilities of military aircraft up to, and then beyond, the almost mythical 'sound barrier.' This is the speed of sound, and for several years in the 1940s it was feared that aircraft could not break through the sound barrier and continue flying. It was found that aircraft approaching the speed of sound would be subject to considerable and very dangerous buffeting, and several test pilots lost their lives trying the break through the sound barrier. Eventually, advances in aerodynamics helped aircraft designers to invent wing and fuselage shapes that allowed aircraft to successfully break the sound barrier without danger. In particular, the swept-wing configuration, developed firstly principally by designers in Nazi Germany, proved to be important in high speed flight. Continuing development led, in the United States in particular, to research programs in which the performance capabilities of manned aircraft were taken to extreme limits. Possibly the most successful of these was the famed North American X-15 program, in which the incredible speed of over Mach 6 (in other words, six times the speed of sound), was achieved.

It is interesting to compare the performance capabilities of aero engines over the years. The power available from aircraft engines had already led to the huge increases in performance capability of civil and military aircraft as the 1930s wore on. The 1,030 hp (horse power) available from the early production Rolls-Royce Merlin inline piston engines that powered initial models of the superlative Supermarine Spitfire and Hawker Hurricane fighters of World War Two, makes an interesting comparison to the power available to the Sopwith Camel, one of the greatest fighter aircraft of World War One. A number of engine types were actually used in the production run of the Camel, but fairly typical were the Clerget rotary engines of 130 hp. By the end of World War Two, the Hawker Tempest Mk.V fighter was fitted with the Napier Sabre inline engine of 2,180 hp. In complete contrast, the contemporary Lockheed Martin F/A-22 Raptor tactical fighter is powered by two Pratt & Whitney F119 turbofan engines, of some 35,000 lb st (pounds of static thrust) each with afterburning. Truly a different world altogether. Continuing development had also led to an engine type that is related to the jet engine but which drives a propeller. This is the turboprop, and it has particularly found use for smaller airliners in the decades after World War Two.

The materials that aircraft are made from have also changed over the years. Early aircraft of the pre-World War One era were usually made of wood, covered in doped canvas, and braced with wire. Great advances during the inter-war period took place in aeronautical design and construction, one of the most important of these being the large-scale adoption of metal in aircraft construction, for the structure of the aircraft and eventually for the aircraft's skin as well. Thanks to pioneering work by Junkers, Dornier and others, the all-metal aircraft in fact had started to become a reality long before the beautifully streamlined all-metal stressed skin fighters of the Second World War era. It eventually became a type of construction that was enthusiastically taken up by aircraft designers and manufacturers, (although some embraced it more rapidly than others did), and by the dawn of the jet era most aircraft were made of metal. Nowadays, there are many different types of material that are used in aircraft construction. Much of this has to do with strength and weight. The increasing development and refinement of so-called 'composite materials' has brought about the use of this type of material in aircraft construction. Composite materials are strong and light, and are made from many different substances. Plastics of various types, and carbon fibre, are two important materials that are often used. Metal continues to be of great importance, however, and will probably never be replaced entirely by advanced composite materials in aircraft construction.

There were many other important advances in aircraft design and operations in the post-World War Two period. One of these was the development of guided air-to-air and air-to-ground missiles. Again this concept had been pioneered particularly in Nazi Germany, but it was some time after the end of the war that guided missiles were developed to such a form that they became viable weapons for widespread use. In some countries that resulted in the traditional gun or cannon armament of fighter aircraft being removed in

favor of unguided air-to-air rockets fired in salvoes against enemy bombers, or in the later widespread introduction of air-to-air missiles. In fact the loss of the gun armament from fighter aircraft proved to be a mistake, because air-to-air missiles do not always work properly and there are conditions in which they cannot be fired; in any case, most early missile-armed fighters could only carry a limited number of missiles. Nowadays most fighter aircraft are fitted with an internal cannon in addition to their guided missile armament. One casualty of continuing armament development, however, has been the manned gun turret. This piece of machinery was first developed and placed in production aircraft in the 1930s, and was an important feature of heavy bomber armament in particular during the course of World War Two. Nowadays there are no manned gun turrets on any military aircraft – a few bomber types continue to retain gun turrets, but these are remotely-controlled and fired.

The initial introduction of radar in the 1930s was a further important step forward that was to have great implications for warplane development. During World War Two there was a major distinction between day fighters such as the Supermarine Spitfire, North American P-51 Mustang and Messerschmitt Bf 109, and the radar-equipped night fighter such as the de Havilland Mosquito and Northrop P-61 Black Widow (all of these types are covered in detail in the second Volume of *The Complete Encyclopedia of Flight*). In the post-war years, 'all-weather' radar-equipped jet fighters were developed (by 'all-weather,' we mean able to fly and fight at night and in bad weather

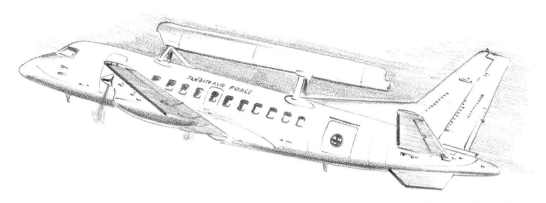

Military aircraft come in all shapes and sizes. This is a Swedish-designed and –manufactured Saab 340. Normally a short-range turboprop-engined airliner, a small number have been converted for military use as shown in this illustration with the mounting of a distinctive radar installation above the fuselage.

conditions). However, gradually the distinction between this type of aircraft and the day fighter became blurred as more and more warplanes were fitted with radar. Nowadays, most if not all front-line warplanes have some type of radar fitted, and are expected to perform as well during the night and in bad weather as they are able to do in clear daytime conditions.

In civil aviation, the introduction of the jet engine had profound effects just as it did for military warplane development. Alongside developments in aerodynamics, commercial aircraft were finally able to fly over increasingly long ranges. This gave new generations of airliners truly intercontinental range, something that aircraft designers in the 1930s were forever striving to achieve. In conjunction with these improvements came the widespread use of innovations such as pressurisation, which allowed transport aircraft to fly higher (and therefore more efficiently and effectively) while keeping their passengers in the comfort that they would normally experience at much lower altitudes.

The post-World War Two period also witnessed the demise of a type of passenger aircraft that had been widely accepted during the inter-war years. This was the passenger flying-boat, which went out of use altogether as a major means of passenger transport during the 1950s.

It is not just the flying-boat as a means of long-range passenger transport that has disappeared in the post-war period. Sadly, many of the famous aircraft companies that had been so much a part of the development of aviation during and after World War One and in the Second World War disappeared in the years after World War Two. This has come about for many reasons that are too complicated to explain in detail here. However, such factors as dwindling defence orders in times of relative peace, bad decision-making, poorly thought out official requirements, and the escalating cost of developing new aircraft types, have all played a part in the demise of many famous companies. The continuing domination of the world's aircraft industry by the United States has not even guaranteed the survival of all the famous American companies that were making aircraft in the time of huge military orders during World War Two. Indeed, a round of take-overs and mergers in the 1980s and 1990s saw the disappearance of several famous American companies – the most well-known and lamented of these being McDonnell Douglas.

Total War

We have already seen in the second Volume of *The Complete Encyclopedia of Flight* that the Second World War was the most extensive and costly armed conflict in the history of the world, and that it eventually embroiled the great majority of the countries of the world. It was fought simultaneously in several major theatres of war around the world, and it cost approximately 55 million lives – exact figures will never be known. In its simplest terms, the war was fought between two groups of powers. The first of these was the eventually victorious alliance of Britain and the British Commonwealth (formerly the British Empire), together with (eventually) the United States, the Soviet Union (which started out on the opposing side), various Chinese groupings, and countries such as Czechoslovakia, France, Poland, and other European nations that were taken over before or early in the war by Germany, and some of whose nationals fought on alongside these powers. Collectively they were known as the Allies. Opposing them was the side that started the conflict, known as the Axis powers due to the Axis alliance that was signed prior to the war between Germany and Italy, and later extended to include Japan. It contained the alliance of Nazi Germany under Adolf Hitler, Fascist Italy under Benito Mussolini, and Japan under

an Imperial dynasty led by Emperor Hirohito. This grouping also had the support of other smaller nations, and nationals of various other countries also fought for the Axis. These included fighting men from countries overrun by the Germans, who nevertheless saw this as the opportunity of freeing their homelands from previous oppressors. Most of the fighting during the Second World War took place in and around Europe, in North Africa where several European powers had colonies which also became embroiled in the fighting, and in the Pacific theatre across the vast distances of the Pacific Ocean and in East Asia.

The war commenced with the German invasion of Poland on 1 September 1939. It ended virtually six years later with the total defeat of the Axis powers. Fascist Italy was defeated in 1943, Nazi Germany in May 1945, and imperialist Japan in August 1945 (although the final Japanese surrender actually took place in September 1945). The stubborn fanaticism of the Japanese had convinced many planners that an invasion of Japan itself would be a very costly venture. The Americans, however, held a trump card that was to transform the whole face of warfare, and lay the foundations for confrontation in the post-war years. For some years American scientists had been working on nuclear fusion, with a view to creating a powerful bomb that would benefit not from standard and established high explosive, but from the splitting of the atom. They were aided in their work by scientists who had fled persecution in Nazi Germany, and eventually the world's first atomic weapons were created under the 'Manhattan Project.' The only bomber capable of carrying the resulting very large and very heavy bomb was the Boeing B-29 Superfortress, and it was this aircraft that was to end the Second World War at a stroke. The first-ever atomic bomb to be used in war, nicknamed 'Little Boy,' was dropped from the B-29 'Enola Gay' on 6 August 1945. It destroyed much of the industrial town of Hiroshima. On 9 August 1945, over Nagasaki, another atomic bomb, 'Fat Man' was dropped by the B-29 'Bock's Car.' The use of these two hugely destructive weapons has become mired in controversy virtually ever since, but at the time it had the immediate effect of concentrating minds amongst the Japanese leadership. The Japanese surrendered on 14 August 1945, and signed amid great publicity the actual surrender documents on 2 September 1945 aboard the battleship U.S.S. Missouri in Tokyo Bay.

So the most famous war in history came to an end. Aerial bombardment had achieved what has sometimes been subsequently called an 'airpower victory,' and the face and tactics of warfare had been completely re-written. Unfortunately, hopes that the post-war world would be a better place were soon irrevocably compromised. Much of Europe was in ruins, the results of aerial bombing by heavy bombers and massively destructive ground warfare added to by the use of tactical ground attack aircraft. Civilians had been targeted by bombing in their own homes, a process that had started during World War One but which had been pursued with the utmost vigor during World War Two. Indeed, it had become quite normal by the end of World War Two that the battlefield extended wherever an aircraft could fly. The Second World War also saw a complete re-drawing of the map of which countries were the real powers in political and military terms for the post-war world. In particular, the United States finally came out of its so-called 'isolationism' to become a dominant world power both politically and militarily. The defeat of Germany and Japan saw these two powers shake off their former totalitarian and absolutist rule, and even-

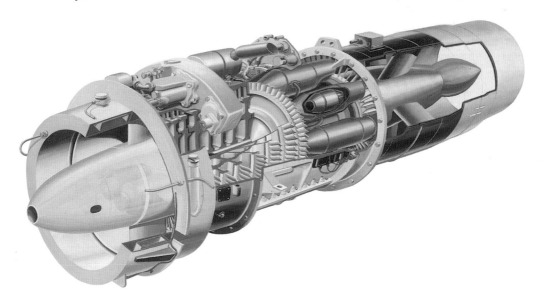

tually witnessed both of these two countries rebuilt into major industrial powers. With massive financial assistance from the United States under the famed Marshall Plan, Western Europe was rebuilt and many of the formally defeated powers emerged as important constituent members of the North Atlantic Treaty Organisation western military alliance during the 1950s. Colonial powers such as Britain lost much of the influence that they had enjoyed prior to the war, the many defeats that Britain had suffered prior to the final victory causing a massive reduction in Britain's prestige and influence in the post-war world. The successful development of the atomic bomb, and the emergence of the United States and the Soviet Union as global superpowers with widespread nuclear and chemical arsenals, and large military infrastructures, were hugely important developments that shaped the following decades. The so-called Cold War that developed quickly in the post-war years saw the United States and its Allies in Western Europe and elsewhere ranged against a new grouping in Central and Eastern Europe that was dominated by the Soviet Union. This influenced many military trends in the coming decades. The war also directly led to the creation of the international body known as the United Nations, which was founded by the victorious Allies partly to prevent such a large, disastrous and destructive conflict from ever breaking out again – something that, thankfully, it has so far proven able to achieve. Nevertheless, smaller but no less deadly conflicts have flared in many parts of the world following the end of World War Two, and in these wars aviation has played a major part on many – if not all – occasions.

A Lack of Peace

It was no doubt a considerable disappointment to many people that the end of the Second World War did not witness an end to major, widespread warfare. Indeed, it can be argued that the period after 1945 up to the present has been one of the most violent in world history, with destructive wars and smaller conflicts taking place in many parts of the world. The type and nature of these wars has been very diverse, from full-scale wars like that in Korea, to colonial wars and so-called wars of independence. The most important of them all, however, was not a 'war' at all in the normal way. This was the Cold War, the forty-year stand-off between the Soviet Union and the Western World. The Soviet Union, under Communism and a succession of dictators of which the best known was Josef Stalin, held in its grasp the countries of Eastern and Central Europe following the war. These were brought together in a number of economic and military groupings, the most important being the Warsaw Pact. For a time the Soviet Union was also allied to Communist China, and there were many states around the world which claimed the Soviet Union as their friend. By the 1950s the Soviet Union was developing its own nuclear arsenal to rival that of the United States, and the possibility for a war even more destructive than the Second World War was an ever-present danger. It was the potential nuclear confrontation between East and West, in which each side eventually held enough nuclear weapons to destroy civilisation many times over, that characterised the decades following the end of the Second World War.

There were many facets to this stand-off, and a number of significant incidents during the Cold War. One of these was the Cuban missile crisis of 1962, when the world came alarmingly close to nuclear war. In 1948, the Soviet Union tried to establish a blockade on the city of Berlin, the former Nazi German capital which had been partitioned after the war and which lay deep within the Communist-dominated East Germany. Fortunately, although the land routes in and out of Berlin were sealed off by the Soviets, air routes remained open. This led to the Berlin Airlift, in which Allied transport aircraft kept the beleaguered Western part of Berlin from being taken over by the Communists. The airlift lasted well into 1949, when the Communists finally backed down and opened once more the land routes into Berlin, although the air supply continued after that time in a diminished form. In 1961 the Communists began the construction of the Berlin Wall, which was built not to keep the West out, but to stop the many disaffected East Berliners from fleeing to the West from the hopeless living conditions that they faced under Communist rule in the East.

Finally, however, after four decades of the Cold War, the West prevailed. The coming to power in the Soviet Union during the 1980s of Mikhail Gorbachev signalled a massive shift in Soviet thinking, and led to the process in which the brave peoples of Eastern and Central Europe rose up peacefully but effectively against the dictatorship of the Soviet Union. Firstly in Poland with the 'Solidarity' movement, and then in other coun-

Aircraft carriers first came to real prominence during World War Two. Their importance in that conflict was considerable, and during the post-war era they have grown in significance. Several countries, notably the United States, France, and Britain, have operated aircraft carriers in the years after World War Two, and have sometimes used them in conflict. By far the largest user is the United States, which nowadays maintains a number of aircraft carriers as a major part of its naval strength. These have seen combat from Vietnam to the recent air operations over the former Yugoslavia, Iraq, and Afghanistan. Illustrated here is a Nimitz Class aircraft carrier, a nuclear-powered carrier that has an air group of some 78 aircraft and helicopters – virtually a small air force in its own right. The United States' aircraft carriers are a form of force projection, conveying American foreign policy wherever they go, and always ready for combat if it is required.

tries dominated by the Soviet Union like Hungary and Czechoslovakia, the Soviet rule was eventually successfully – and peacefully – challenged. This was particularly important in East Germany, where the Berlin Wall that had walled-in German citizens in the Soviet-dominated parts of Berlin had become a symbol of the Soviet Union's intransigence and unwanted domination over Central Europe. The destruction of the Berlin Wall by popular protest in late 1989 signalled the true beginning of the end of the world order of the Cold War, and a new era. Unfortunately, that new era has proven to be no less warlike than its predecessors.

It is beyond the scope of this book to discuss in detail the many wars that have taken place in the post-Second World War period. However, the following brief summary will give some idea as to the number and scale of those many diverse conflicts. Even as the Second World War was ending, unrest was starting to gather momentum. In Greece, a civil war took place in which, fortunately, a Communist uprising was defeated. Much greater trouble was developing in the overseas colonies of several of the European colonial powers, however. In particular, the prestige of Britain as a world power had been broken by the war. Large areas of the former British Empire had fallen to the Japanese in the Far East, and colonial troops had been very important in helping Britain to ultimately defeat both Japan and Germany. The move for independence within many of the former colonial powers became irresistible after the war had ended. In some places peacefully, but in others through conflict, many of the colonial powers like Britain had eventually to give up their overseas possessions.

Out of these independence movements grew new states such as India and Pakistan, but some of these newly-independent countries were unable to get along peacefully with their neighbors. India and Pakistan, for example, have subsequently fought two major wars. Both now possess nuclear weapons, with the danger that these could be used in the future if tensions between the two ever become irreversibly out of hand. It was not just Britain that lost territories, however. France fought a long but ultimately unsuccessful war to hang on to Algeria in North Africa, and equally disastrously lost her colonies in Southeast Asia in the 1950s. Other colonial powers such as the Netherlands and Belgium also had to give up their overseas possessions. In many cases the newly-independent countries resulting from the colonial break-up in Africa and elsewhere in the world have subsequently made a complete mess of running their own affairs, and have sometimes descended into civil war or unnecessary conflicts against their neighbors.

The most significant war of the immediate post-Second World period was the Korean War. During World War Two much of Korea had been occupied by the Japanese. Following the end of the war, Korea was divided into Communist-led North Korea, and South Korea which was friendly towards the West. In June 1950 North Korean forces invaded South Korea to impose their will and ideology onto their neighbor. This was the first real test for the United Nations, and the response of this international organisation was to send forces from several countries to help the South Koreans to defend themselves. This was only possible because the Soviet Union was boycotting the United Nations' Security Council at the time. The United Nations forces were dominated by the United States, but other countries such as Britain and Australia, as well as the South Koreans themselves, also played an important part. After three years of bitter fighting, the war ended in a stalemate during 1953, and the tensions between South Korea and North Korea remain to this day.

The 1950s also saw several other important conflicts. One of these was in 1956, when troubles in the Middle East began to gain international importance. The creation of the state of Israel in the later 1940s had taken place against a backdrop of considerable violence in the Middle East. Britain had been the dominant power in that region during World War Two, and had successfully fought off the Italians and Germans who had sought to take over North Africa. The terrible persecution that the Jewish people had faced in Nazi Germany before and during World War Two helped lead to the creation of an independent Jewish state in the Middle East after the war. Jewish terrorism against British forces eventually led to the British withdrawal from the area, but at once the newly-created state of Israel had been attacked by her Arab neighbors. This was the first of several major conflicts between Israel and the Arab world, and this problem is the most serious predicament that continues to face the world in our own time. In 1956 the Egyptian dictator President Nasser attempted to take over the Suez Canal, which is the main waterway from Europe and the Mediterranean through the Middle East to the Indian Ocean. The response was a joint British-French-Israeli operation to try to capture the Canal and to keep it open for international traffic. Although the air and ground operations by these three countries against the Egyptians were successful, American opposition led to the abandonment of the whole operation. It was the first of several occasions during the post-war period when Britain's foreign policy was totally and detrimentally taken over by the Americans.

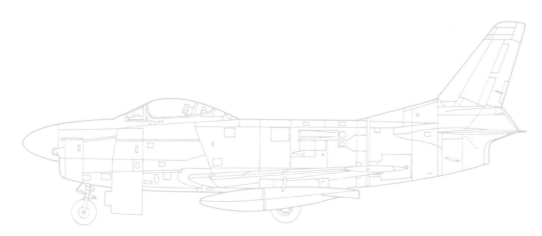

The North American F-86 Sabre was outstanding in its field as one of the best jet fighters in the air.

The Sikorsky S-55 series helicopters were the first really internationally-operated helicopters, and truly established the lasting significance of the helicopter in civil and military operations. This is a Royal Canadian Navy-operated Sikorsky HO4S derivative.

The United States did not have foreign policy all its own way during the Cold War period, however. Following the French withdrawal from Southeast Asia in the 1950s, several newly-independent countries in that area had come increasingly under Communist influence. Vietnam in particular had been partitioned into a Communist north, and a Western-supporting south – exactly the same situation that had led to so much trouble in Korea. From the late 1950s onwards, the Communists attempted to spread their influence over the south of Vietnam. The South Vietnamese resisted these attempts, and the United States began to give aid in the form of military equipment and so-called advisors. Soon, however, as the situation became increasingly out of hand, the United States began to send its own military forces. This was carried out covertly at first, but eventually American forces on land and in the air became openly involved. This conflict was the famous – some would say 'infamous' – Vietnam War. It continued in several bitterly-fought stages until 1973

when a very poor peace settlement was concluded. This led to renewed aggression from North Vietnam, and following the withdrawal of American forces the South was taken over and the whole of Vietnam unified under Communist rule in 1975. One of the first tasks of the new unified Vietnam was to perform a very necessary invasion of its neighbor Cambodia (Kampuchea) to remove from power the murderous Pol Pot regime, which was killing many innocent people within that country.

In other parts of the world, peace was similarly proving difficult to find. In early 1982 Argentine forces took over the British territories in the South Atlantic of South Georgia and the Falkland Islands. Massive defence cuts in Britain had led the Argentine leader General Galtieri to conclude that Britain would not fight to defend the islands, which Argentina considered to be its own territory. Britain did respond, however, and sent a naval task force to successfully retake the islands later in 1982. This was just one of many small but nevertheless important conflicts in which, just as in the larger wars, aircraft played a significant role.

Small-scale but no less brutal wars were successfully fought by Britain against Communist aggression in Malaya and against so-called freedom fighters in Kenya during the Mau Mau terrorist uprising, both during the 1950s. Amongst the more unusual conflicts that have taken place, in 1969, the South American countries of Honduras and El Salvador fought a short and completely unnecessary war that was sparked by the sporting contest between the two countries in the qualification for the 1970 football World Cup. Aviation played its part in that conflict too.

The end of the Cold War was heralded by many as the end of major conflict, and a real possibility for peace across the globe. Those who held a more knowledgeable and intelligent view of the world knew differently, and indeed the situation that exists nowadays is just as uncertain as it was at the height of the Cold War. In fact, it can be argued that the general situation in the world now is actually more dangerous than it was twenty years ago. The former Soviet Union broke up during the

early 1990s, and many of its former constituent republics are now independent countries. This is a good thing, but unfortunately the possibility has existed for military equipment or even materials to make nuclear weapons to fall into the hands of terrorists or rogue states due to the large amount of this material that became surplus and available as the Soviet Union disintegrated.

During the 1980s, in what was known at the time as the Gulf War but which has since been re-named the Iran-Iraq War, the Iraq of Saddam Hussein was at war with the Islamic fundamentalist state of Iran. Saddam Hussein has since become a figure of immense proportions, whose actions and eventual downfall have dominated world affairs for over a decade. In 1990 his Iraqi dictatorship invaded and conquered the neighboring state of Kuwait. A huge international response to this unprovoked action culminated in the Gulf War of 1991. In Operation 'Desert Storm' the forces of an international coalition led by the United States drove the Iraqi forces from Kuwait. Unfortunately, the overwhelming coalition victory in this war foolishly left Saddam Hussein in power in Iraq.

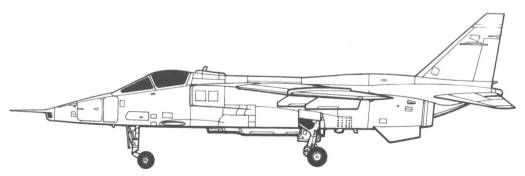

A Sepcat Jaguar, which is an attack aircraft that was designed by a French and British consortium – an example of the growing need in aviation for countries to work together to share the huge cost of designing and building modern combat aircraft.

After years of further troubles, including the persecution of opposition factions in Iraq, a further war was mounted against his régime in 2003. This principally involved the United States and Britain, and was named Operation 'Iraqi Freedom' (the Royal Air Force's involvement went under the name of Operation 'Telic'). The campaign successfully drove Saddam Hussein from power, but has since led to a disastrous breakdown of law and order in various parts of Iraq, where terrorism has continued to claim many lives.

Indeed, it is terrorism that has now become one of the greatest pre-occupations of military planners and politicians the world over. The disastrous terrorist attacks in New York on 11 September 2001 resulted in a successful American-led campaign to force from power the brutal terrorist-sympathising Taleban régime in Afghanistan. There have been other incidents since, including an attack on suspected terrorists in Yemen by an American-operated unmanned aerial vehicle (UAV). Indeed, the increasing use of UAVs by military forces in several countries during the past few years has started to transform the battlefield itself, for these unmanned remote-controlled flying machines are capable of per-forming many of the tasks that hitherto manned aircraft have been expected to perform. It will be interesting to see in the years to come just how far UAVs actually take over from manned aircraft.

This fascinating aeronautical story of aviation after the Second World War, during the Cold War era and up to the present day, brings this three-volume encyclopedia to a close. In the telling of any historical narrative, authors and artists are indebted to many historians and colleagues for their assistance and practical help. As ever, it is a pleasant exercise to acknowledge friends and experts whose assistance and advice have been such an invaluable contribution towards the piecing together of much of the information and photographic content of this third and final Volume of *The Complete Encyclopedia of Flight*. Particular recognition must go to Tony Blake, Derek Foley, Martin Hale, Jack Harris, my father Victor Lowe, Jim Smith, Derek Spurgeon, Gordon Stevens, and Paul Tuckey, for their assistance with information and illustrations, together with many overseas colleagues including Christian Durand, Philippe Jalabert, Miroslav Khol, Hans Meier,

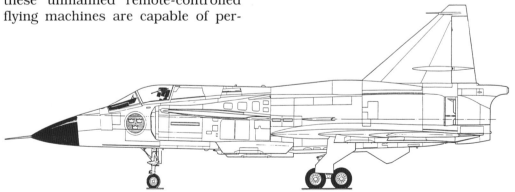

The big, powerful Saab AJ 37 Viggen from Sweden is proof that countries other than the superpowers can design and build capable and successful modern warplanes.

Michal Ovcacik, and Peter Walter. Particular thanks to David Willis for his assistance with information and text summaries, especially for many of the British and American aircraft from the mid-1950s onwards. Special recognition must additionally go to Chris Slocock of Publishing Solutions (www) Ltd. They have all been an important help in the telling of the story in this book. Aviation has been of vital importance in the decades since World War Two. It continues to be of great significance in our own time, and it will remain vitally important well into the future.

Author's Note
This book sets out to give the most accurate figures available for specifications, based where possible on manufacturer's or service data. However, there remain a number of aircraft types (as was also the case in Volumes 1 and 2 of The Complete Encyclopedia of Flight) where more information is needed – or might eventually be unearthed – regarding their specifications, or where contemporary sources seriously disagree. The same is true where metric dimensions have been translated over the years into Imperial specifications, and vice versa, with the attendant loss of specificity that such calculations often create. In similar fashion, there exist serious differences of opinion in a number of historical cases over such facts as first flight dates. Again those quoted in this book are the ones that, where possible, stand up to the data of the time – or acknowledged later sources which draw on information from the era when the particular aircraft in question was being built. In addition, the end of the Cold War has allowed Western historians the opportunity to find out much more than was previously known about aircraft that were designed and manufactured in the Soviet Union, and therefore much of the recently-published material on Russian aircraft has proven to be much more accurate than that published through the 1980s.

Miles M.52

The performance capabilities of combat aircraft moved ahead in leaps and bounds during the World War Two period. Piston engine development gave ever-increasing performance improvements to propeller-driven aircraft. Eventually the conventional piston engine came to virtually the limits of its power output and development potential, but by then the new era of jet propulsion was dawning as the future of front-line combat aircraft power. These increasing performance capabilities opened up the possibility of aircraft flying so fast that they would break the 'sound barrier' (760 mph [1,223 km/h] at sea level), a capability that some fast-flying propeller-driven and early jet aircraft had neared on a number of occasions during and after the war. Their disconcerted pilots had encountered compressibility (severe buffeting) during these encounters, and some aircraft

had broken up as a result. This gave the sound barrier almost mythical proportions, and efforts were made to find the right type of design to safely pass through the sound barrier and into the higher speeds beyond it. Research took place in Nazi Germany, Britain and the United States into the best design layouts to successfully break the 'sound barrier,' and after the war much captured German data became available on this subject to the victorious Allies. In Britain, Specification E.24/43 was issued to cover the development of what would be the world's first manned supersonic aircraft, able to fly at 1,000 mph (1,609 km/h) at 36,000 ft (10,973 m). The small but innovative Miles company was tasked with the development of a research aircraft to this requirement, and it created

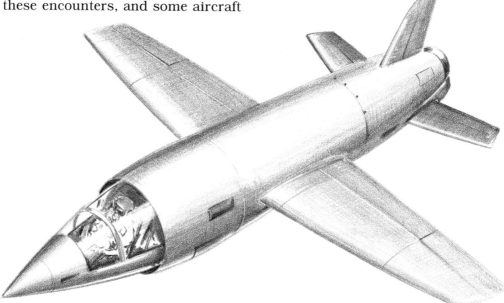

The Miles M.52 was an advanced design, the best aspects of which were passed to the Americans for their own supersonic research programs. Note the pilot's position in the nose under the glazing, and the air intake around the cockpit pod. Under Operation 'Neptune,' an air-dropped model of the M.52 was successfully launched several years after the M.52's cancellation.

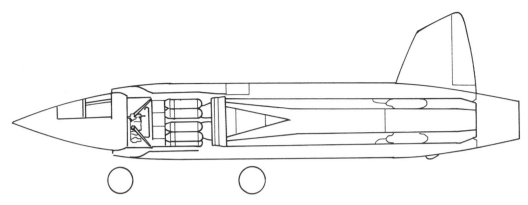

The Miles M.52's jet engine within the fuselage would have been fed by air from the annular intake duct around the fuselage behind the cockpit. An afterburner would have been fitted in the rear fuselage for more thrust. The M.52 was never built.

the M.52 design. With a configuration drawing from some aspects of ballistics (bullet and other projectile design), the M.52 was a straight wing streamlined projectile-like design with its pilot positioned in the nosecone within a jettisonable container. To cut down on weight a conventional undercarriage was not to be fitted, the M.52 instead being planned to land on a retractable skid after being air-launched from a 'mother ship' aircraft. Power was to be provided by the most powerful turbojet available, although an advanced turbojet with the then-new concept of an afterburner was planned for the future. Unfortunately, after much design work had been performed, the whole project was can-

celled by the British government in February 1946. It was claimed that the planned aircraft was too dangerous for its test pilot (but its planned pilot, Captain Eric Brown, later said that he wanted to be given the chance to fly it). Much of the M.52's ground-breaking technology was instead given to the Americans, who used some of the advanced ideas on the Bell X-1 (see pages 46 to 47), which became the first aircraft to 'officially' break the sound barrier in October 1947. This was a crippling blow to Britain's aircraft industry, and it ensured that in the post-war period the Americans would take an unassailable lead in jet fighter design.

Specifications – Miles M.52 (some data estimated)

Wingspan	27 ft (other dimensions were examined)
Length	28 ft 7 in
Maximum speed	approximately 1,000 mph
Maximum take-off weight	7,710 lb
Service ceiling	approximately 36,000 ft
Engine	One Power Jets W.2/700 turbojet engine with augmentor and afterburner, of 2,000 lb st
Crew	One

Avro Lancastrian and York

The American aviation industry provided many of the long-range (and shorter-range) transports that were so important to the Allied war effort during the latter stages of World War Two. Nevertheless, some of Britain's aircraft companies were able to produce a number of interim and to an extent makeshift types during the war that also had the possibility of civil transport use after the war – until purpose-designed commercial passenger aircraft like those proposed by the wartime Brabazon Committee could be designed and manufactured. Due to their long-range capabilities, the natural choice as the basis of these passenger-carrying and cargo makeshift conversions were the new generation of heavy bombers in production in Britain. These included the Handley Page Halifax, from which was developed the Halton transport; and the Avro Lancaster, which formed the basis of several major developments and conversions, including ad hoc transports during the war as well as the more finely developed Lancastrian and York. The first

Lancaster cargo and passenger-carrying conversions were pioneered by the Canadians, who had the need for a transatlantic-capable transport for mail and people in the mid-war years. The Canadian conversion program was so successful that the type's manufacturer, Avro, used this initial work as the basis of what became a successful series that eventually took the name Lancastrian. Initial Lancaster transport conversions were very austere, with few creature comforts for their passenger. Some had the positions usually occupied by gun turrets on operational Lancasters simply sheeted over. Later, with the creation of the Type 691 Lancastrian, the interiors were more finely appointed. In addition, neat nose and tail extensions were adopted which gave a more streamlined appearance to the aircraft. Several were initially ordered by Trans Canada Air Lines from the Canadian Lancaster licence-producer Victory Aircraft. In Britain, Lancastrians were built

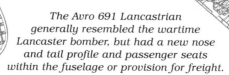

The Avro 691 Lancastrian generally resembled the wartime Lancaster bomber, but had a new nose and tail profile and passenger seats within the fuselage or provision for freight.

The Avro 685 York was a passenger adaptation of the Avro Lancaster bomber with a new passenger-carrying fuselage. Registration G-AGNL was named 'Mersey' by BOAC and survived until 1954 when it was scrapped.

for military (to Specification C.16/44) as well as civil use, with seating usually for nine or thirteen passengers. The major British airline BOAC used the type as a civil transport from May 1945, and Lancastrians were operated in the Berlin Airlift of 1948-1949 while others were employed as engine test-beds. Just over ninety of all versions are believed to have been produced. A more major adaptation of the Lancaster for passenger-carrying was the Type 685 York, which featured a completely new fuselage and other changes. Originally devised to Specification C.1/42 for Royal Air Force transport service, the initial aircraft flew on 5 July 1942. Manufactured up to 1948, 256 Yorks were built in Britain, some of them post-war. The type served extensively with the R.A.F., but from 1944 BOAC also operated Yorks for war-related transport duties. One was used by Britain's Prime Minister Winston Churchill as a special transport. Yorks were later employed extensively by various civil operators post-war, with a variety of seating arrangements (sometimes as 21 or 24 passenger transports), and the type also operated during the Berlin Airlift.

Specifications – Avro 691 Lancastrian Mk.1

Wingspan	102 ft
Length	76 ft 10 in
Maximum speed	315 mph at 12,000 ft
Maximum take-off weight	65,000 lb
Range	4,100 miles (with nine passengers)
Service ceiling	24,300 ft
Engine	Four Rolls-Royce Merlin T.24/2 inline piston engines, of 1,620-1,635 hp each
Crew	Four or five crew, nine or thirteen passengers

Early Soviet Jet Fighters

In common with countries such as Britain, Germany, and the United States – as described elsewhere in this book – the Soviet Union attempted to embrace the new advances in aerodynamics, materials and propulsion that were made in the Second World War period. As far as jet propulsion was concerned, the Soviet Union lagged seriously behind Britain and Germany, although some limited experimentation into jet engine development had taken place in the Soviet Union during the later 1930s. Soviet planners realised, as was the case in other countries, that the jet engine was going to be highly significant in the post-war period. Fortunately for the Russians, the advancing Soviet army in the latter stages of World War Two captured German jet aircraft and engines and their related technology. Much of this captured material formed the basis of the Soviet Union's initial jet technology. In particular, the German Junkers Jumo 004 and BMW 003 axial-flow turbojets were eventually copied and manufactured in the Soviet Union as the RD-10 and RD-20 respectively. During 1945 several Soviet aircraft design organisations were diverted to create a new, first generation of jet aircraft for the Soviet Union. A captured German Messerschmitt Me 262 jet fighter was tested in the Soviet Union in the latter half of 1945, and this helped towards the creation of several Russian jet aircraft. The design bureaux of Yakovlev, Mikoyan-Gurevich (MiG), Lavochkin, Sukhoi, and Alekseyev, all designed new jet fighters, the first three of these being well-known for their piston-engined Second World War Soviet combat aircraft. The new jet designs by Sukhoi, Lavochkin, and Alekseyev did not subsequently reach wide-scale production or service, but Yakovlev and MiG both created relatively successful designs. MiG's aircraft was the I-300, an all-metal tricycle undercarriage twin-engined RD-20 powered straight-wing fighter, with its two jet engines mounted low down in the fuselage in a 'stepped' layout. Yakovlev's straight-wing all-metal Yak-Jumo was eventually powered by the RD-10, with its single engine mounted in a stepped fuselage but with a tailwheel undercarriage layout.

Much more information has subsequently come to light about the Yakovlev Yak-15 since drawings like this of the well-known 'number 20' proliferated during the Cold War. Although a significant type, the Yak-15's modest performance limited it to training and familiarisation purposes.

It's that famous 'number 20' again! In fact around 280 Yak-15s were actually built (not just the one illustrated), eventually receiving the NATO reporting name 'Feather,' which they appear to have shared with a tricycle undercarriage development called the Yak-17.

It was basically a piston-engined Yak-3 Second World War fighter design, modified with its piston engine replaced by the re-located jet engine. The prototypes of these two designs both officially flew on 24 April 1946 (although the Yak may have flown earlier). Both later entered production and service in the Soviet Union. The MiG design grew into the MiG-9 (NATO reporting name 'Fargo'), which served with the Soviet air force and also later with that of Communist China. The Yak design became the Yak-15, which apparently gained the NATO identification 'Feather,' which is also attributed to a later tricycle undercarriage development called the Yak-17. Both the MiG-9 and the Yak-15 suffered with comparatively limited performance and high fuel consumption. Some 600 (possibly considerably more) MiG-9s were built, and 280 Yak-15s (plus a two-seat trainer called the Yak-21). Further development led to much more capable fighters being designed, and with British engine technology added, MiG created the world-famous MiG-15 – see pages 58 to 59.

Specifications – Yakovlev Yak-15 (early production aircraft)

Wingspan	30 ft 2.25 in
Length	28 ft 6.5 in
Maximum speed	488 mph at 16,405 ft
Maximum take-off weight	6,045 lb
Range	317 miles
Service ceiling	approximately 43,799 ft
Armament	Two nose-mounted 0.9 in (23 mm) cannons (not fitted to some early aircraft)
Engine	One RD-10 turbojet engine, of approximately 1,984 lb st
Crew	One

Hawker Sea Fury

During World War Two a number of outstanding aircraft were built in Britain by the Hawker aircraft company. These included the Hurricane, which was one of the main British fighters in the Battle of Britain during 1940. A little after the Hurricane, Hawker designed the powerful and ultimately successful Typhoon and Tempest, the latter being one of the fastest piston engined fighters of the late Second World War period. All these famous types are covered in the second Volume of *The Complete Encyclopedia of Flight* relating to World War Two. Continuing development by Hawker led to proposals to create a smaller and lighter Typhoon/ /Tempest derivative, and by a long process of evolution and a variety of official Specifications the new design evolved as the Hawker Fury/Sea Fury. Much of this development work was under Specification F.2/43, and the original intention was for a land-based fighter for the Royal Air Force named Fury, and a navalised derivative called Sea Fury. Eventually the land-based version was cancelled, but design work and prototype construction continued for the naval derivative. The first aircraft flew on 21 February 1945. After a number of design alter-ations, particularly to make the aircraft suitable for aircraft carrier operations, the type entered production as the Sea Fury F.Mk.X fighter. The first production example flew in September 1946 – too late for service in the Second World War. In the event only 50 Mk.X were built, because continuing development had already led to the more powerful and capable fighter-bomber FB.Mk.11. Eventually 615 of this mark were produced, and alongside other piston engine types like the de Havilland Hornet and Sea Hornet (see pages 62 to 63) they represented the final service of high-performance piston engine front-line aircraft in Britain prior to the general introduction of jet-powered aircraft. In fact the Sea Fury was one of the finest piston engine fighters, and it served front-line with Britain's Royal Navy from 1947 to 1953. It additionally saw considerable combat in the Korean War, Sea Furies being in action mainly as ground attack aircraft for United Nations forces, initially with No. 807 Naval Air Squadron. Sea Furies were also com-

The Hawker Sea Fury was a big, powerful naval fighter-bomber that was at the end, and the zenith, of piston engined fighter design. A Sea Fury FB.11 is shown in this illustration.

It is unusual for a piston engined fighter to shoot down a jet aircraft. In August 1952 during the Korean War, Lieutenant Peter Carmichael flying a Sea Fury FB.11 of No.802 Squadron, Fleet Air Arm from H.M.S. Ocean, succeeded in shooting down a Communist-flown MiG-15 jet. One of H.M.S. Ocean's Sea Furies is shown here, but not the aircraft that Carmichael flew on that occasion.

paratively widely exported. Australian-operated examples similarly flew in action over Korea, while Canada, the Netherlands, Pakistan, Egypt, Burma, and Cuba additionally flew the Sea Fury (some of these only from land bases), while Iraq flew single and two-seat de-navalised Fury derivatives. A two-seat Sea Fury development was the dual-control Sea Fury T.Mk.20 trainer, 60 being built for land-based Royal Navy use although several were later exported and some were used by West Germany as target-towers.

Specifications – Hawker Sea Fury FB.Mk.11

Wingspan	38 ft 4.75 in
Length	34 ft 8 in
Maximum speed	460 mph at 18,000 ft
Maximum take-off weight	14,650 lb
Range	700 miles
Service ceiling	35,800 ft
Armament	Four wing-mounted 0.787 in (20 mm) cannons, two bombs of up to 1,000 lb, up to 12 unguided rockets
Engine	One Bristol Centaurus 18 radial piston engine, of 2,480 hp
Crew	One

Bell P-59 Airacomet

There is no doubt that the United States benefited greatly during and after World War Two from aviation technology that was transferred to its aircraft companies by its chief ally, Britain, and (after the war) from the defeated Nazi German aviation industry. As pointed out on pages 46 to 47, the American achievement of being the first to safely break the 'sound barrier' was helped by British innovation, and the same was also true of jet engine development. Both Britain and Germany led the world in the 1930s and early in World War Two in the development of practical jet engines for front-line combat aircraft, and both countries were able to deploy successful operational jet aircraft before the end of the Second World War. These achievements are described in the previous Volume of *The Complete Encyclopedia of Flight* describing World War Two. In the United States, the development of practical jet-powered combat aircraft was much slower than in oth-

er countries – which is a surprising fact in itself, especially when one remembers that the American aviation industry eventually led the world in jet aircraft design and quantity manufacture. During 1941 the Americans successfully obtained the rights for the construction and development of the Frank Whittle-inspired turbojet already well under development and manufacture in Britain. This allowed the American General Electric company to become the American leader in turbojet development, and in 1941 the Bell company was designated to design and build America's first jet-powered fighter. This company was already producing the piston-engined P-39 Airacobra single-engined fighter, but this aircraft was not one of World War Two's best fighters. The new Bell jet aircraft also proved to be unremarkable, except that it was America's first true jet fighter. Known as the P-59 Airacomet, it first flew on 1 October 1942. Three XP-59A prototypes were built, followed by 13 development and service test YP-59A examples. These

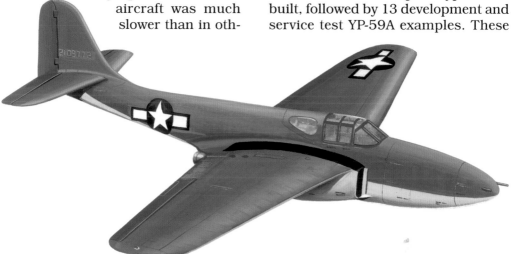

The Bell P-59 Airacomet was the United States' first practical jet fighter, but its performance was hardly outstanding and the type performed only training and familiarisation duties for America's first jet fighter pilots. This drawing shows one of the 13 YP-59A development aircraft, serial number 42-108772, which preceded the actual series production Airacomets.

Two photographs of one of the early development Bell Airacomets. The type was of straightforward conventional design, and never flew in combat (Photos: U.S. Army Air Force).

did not show particularly good performance, several of America's wartime piston-engined fighters such as the superb North American P-51 Mustang being faster. The Airacomet also proved to be a below-par gun platform, suffering from poor directional stability at higher speeds, despite usefully having all its guns concentrated in the fuselage nose. One example was passed to Britain in return for a Gloster Meteor, Britain's more advanced and more capable contemporary jet fighter. The decision was later made that the Airacomet would be a non-operational introduction to jet fighter operation for the U.S. Army Air Force, and the initial, comparatively large orders were cut back. Eventually only 20 P-59A initial production aircraft and 30 slightly improved P-59B were built. Only one fighter unit, the 412th Fighter Group, flew the production Airacomets – and did not see combat. A number of Airacomets were later used as drones or drone-controllers in experimental programs, at least one having a specially-modified nose fitted with a seat for a second occupant.

Specifications – Bell P-59A Airacomet

Wingspan	45 ft 6 in
Length	38 ft 1.5 in
Maximum speed	409 mph at 35,000 ft
Maximum take-off weight	up to 13,000 lb
Range	240 miles on internal fuel
Service ceiling	46,200 ft
Armament	One 1.456 in (37 mm) cannon and three 0.5 in (12.7 mm) machine guns in fuselage nose
Engine	Two General Electric I-16 (J31-GE-3) turbojet engines, of 1,650-2,000 lb st each
Crew	One

Vickers Viking

With increasing Allied success in World War Two and the end of the war in sight, many planners began to think in terms of how civil aviation could be reinstated and developed in the coming post-war world. As explained on Page 122, an influential body in Britain that looked at this problem was the Brabazon Committee. The discussions of this group led to the general framework in which several aircraft such as the Vickers Viscount airliner (see pages 80 to 81) were created. However, the Brabazon Committee did not give much consideration to the creation of interim types to fill the gap between the end of the war and the development of all-new airliners for the post-war years. Fortunately several manufacturers in Britain were already seriously considering this

problem. Somewhat makeshift but nonetheless effective types such as the Avro Lancastrian and York described on pages 26 to 27 were by then already in existence, but another interim type that was developed at that time was the Vickers-Armstrongs Viking. During World War Two Vickers produced the famous Wellington twin-engined bomber, which was well-known for its unusual geodetic construction and is described in the second Volume of *The Complete Encyclopedia of Flight*. Vickers used the Wellington design for their new airliner layout, mating the fabric-covered geodetic Wellington wings with a new all-metal fuselage and more powerful engines. Designed to Specification 17/44, and designated VC1

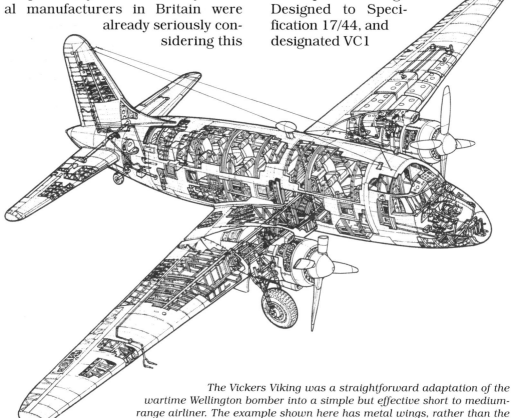

The Vickers Viking was a straightforward adaptation of the wartime Wellington bomber into a simple but effective short to medium-range airliner. The example shown here has metal wings, rather than the fabric-covered geodetic construction of the earliest Vikings.

An important operator of the Vickers Viking airliner was Cunard Eagle Airways. The aircraft illustrated, registration G-AJPH, was at one time experimentally fitted with two Rolls-Royce Nene turbojet engines as Britain's first jet-powered commercial transport.

(Vickers Commercial One), the Model 491 Viking first flew on 22 June 1945 – only several weeks after World War Two in Europe had ended. The first production model was the Viking Mk.1A, which retained the fabric-covered wings, and the first Viking commercial service opened between London (Northolt) and Copenhagen with British European Airways in September 1946. Further development led to the Viking Mk.1 with new, all-metal wings. The main production Viking version was, however, the Viking Mk.1B with a slightly lengthened fuselage, of which 113 were completed. Vikings operated with various airlines in many parts of the world, and the type also had several military spin-offs. These were the Valetta troop and paratroop transport and freighter for Britain's Royal Air Force, and the completely revised R.A.F.-operated Varsity with a tricycle undercarriage layout. Several Vikings themselves served with the R.A.F. for trials work, general transport and VIP transport, and cargo operations. A unique Viking conversion involved the installation of two Rolls-Royce Nene turbojet engines in place of the usual Hercules radial engines. This aircraft first flew on 6 April 1948, and has been claimed as the first completely jet-powered commercial aircraft to fly in the world, but it did not enter production. As usual, reputable sources disagree as to how many Vikings were built, the manufacturer's own records suggesting 172, but 167 and 163 have also been accepted in the past.

Specifications – Vickers Viking Mk.1B

Wingspan	89 ft 3 in
Length	65 ft 2 in
Cruising speed	210 mph at 6,000 ft
Maximum take-off weight	34,000 lb
Range	520 miles plus
Service ceiling	23,750 ft
Engine	Two Bristol Hercules 634 radial piston engines, of 1,690 hp each
Accommodation	Four or five crew, up to 27 (or in some cases 36) passengers

de Havilland D.H.100 Vampire

Both Britain and Germany achieved the breakthrough of placing jet-powered combat aircraft into front-line service before the end of World War Two. Britain's first jet combat aircraft was the Gloster Meteor, the initial versions of which were covered in the second Volume of *The Complete Encyclopedia of Flight*. The later, post-war developments of the Meteor are described on pages 90 to 91 of this book. The second British jet fighter was already well progressed in its development before the end of the Second World War. This was the de Havilland Vampire (originally intended to be called Spider Crab), a somewhat unconventional twin-boom single-engined light fighter with mixed metal and wood construction. Wood is certainly no longer used in jet fighter construction, but the Vampire and its later derivatives gave valuable service to Britain's Royal Air Force and many other air arms around the world. The de Hav-illand company had the advantage of not only being a world-famous aircraft manufacturer, but also being involved in jet engine development. It worked closely with the jet engine pioneer Frank Halford whose centrifugal-flow turbojets were later developed into several significant types including the Goblin engine for the Vampire. The Vampire was designed to Air Ministry Specification E.6/41, the first prototype flying on 20 September 1943. The initial production version was the F.Mk.1, which entered R.A.F. service in the spring and summer of 1946. This was a very basic combat aircraft, but it was the R.A.F.'s very first single-engine jet fighter. Further development led to a long succession of production versions as fighters or fighter-bombers for British and export use, there being many export buyers of the Vampire. Indeed, licence-production or assembly was also carried out in France (some French versions being

The de Havilland Vampire was a simple but effective first generation jet-powered fighter and fighter-bomber. Its centrifugal-flow turbojet engine can be seen here within the fuselage pod behind the cockpit.

The first de Havilland Vampire F.Mk.1s entered R.A.F. service with No.247 Squadron in 1946, one of whose Vampires is seen here. The unit was based for a part of that period at R.A.F. Odiham in Hampshire, southern England.

called Mistral), Australia, Italy, Switzerland and India. A two-seat, side-by-side seating radar-equipped night fighter Vampire with a modified fuselage pod existed as the D.H.113 Vampire NF.Mk.10, and this seating arrangement was additionally employed for the dual-control D.H.115 Vampire Trainer, which served with the R.A.F. as the T.Mk.11. Single-seat navalised Sea Vampires were the first (but non-operational) jet fighters for Britain's Royal Navy, and the navalised two-seat trainer version was the Sea Vampire T.22. Vampires were involved in combat during several conflicts, including R.A.F. aircraft in the Malayan Emergency, and Rhodesian-operated examples flew against terrorists during the 1970s in that country. Company records suggest that 1,565 Vampires were built to R.A.F. or Royal Navy order, including some for export, but the overall total including foreign licence manufacture is much higher. Further development of this successful, austere early jet combat aircraft led to many other derivatives described on pages 94 to 95

Wingspan	40 ft
Length	30 ft 9 in
Maximum speed	531 mph at 10,000 ft
Maximum take-off weight	11,970 lb
Range	1,145 miles with underwing fuel tanks
Service ceiling	43,500 ft
Armament	Four lower nose-mounted 0.787 in (20 mm) cannons
Engine	One de Havilland Goblin 2 turbojet engine, of 3,100 lb st
Crew	One

Supermarine Spitfire/Seafire Late Marks

The Supermarine Spitfire is one of the classic warplanes of all time. It is also one of the best-known aircraft types ever produced, and its highly important service during World War Two is described in the second Volume of *The Complete Encyclopedia of Flight*. The Spitfire's service life did not finish with the end of the war, however, and Spitfires continued in Royal Air Force service in the post-war period. The final R.A.F. Spitfires were three photo-reconnaissance Spitfire PR.Mk.XIX which were finally retired in the later 1950s. Spitfires were also flown post-war by many other air arms, including those of France, the Netherlands, Czechoslovakia, and Israel. Total Spitfire production extended to over twenty thousand three hundred. An important derivative of the Spitfire was the Supermarine Seafire, which was a navalised development that saw service especially from British aircraft carriers during and after World War Two. The Seafire came about due to an increasing need by Britain's Royal Navy for a modern carrier-based fighter able to operate on even terms with the best-available German

warplanes. In fact the creation of the Seafire was something of a stop-gap until more suitable fighters from the United States became available later in World War Two. The narrow track (the distance between the mainwheels) of the Spitfire/Seafire undercarriage was a large disadvantage for aircraft carrier operations, so too was the restricted view forward. In any case, the Spitfire's airframe had not been originally designed for the tough operating circumstances of an aircraft carrier, and was thus rather 'dainty' for this type of operational environment. Nevertheless, the development of the naval Seafire progressed quickly. Initially most early Seafires were converted Spitfires, but the first major Seafire new-build version was the Mk.II series. Seafires entered combat in 1942, and were prominent for the first time dur-

Serial number VP441 was a Supermarine Seafire Mk.47, which was the last of the Seafire production marks. This version flew combat missions over Malaya and in the Korean War

Like most aircraft carrier-based warplanes, many versions of the Supermarine Seafire had folding wings so that they could fit into the confined space of the ships' below-deck hangars. This is a late-mark Griffon-engined Seafire, illustrating the pilot's restricted view forward and the narrow track of the Seafire's main undercarriage (Photo: Vickers-Supermarine).

ing the North African invasion in November 1942 (Operation 'Torch'). Continuing development led to a variety of Seafire versions which were developed alongside the land-based Spitfires. Early Seafires were Rolls-Royce Merlin-powered, later models (from the Mk.XV onwards) were Griffon-powered. The final Seafire version was the Mk.47. Fleet Air Arm Seafires flew with varying degrees of success during World War Two, and even the Mk.47 saw combat, over Malaya in 1949 and in the initial stages of the Korean War in 1950. Seafires also operated with the French and Canadian naval air arms, and (land-based) with Burmese and Irish forces. Overall, 2,568 (possibly more) Seafires are believed to have been built or converted, the final Royal Navy examples being retired in November 1954.

Specifications – Supermarine Seafire F./FR.Mk.47

Wingspan	36 ft 11 in
Length	34 ft 4 in
Maximum speed	452 mph at 20,500 ft
Maximum take-off weight	12,530 lb
Radius of action	approximately 200 miles
Service ceiling	43,100 ft
Armament	Four wing-mounted 0.787 in (20 mm) cannons, up to three 500 lb bombs or eight 60 lb unguided rockets
Engine	One Rolls-Royce Griffon 88 inline piston engine, of 2,350 hp
Crew	One

Northrop XP-56

It is very often the case in aviation that the eccentric and unusual do not find much favor amongst military and civil operators. One of the most significant exceptions to this 'rule' is the flying wing, an unorthodox design layout that has nonetheless had sufficient adherents and modest successes over the years to result in several aircraft being designed in this way. One of the principal exponents of the flying wing was John K. Northrop, an American pioneer whose company has been responsible for many of the flying wings that have so far been built (the Horten brothers in Germany during the 1930s and 1940s were also active in this area). Northrop began his work in earnest on flying wings in the 1920s, and created several designs that culminated in the N-9M flying wing of the early 1940s. This successfully proved the concept of the flying wing, and Northrop subsequently built the bomber designs B-35 and B-49 (see pages 98 to 99), and an experimental fighter design (the XP-56). The unconventional XP-56 arose from an innovative and open-ended U.S. Army Air Corps design requirement of 1940 intended to stimulate advanced concepts from American fighter designers. Northrop enthusiastically delegated the flying wing layout to his proposal to meet this official requirement. The resulting XP-56 flying wing had no real tailplane, the actions of a conventional aircraft's elevators being performed on the XP-56 by elevons in the wing trailing edges. The XP-56 was intended to be powered by an equally innovative new engine, the Pratt & Whitney X-1800 liquid-cooled inline engine of H-configuration. This power plant was eventually abandoned, so the XP-56 was re-engined with a specially-modified R-2800 Double Wasp radial engine buried inside the aircraft's fuselage pod with complicated cooling installed and a contra-rotating propeller assembly to use the output of the powerful engine. The first prototype XP-56 made its initial flight on 30 September 1943 (some historians claim 6 September), but was found to have handling problems and was later wrecked when it turned over on the ground. The much-modified second prototype flew in March 1944, but was similarly unsatisfactory and its testing was never completed. It failed to out-pace its contemporary conventional production piston-engined American fighters such as the North American P-51 Mustang, and the coming of jet power rendered its

Unconventional due to its tail-less flying wing layout and magnesium construction – plus other odd features – the Northrop XP-56 was named Black Bullet by Northrop for unknown reasons. This is the second prototype.

The left-hand photograph shows the first prototype Northrop XP-56, the right-hand picture illustrates the second prototype with its revised vertical surfaces and other alterations (Photos: U.S. Army Air Force).

unconventional layout of little purpose. Nevertheless, Northrop subsequently had more success with flying wing jet bombers, as described later in this book.

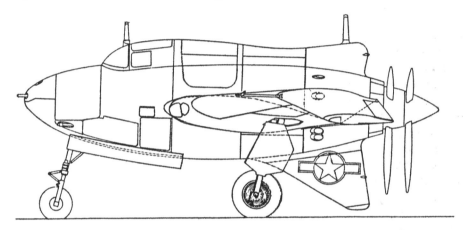

Only two examples of the Northrop XP-56 were built. This drawing shows the first prototype.

Specifications – Northrop XP-56 Black Bullet (Second Prototype)

Wingspan	42 ft 6 in
Length	27 ft 6 in
Maximum speed (intended)	465 mph at 25,000 ft
Maximum take-off weight	12,145 lb
Range	c. 660 miles
Service ceiling (intended)	33,000 ft
Armament (intended	Two 0.787 in (20 mm) cannons plus machine guns in the fuselage nose
Engine	One Pratt & Whitney R-2800-29 Double Wasp radial piston engine, of 2,000 hp
Crew	One

Bell 47

It took a long time for successful and safe helicopters to be developed. This was eventually achieved some time after the successful creation of man-carrying aircraft, and important aspects of the long and difficult helicopter development story are related to in the first Volume of *The Complete Encyclopedia of Flight*. By the end of World War Two, a number of helicopter types had been produced in modest numbers and were starting to prove the worth of helicopters. It was in the period after World War Two that the helicopter literally 'took off,' however, both in capability and in widespread manufacture and service. Several companies such as Sikorsky and Bell in the United States emerged in the post-war years amongst the leaders in the helicopter field. Sikorsky was one of the pioneers in helicopter development, while Bell had a pedigree in producing warplanes – including the P-59 Airacomet early jet fighter (see pages 32 to 33). During 1943 Bell started to move into the helicopter business by developing the Model 30, a rudimentary but basically sound helicopter design that was to lead to great things. The Model 30 did not enter widespread production, but it taught Bell many lessons. On 8 December 1945 was the first flight of a true world-beater, the Model 47 helicopter. This was to grow into the world's first widely-produced helicopter, one of the first to see widespread military service, and the first to be manufactured in large numbers for private customers. It was the first helicopter type to gain a civil Approved Type Certificate in America, and military interest in the Model 47 ensured its worldwide service for many different air arms. The U.S. Army Air Force initially ordered a batch as the YR-13 in 1947, but it is as the H-13 that the Model 47 is best known. Early examples, as the HTL-1, also served with the U.S. Navy. The U.S. Army saw the type's great potential and used H-13s extensively for observation, liaison, and training. Famously, some were employed in the Korean War of 1950 to 1953 as medevac (medical evacuation) helicopters – these were later immortalised in the popular television drama series M*A*S*H*. The Model 47 was built in a large number of versions and sub-types, the Model 47G series being the best of the later developments, and Bell's own manufacture lasted until 1973/1974. By then licence-production had taken place elsewhere. The first Agusta-Bell example flew in Italy in 1954, and the type was also built in Japan, and in

A large number of military users have flown the Bell 47 in various different versions. This is U.S. Army-operated H-13 series example.

The Bell 47 was an outstanding helicopter that saw widespread production and service. A later production Model 47G-series example is shown here (Photo: Bell Helicopter Textron).

Britain by Westland. The British examples, of which at least 231 were Westland-manufactured, were named Sioux and flew with Britain's Army Air Corps. Well over five thousand (possibly more than six thousand) Bell 47 of all types by all manufacturers were built. The type continues to fly in several countries, although numbers are now dwindling of this famous early helicopter.

Specifications – Bell 47G-5A

Main Rotor Diameter	37 ft 1.5 in
Fuselage Length	31 ft 7 in
Maximum speed	105 mph at sea level
Maximum take-off weight	2,850 lb
Range	256 miles
Service ceiling	10,500 ft
Engine	One Lycoming VO-435-B1A inline piston engine, of 265 hp
Accommodation	One pilot, two passengers

Vickers-Supermarine Seagull

An unfortunate aspect of Britain's once very large aircraft industry was its ability to sometimes go down blind alleys that turned out to be developmental and commercial dead-ends. As described elsewhere in this book, many innovative designs, prototypes, development and research aircraft were built and flown in Britain following World War Two – but many of these did not lead to long-lasting successful production aircraft. One of these less than auspicious types was the Supermarine Seagull amphibian. During World War Two some excellent service had been performed by the Vickers-Supermarine Walrus amphibious flying-boat for Britain's Royal Navy and Royal Air Force, especially in picking up downed Allied airmen from the sea. The Walrus was a biplane amphibian, configured with a pusher engine layout. Its potential replacement, the biplane Supermarine Sea Otter, retained this general configuration (aside from its more conventional tractor engine layout), but did not

replace very successfully the redoubtable Walrus and was not as successful. In the early part of the Second World War, the Specification S.12/40 was issued by Britain's Air Ministry for a more modern replacement for these types, able to perform ship-borne reconnaissance and rescue missions for the Royal Navy. Supermarine's design to this Specification was eventually built as the Type 381 Seagull, with a streamlined monoplane amphibian layout and some unusual features. One of these was its high-set monoplane wing, the incidence of which could be altered. This was an unusual innovation that is little used in aircraft design, although it allowed the Seagull to have a level fuselage when making its landing approach (and so gave the pilot a good view forward) rather than the somewhat nose-high landing attitude of most aircraft. Three prototypes were ordered to the revised Specification S.14/44, although only two were completed. The first of these initially flew

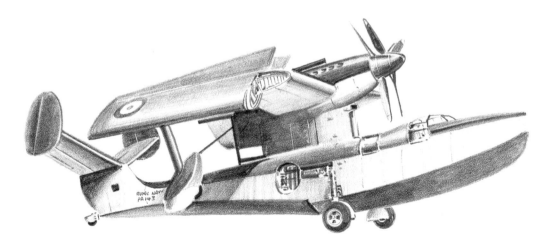

Of unconventional design but nicely streamlined, the Supermarine Seagull had folding-wings for its originally-intended ship-borne reconnaissance role. It was later diverted to land-based general utility and particularly SAR duties, for which it was unsuitable.

in the summer of 1948. Eventually the role of the Seagull was altered from fleet ship-based reconnaissance to land (or water)-based Search and Rescue (SAR), the old wartime air-sea rescue, but the type's fuselage was far too cramped for this task. Unfortunately the Seagull was also found during flight testing to suffer important problems, including some handling difficulties when landing in windy conditions, a tendency to skip during water landings, and an inability to turn at all in the water when it was windy. The Seagull was eventually cancelled, and its final intended role of SAR was later assumed by helicopters such as (in later years) the Westland Wessex. An American equivalent of the Seagull was the Grumman Albatross (see pages 120 to 121), which was more conventional in design and layout, and far more successful.

The Supermarine Seagull was an amphibian (a flying-boat with a retractable conventional land undercarriage), and had contra-rotating propellers to use the considerable power of its Griffon engine with a small propeller diameter.

Specifications – Vickers-Supermarine Seagull
(prototype layout, intended production performance)

Wingspan	52 ft 6 in
Length	44 ft 1.5 in
Maximum speed	260 mph at 11,800 ft
Maximum take-off weight	14,500 lb
Range	875 miles plus
Service ceiling	23,700 ft
Engine	One Rolls-Royce Griffon 29 inline piston engine, of 1,815-2,055 hp
Crew	Two or three

Bell X-1

There are a number of landmark events in the history of aviation that helped to significantly push forward the boundaries of what is achievable and safe. One of these was the successful passing through what had become known as the 'sound barrier.' As pointed out on pages 24 to 25, the advent of jet propulsion and the expanding understanding of aerodynamics for high-speed flight raised the possibility of increasing performance capabilities for military and civil aircraft. As potential speeds increased, so the mythical 'sound barrier' was more and more likely to be encountered. For a time this so-called barrier was feared to be a highly dangerous point that aircraft could not safely pass on their way into supersonic flight. Although Britain had the possibility of breaking the sound barrier first, with the Miles M.52 project which was instead cancelled, it was the United States that eventually achieved the goal of supersonic flight. However, this achievement was managed with a small, air-dropped, rocket-powered research aircraft called the X-1, but it nevertheless taught a lot about what was needed for con-

ventional jet-powered aircraft so that they too could safely achieve supersonic speeds. The task of building the X-1 was contracted to Bell, which had already become involved in other important programs like the P-59 Airacomet (see pages 32 to 33) and which later became a major helicopter manufacturer. Design of the Bell X-1 (originally called the XS-1) had inputs from several agencies including the important research body the National Advisory Committee for Aeronautics (NACA, nowadays the well-known NASA). The X-1 design involved a bullet-shaped fuselage (bullets after all fly very fast), but otherwise it had various conventional features like a straight-wing. It was designed to be air dropped from a specially-converted Boeing B-29 Superfortress bomber 'mother ship,' then its liquid-fuel rocket motor started, followed by a fast run to supersonic speed or beyond. The program commenced in earnest during early 1945, and three X-1 were ordered.

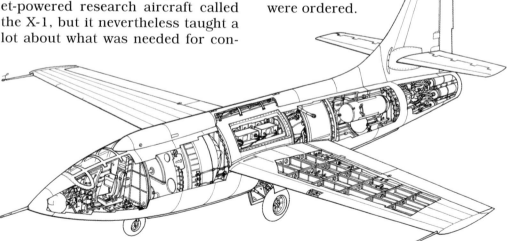

Despite their ground-breaking achievements, the Bell X-1 series aircraft were quite straightforward in design and construction. The rocket motor was housed in the rear fuselage.

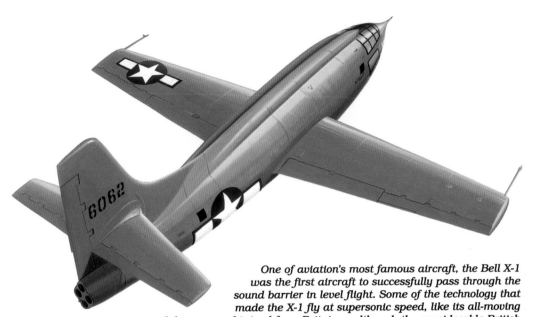

One of aviation's most famous aircraft, the Bell X-1 was the first aircraft to successfully pass through the sound barrier in level flight. Some of the technology that made the X-1 fly at supersonic speed, like its all-moving tailplane, was obtained from Britain – although the considerable British help with this program has never been acknowledged by the Americans.

The first made its initial, un-powered drop from its 'mother ship' in January 1946. After a number of test and proving flights, the historic sound barrier-breaking flight was made with rocket-power on 14 October 1947. The X-1 involved reached Mach 1.015 on that flight, its pilot being American fighter pilot Charles 'Chuck' Yeager. Continuing testing led to the construction of three slightly modified additional aircraft, and the small test fleet pushed speeds and altitudes

onwards and upwards – in December 1953, for example, one of the later aircraft reached well over Mach 2. None of these speeds, however, were official aircraft speed records, because the X-1 series were air-dropped rather than taking-off from land. The X-1 was the first in a series of famous American 'X-Planes' that subsequently explored many of the boundaries of the attainable in aviation – see also pages 154 to 155.

Specifications – Bell X-1

Wingspan	28 ft
Length	31 ft
Important flight speed	Mach 1.015 (on 14 October 1947)
Maximum launch weight	approximately 13,400 lb
Engine	One Reaction Motors XLR-11-series liquid-fuel rocket motor, of some 6,000 lb st
Crew	One

French Experimentals

The liberation of France from German occupation in the latter stages of World War Two allowed the French aircraft industry the chance to recover and rebuild itself after four years of German domination. Historically, during the First World War era and well into the inter-war period France had been fortunate to have one of the largest and most important aircraft industries in the world. Sadly a number of factors, including nationalisation during the later 1930s, had led to this once great industry being poorly-equipped to re-arm the French air force in time for the Second World War. German domination of the French factories from 1940 to 1944 after France's defeat subsequently did nothing to further the French aeronautical tradition. However, the period after 1944/1945 saw a very vibrant aircraft industry reborn in France, and many parts of this significant enterprise exist to this day. In the post-war period France became one of the countries in which the potential of jet propulsion was fully explored, togeth-er with the associated advances in aircraft design and aerodynamics as well as other sources of power such as ramjets and rockets. Although the development of indigenous jet engines was slow in France, many futuristic experimental aircraft were built by a variety of companies. Some of these were important in pushing forward supersonic aircraft design and performance. France's first turbojet-powered aircraft was the Sud-Ouest Triton (initially powered by a World War Two-era German turbojet, later by a British engine), which first flew in 1946. The supersonic mixed-powerplant (jet and rocket) Sud-Ouest Trident broke several world records in the later 1950s and almost led to a production series, the same being true for the Mach 2-capable mixed-powerplant Nord Griffon. Both of these types lost out to the Dassault Mirage (see pages 182 to 183) for production orders. The most radical of France's dynamic experimental post-war jets was the Leduc ramjet series. The brainchild of ramjet pioneer René

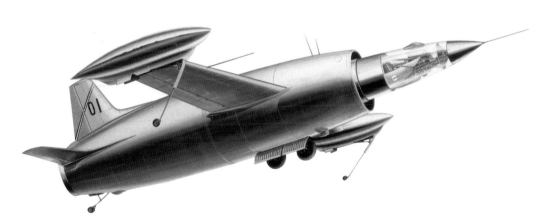

The Leduc 021 was an amazing, space-age design reminiscent of the futuristic flying machines in comic-books of that era. Its intrepid pilot was positioned in the clear-glazed pointed cone that protruded from the front of the main fuselage.

The Leduc was carried aloft to its launching altitude above a specially-configured Sud-Est Languedoc radial-engined transport. The Leduc 021 No.01 is seen here above the Languedoc registered F-ZLAV while being prepared for a show-stopping flight demonstration at the Paris air show of 1955 (Photo: Musée de l'Air).

Leduc, these amazing craft were built in several distinct series (the 010, 021, and 022). Each of the several examples constructed featured a cylindrical fuselage housing the fuel injectors and burners for the simple ramjet layout, plus a small turbojet to give airflow to light the whole contraption. This simple but effective arrangement worked comparatively well, but has nevertheless received little interest from aircraft designers subsequent to the 1960s. The early Leducs were designed to be air-launched from a flying launch platform (a converted Sud-Est Languedoc transport aircraft), landing back on their home airfields on small retractable undercarriage components. The initial Leduc 010 flew on its ramjet power on 21 April 1949, arguably the first aircraft ever to fly with ramjet propulsion in this configuration. The more refined Leduc 021 first flew in 1953, and the Mach 2-capable Leduc 022 flew in 1956. The latter could have led to a very high-performance operational point-defence interceptor, but defence cutbacks led to the cancellation of the whole program in the later 1950s.

Specifications – Leduc 021

Wingspan	38 ft 1 in
Length	41 ft 1 in
Maximum speed	Mach 0.85
Maximum take-off weight	13,228 lb
Endurance	15 minutes to one hour
Service ceiling	65,000 ft
Engine	One Leduc ramjet (thermo-propulsive fuselage construction), of some 13,200 lb st (started by one Turboméca Artouste turbojet engine)
Crew	One

Douglas DC-6 and DC-7

The World War Two period saw a large increase in the need for long-range transport aircraft. Fortunately, during the 1930s the range capabilities of airliners had increased considerably, and one of several major companies involved in commercial aircraft production was the famous Douglas Aircraft Company of Santa Monica, California. Douglas is well-known for its civil as well as military aircraft designs, and prior to World War Two it created the famous twin-engined DC-3 airliner (the military C-47 Dakota/Skytrain of World War Two fame), as well as the longer-range and larger four-engined DC-4. Both of these aircraft are covered in the second Volume of *The Complete Encyclopedia of Flight*. The DC-4 was a successful military transport as the C-54 (R5D to the U.S. Navy), and also went into civil airline service after World War Two. Douglas, however, improved the unpressurised DC-4 to meet the likely growing immediate post-war demand for long-range civil transports. The

result was the DC-6, which became one of the classic piston-engined transports of the 1950s. The type was at first developed as a military transport, and was initially flown on 15 February 1946 as the XC-112A for the U.S. Army Air Force. The ending of World War Two, however, reduced the need for large numbers of military transports, and the C-112 layout was instead successfully developed for civil operations. The resulting DC-6 had a new, lengthened and pressurised fuselage compared to the DC-4, plus other changes. Interest from major airlines was considerable, and the type's first commercial service was flown by American Airlines in April 1947. Further development led to the longer-fuselage and more powerful DC-6A cargo version and the DC-6B passenger carrier. The DC-6B first flew in February 1951, and production totalled some 288 with manufacture ending in late 1958. The type combined reliability with comparatively low operating costs, and further develop-

The Douglas DC-6 served comparatively widely as a military transport, in addition to its civilian operations. Illustrated is a U.S. Air Force C-118A Liftmaster, the type was also used by the U.S. Navy as the R6D.

ment resulted in a convertible passenger/freight model called the DC-6C. DC-6 derivatives also served with the U.S.A.F. as the C-118A, and the U.S. Navy as the R6D, 166 being built. The DC-6 was a direct competitor with the Lockheed Constellation (see pages 64 to 65), and in 1951 American Airlines approached Douglas for an improved DC-6 to counter Lockheed's then-new Super Constellation development. Douglas therefore further lengthened and altered the DC-6's fuselage, and introduced Wright R-3350-series Turbo-Compound Duplex Cyclone engines for more power. The result was the DC-7, which first flew on 18 May 1953. The initial DC-7 was followed by the longer-range DC-7B. The final derivative was the DC-7C, with increased range for intercontinental operations (the famous 'Seven Seas' airliner). The type first flew on 20 December 1955, and some 120 were built up to 1958. Like the Constellation, DC-6 and DC-7 examples flew with many small airlines (sometimes as pure freighters) after being replaced by jet airliners in the major airlines. Approximately 1,041 of all marks were built.

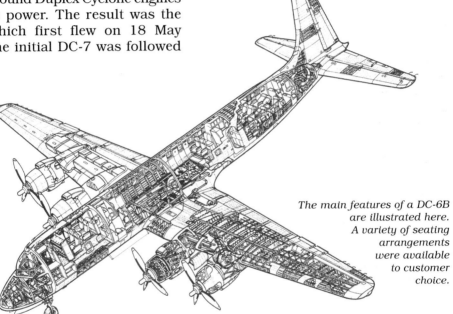

The main features of a DC-6B are illustrated here. A variety of seating arrangements were available to customer choice.

Specifications – Douglas DC-6B

Wingspan	117 ft 6 in
Length	105 ft 7 in
Cruising speed	315 mph at over 20,000 ft
Maximum take-off weight	107,000 lb
Range	3,005 miles
Service ceiling	25,000 ft
Engine	Four Pratt & Whitney R-2800-CB17 Double Wasp radial piston engines, of 2,500 hp each
Accommodation	Three or four crew plus stewards/stewardesses, 54 passengers (over 80 in some seating arrangements)

Lockheed P-80 (F-80) Shooting Star

The Lockheed P-80 (F-80 from 1948) Shooting Star was the first successful American jet fighter, following on from the less successful Bell P-59 Airacomet (see pages 32 to 33). The prototype XP-80 was produced in only 143 days following the initial U.S. Army Air Force order for the type. It was powered by a British centrifugal flow turbojet of Halford type – another example of British jet technology being used by the Americans. The prototype XP-80 made its first flight in January 1944. By VE-Day (the end of World War Two in Europe, in May 1945) two YP-80As were in Italy being readied for combat missions, another pair were under test in England and 12 others were flying – but none saw combat in World War Two. Development continued post-war, resulting in the P-80A, P-80B and C-models, powered by an Allison J33 turbojet (or General Elec-

tric-built J33 in some examples). A reconnaissance version was built as the F-14A (later FP-80A or RF-80A). A specially-configured one-off XP-80R set a world speed record of over 623 mph (1,003 km/h) at Muroc Dry Lake, California, in the summer of 1947. Production of single-seat versions was probably 1,714 (some historians quote different figures, including 1,639). A two-seat trainer developed as the TF-80C entered production as the T-33, later forming the basis of the two-seat F-94 Starfire all-weather interceptor and T2V SeaStar two-seat naval trainer. The T-33 became one of the world's classic two-seat early jet trainers, well over five thousand being built by Lockheed plus 210 in Japan and 656 in Canada by Canadair. The U.S. Navy also flew 50 single-seat F-80Cs as TO-1 (later TV-1) advanced

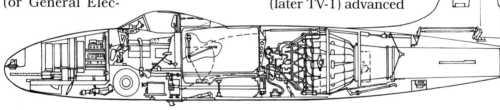

A cutaway side view of a Lockheed F-80 Shooting Star.

A Lockheed F-80B Shooting Star of the 94th Fighter Squadron, U.S. Air Force, wearing high-visibility markings while deployed to Alaska.

52

A photograph of a preserved Lockheed T-33 two-seat trainer in the United States (Photo: John Batchelor).

trainers. Shooting Stars provided the U.S. Air Force's fighter community with its initial jet experience, several squadrons flying the type in the Continental U.S., Alaska and Japan by the late 1940s. When North Korean forces crossed into South Korea in 1950, one of the first American types to be committed to what became the Korean War was the F-80. Shooting Stars proved to be effective against North Korean piston-engined aircraft, but when China entered the conflict – equipped with the MiG-15 (see pages 58 to 59) – it was outclassed as a fighter and was switched to the ground attack role. Nevertheless, F-80s also scored important air-to-air successes – Lieutenant Russell Brown was credited with destroying a MiG-15 in the world's first-ever jet-against-jet air combat victory, in an F-80C during November 1950. Soon replaced in the U.S. Air Force, the F-80C survived in the Air National Guard until 1958, while reconnaissance RF-80As and QF-80 target drones soldiered on some time after. F-80s were supplied under U.S. military assistance arrangements to several South American countries.

Specifications – Lockheed F-80C Shooting Star

Wingspan	38 ft 9 in
Length	34 ft 5 in
Maximum speed	601 mph at sea level
Maximum take-off weight	16,856 lb
Range	825 miles
Service ceiling	46,800 ft
Armament	Six 0.5 in (12.7 mm) machine guns in the lower nose, provision for two underwing bombs of up to 1,000 lb or eight 5 in unguided rockets
Engine	One Allison J33-A-35 turbojet engine, of 5,400 lb st
Crew	One

Westland Wyvern

Although the turboprop engine has been much used since the 1950s for smaller civil transport aircraft, some military transports and aircraft such as long-range patrol types, it has rarely been used as the power plant for front-line combat aircraft. The few exceptions include the Westland Wyvern, a large naval strike aircraft of the 1950s. The Wyvern was also unusual for a turboprop-powered front-line aircraft by actually flying in combat, and it was additionally the last fixed-wing aircraft manufactured by Westland before this famous aviation company concentrated solely on helicopter design and manufacture (see pages 160 to 161). The Wyvern was developed from a 1944 requirement for a new attack aircraft, and at first both Britain's Royal Air Force and Royal Navy were interested in the resulting Westland design studies. Eventually, however, the Wyvern developed solely as a naval strike

aircraft around Specification N.11/44, and the first prototype initially flew in December 1946. It was powered by a Rolls-Royce Eagle inline piston engine of H-configuration. This new power plant was intended for production Wyverns, but the Royal Navy's interest in the new technology of jet engines and turboprops (the latter being a hybrid jet-type engine driving a propeller or propellers) resulted in Rolls-Royce abandoning the Eagle piston engine (which only ever flew in early Wyverns). Instead Rolls-Royce concentrated on developing two turboprop engines for the Wyvern, the Clyde and the Python. The initial Clyde-powered Wyvern first flew in January 1949, but this engine too was discontinued. Wyvern development instead concentrated on the Python-powered version, and this was eventually built as the Wyvern S.Mk.4. The first Python-engined Wyvern flew in March 1949, but a large amount of devel-

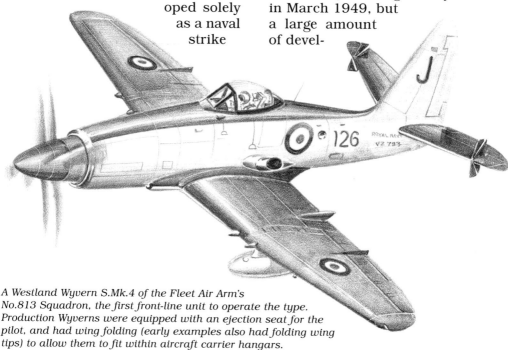

A Westland Wyvern S.Mk.4 of the Fleet Air Arm's No.813 Squadron, the first front-line unit to operate the type. Production Wyverns were equipped with an ejection seat for the pilot, and had wing folding (early examples also had folding wing tips) to allow them to fit within aircraft carrier hangars.

54

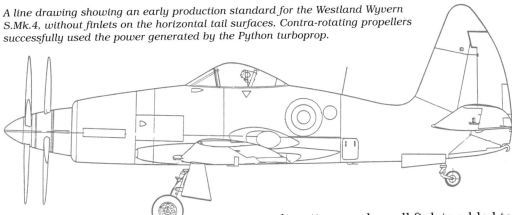

A line drawing showing an early production standard for the Westland Wyvern S.Mk.4, without finlets on the horizontal tail surfaces. Contra-rotating propellers successfully used the power generated by the Python turboprop.

opment work was needed with this engine as it sometimes suffered from sudden surges in power as well as other difficulties. Some re-design of the Wyvern was also needed for the engine to be installed successfully – the S.4 production model looked very different to the original Eagle-powered prototype when it entered production. Eventually 94 production Wyvern S.4 were manufactured (including seven Mk.2 pre-production aircraft brought up to S.4 standard). There were some differences between early and late production S.4 airframes (including cockpit canopy alterations and small finlets added to the horizontal tail), and some retrofitting of early production aircraft to the later standards. The first Royal Navy front-line unit to operate the Wyvern was the Fleet Air Arm's No.813 Naval Air Squadron during 1953/ /1954. Wyverns of No.830 Squadron on the aircraft carrier H.M.S. Eagle successfully flew strike missions during the Anglo-French Suez operations of October/November 1956 against Egyptian targets. Eventually, the final Wyverns were withdrawn from Royal Navy service in 1958. A single two-seat Wyvern Mk.3 was constructed as a prototype for a planned trainer version, which did not enter production.

Specifications – Westland Wyvern S.Mk.4

Wingspan	44 ft
Length	42 ft 0.25 in
Maximum speed	380 mph at 10,000 ft
Maximum take-off weight	24,500 lb
Range	910 miles with external fuel tanks
Service ceiling	28,000 ft
Armament	Four wing-mounted 0.787 in (20 mm) cannons, one 2,500 lb torpedo beneath the fuselage or up to 16 unguided rockets beneath the wings
Engine	One Armstrong Siddeley Python 3 turboprop engine, of 3,670 shp
Crew	One

Ryan FR Fireball

The advent and development of the jet engine in the later 1930s and into the 1940s promised the possibility of enhanced performance capabilities for combat aircraft. In the short-term, however, various early jet engines were of comparatively limited performance and endurance compared to the powerful and efficient jet engines of today, and many early jet-powered aircraft offered performance levels hardly improved compared to those of the best piston-engined combat aircraft of that era. While engine designers worked to improve the power output and reliability of jet engines, several odd compromise aircraft were developed that combined jet and piston engine power in the same airframe. One of the best of these 'mixed power plant' aircraft was the Ryan FR Fireball, a piston engine and jet-powered fighter. Recognising the growing importance of jet power for future combat aircraft, but also realising the problems of early jet

propulsion to give enough power for operations from aircraft carriers, the U.S. Navy launched a program in 1942 to develop a mixed power plant carrier-borne aircraft. The competitor with the best proposals was eventually adjudged to be Ryan. This company was already world-famous for creating the one-off Ryan NYP, in which Charles Lindbergh was the first person to fly non-stop solo across the Atlantic Ocean in 1927 – as described in the first Volume of *The Complete Encyclopedia of Flight*. Ryan's winning mixed power plant proposal was a neat, tricycle undercarriage fighter with its piston engine conventionally-mounted in the nose, and the jet engine buried in the fuselage fed by air from large intakes at the wing roots and exhausting at the tail. This proved to be an effective combination, and folding wings were incorporated for aircraft carrier operations. The prototype XFR-1 first flew on 25 June 1944,

The Ryan FR-1 Fireball was an 'oddball' aircraft, with a jet engine in its fuselage in addition to a normal piston engine in its nose. Landings and cruise were normally made with the piston engine only providing the power, the jet engine being employed mainly for high-speed flight – although the FR-1 was not much faster than standard contemporary piston engine fighters.

A line-up of U.S. Navy Ryan FR-1 Fireballs, illustrating the folding-wing capability of these aircraft and the small jet outlet in the rear of the fuselage (Photo: U.S. Navy).

but only on the power of its radial piston engine (it flew on jet and piston engine power shortly after). Named Fireball, two versions were proposed of the FR-1 first production model, a day fighter (sometimes called FR-1D) and a radar-equipped night fighter FR-1N. Substantial production orders were planned, and the first unit to fly the Fireball, U.S. Navy fighter squadron VF-66, received its initial aircraft in the first half of 1945. The Fireball was not committed to combat, however, and the end of World War Two saw production orders drastically cut – only 66 FR-1 were eventually built. One was converted to FR-2 standard with a more powerful radial engine, and a derivative was the Ryan XF2R-1 (sometimes nicknamed 'Dark Shark,' but only one converted) with an early example of a turboprop engine installed in the nose instead of the Fireball's radial piston engine.

Specifications – Ryan FR-1 Fireball

Wingspan	40 ft
Length	32 ft 4 in
Maximum speed	426 mph at 18,100 ft
Maximum take-off weight	11,652 lb
Range	1,030 miles
Service ceiling	43,100 ft
Armament	Four wing-mounted 0.5 in (12.7 mm) machine guns, provision for underwing unguided rockets or bombs on some aircraft
Engine	One Wright R-1820-72W Cyclone radial piston engine, of 1,350-1,425 hp, and one General Electric I-16 (J31-GE-2 or -3) turbojet engine, of 1,600 lb st
Crew	One

Mikoyan-Gurevich MiG-15

One of the most famous jet fighters of all time, the Mikoyan-Gurevich MiG-15 also has arguably the greatest longevity in service of any jet combat aircraft – some examples remaining active in a small number of countries over fifty years after the type's first flight. The MiG-15 was a product of on-going research work in the Soviet Union into jet fighter development, with reference also to former German studies. Its swept-wing configuration and pressurised cockpit represented major advances in jet fighter technology which were matched in the West at the time only by the North American F-86 Sabre covered elsewhere in this book. The original machine was known as the I-310 or aircraft 'S,' and it first flew on 30 December 1947. It was powered by a British Rolls-Royce Nene turbojet engine, Britain having inexplicably sent a consignment of these secret engines to the Soviet Union which allowed Russian engineers to begin production and improvement of their own turbojets based on British technology. Testing of three prototypes led to design changes and

eventually a production go-ahead later in 1948, the first pre-production 'SV' aircraft flying in late 1948. Contrary to many Western published sources, the MiG-15 did not enter service in 1948. Initial pre-production examples were delivered in the summer of 1949, and the first operational aircraft entered Russian front-line service during the spring or summer of 1950. Russian work on the Nene turbojet led to the RD-45-series turbojet which powered the basic production MiG-15. Further development led to the Klimov VK-1 turbojet, and this was the powerplant for an improved development, the MiG-15bis. In fact the MiG-15 was built in a variety of related sub-types, and there was also a two-seat trainer derivative called the MiG-15UTI. The MiG-15 series operated with Soviet units and a very large number of export users, in the Warsaw Pact, and amongst states elsewhere that were friendly towards the Soviet Union. Licence production took place in Czechoslovakia as the S-102 (MiG-15), S-103 (MiG-15bis) and CS-102 (MiG-15UTI), in Poland as the

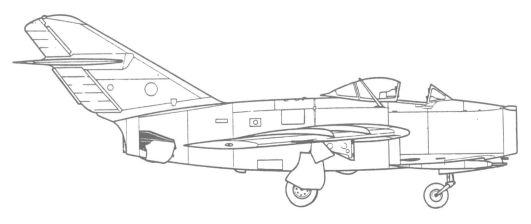

The Mikoyan-Gurevich MiG-15 was a very simple but effective fighter and, later, ground attack aircraft. It was subsonic in performance, featured all-metal construction, and was the first in a line of famous MiG combat aircraft, although it was not the first MiG jet design (see pages 28 to 29).

Many countries around the world that sided with the Soviet Union during the Cold War operated the MiG-15, including several Arab states. The single-seat MiG-15 versions were known to NATO by the uncomplimentary name 'Fagot,' and the MiG-15UTI as 'Midget.'

Lim-1 (MiG-15), Lim-2 (MiG-15bis), as well as two-seat versions, and in China principally as the Shenyang FT-2/JJ-2 (MiG-15UTI). The MiG-15 was operational in the Korean War from late 1950, initially with great success against U.S. forces but the balance was redressed by skilfully flown U.S. Air Force F-86 Sabres, which shot down many MiG-15s flown by North Korean and Chinese pilots – although experienced Soviet pilots fared rather better. MiG-15s also served with some Arab countries in conflict against Israel, and in other smaller wars and skirmishes elsewhere in the world. The exact number of MiG-15s that were built is impossible to verify with a lack of reliable Chinese figures, but otherwise some 8,500 from Soviet, Czech and Polish sources is a possible total.

Specifications – Aero S-103 (MiG-15bis)

Wingspan	33 ft 0.75 in
Length	33 ft 1.75 in
Maximum speed	668.5 mph at sea level
Maximum take-off weight	12,198 lb
Range	826.5 miles (without external fuel tanks)
Service ceiling	50,853 ft
Armament	One 1.456 in (37 mm) and two 0.9 in (23 mm) cannons in the lower forward-fuselage, various small bombs or unguided rockets below the wings
Engine	One Motorlet M-06 (Czech licence-built Klimov VK-1/VK-1A) turbojet engine, of 5,836 lb st
Crew	One

Short Sandringham and Solent

During World War Two one of Britain's most important maritime patrol and anti-submarine aircraft was the Short S.25 Sunderland flying-boat. The history of this famous aircraft is referred to in the second Volume of *The Complete Encyclopedia of Flight* covering the Second World War. The Sunderland was a military follow-on from the civil Short 'C' Class passenger flying-boats of the 1930s, which had served on long-range passenger routes within the former British Empire. During World War Two a need arose for several Sunderlands to be modified into passenger-carrying transports, and the relevant conversions were made from existing Sunderland Mk.III aircraft. Some were duly flown by Britain's international airline British Overseas Airways Corporation (BOAC), which continued to operate on war-related business during the war. The Sunderland conversions proved successful, even though most had rather spartan interiors for their passengers. Eventually many were brought together under the name Hythe to describe the class of flying-boats to which they belonged. For the longer term, the Sunderland's manufacturer Short Brothers identified a possible market post-war for Sunderlands converted into civil transports, and began to develop a civil Sunderland derivative that became the Sandringham. This work was encouraged by an order from Argentina late in World War Two for a handful of civil Sunderland conversions for passenger-carrying work. The first true Sandringham appeared in November 1945, and the aircraft converted to fulfil the Argentine order were finished to Sandringham Mk.2 (45 passenger) and Mk.3 (21 passenger) configurations. With gun turrets removed and faired over, smart and comfortable interiors installed and windows added in various additional locations on the tall fuselage sides, the Sandringhams were impressive aircraft in what was generally an era of post-war austerity. A variety of orders for Sandringhams duly followed, mainly from airlines in South America and the Australias. BOAC also eventually ordered 12 of two different marks, there finally being seven distinct Sandringham versions with various

A reminder of a by-gone age when graceful flying-boat airliners gave passengers a taste of luxury that is now long since just a memory, this Short Sandringham Mk.4 registered VP-LVE flew with a variety of operators world-wide – and survives today in the Southampton Hall of Aviation museum in southern England.

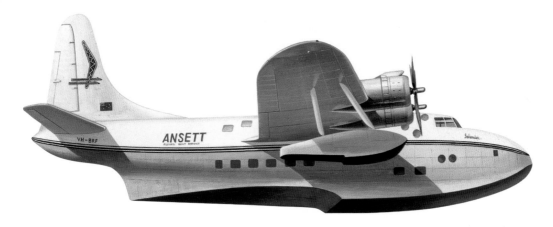

This drawing represents the Short Solent configuration.

seating and sleeper interiors. Some of the final Sandringhams in service soldiered on into the 1970s in Australia and the Virgin Islands, the type having flown literally world-wide for several airlines including service on the picturesque flying-boat routes across the South Pacific. All Sandringhams were converted from former Sunderlands, some being quite tired after service in World War Two. However, much newer was the Short Solent flying-boat airliner. This grew out of the military Short S.45 Seaford, which was built in small numbers for the R.A.F. and itself was developed from a revised, more powerful and heavily-armed Sunderland derivative, the Sunderland Mk.IV. The launch order was for 12 Solent Mk.2 for BOAC, the first of which flew on 1 December 1946. The Solent Mk.3 was several ex-military Seafords civilianised, four of these being delivered to BOAC. Four Solent Mk.4 were also built. Increasingly, however, flying-boats were superseded post-war by long-range land-based passenger aircraft, and no replacements for the Sandringhams and Solents were ever built.

Specifications – Short Sandringham Mk.5 (BOAC 'Plymouth' Class)

Wingspan	112 ft 9.5 in
Length	86 ft 3 in
Maximum speed	204 mph at 7,500 ft
Maximum take-off weight	60,000 lb
Range	2,450 miles
Service ceiling	17,900 ft
Engine	Four Pratt & Whitney R-1830-90C or similar Twin Wasp radial piston engines, of 1,200 hp each
Accommodation	Four or five crew, 22 day or 16 night passengers

de Havilland D.H.103 Hornet/Sea Hornet

The de Havilland Hornet was the ultimate development of the concept that produced the de Havilland D.H.98 Mosquito. The Mosquito was one of the outstanding warplanes of the Second World War, and is covered in the second volume of *The Complete Encyclopedia of Flight*. The Hornet was also one of the most beautiful of piston-engined fighters, and was well-liked by its pilots. Started as a private venture single-seat twin-engined strike fighter in 1942, Specification F.12/43 was written around the design in 1943 to cover prototype construction for Britain's Royal Air Force. The first flight was made on 28 July 1944, and the type soon proved to be faster than even the early Gloster Meteor jet fighters. Ordered for service use in the Pacific, the Second World War was over by the time the first of 60 production Hornet F.Mk.1s was delivered to an operational unit in early 1946.

Directional stability was improved by adding a dorsal fillet to the fin to produce the F.Mk.3, the most widely-produced version. Fuel capacity was also increased in the Mk.3, and it was capable of carrying two bombs or eight rocket projectiles under the wings. The Mk.3 was followed by the F.Mk.4, which had a camera installed in the fuselage, but only 12 were produced. The Mk.3 additionally served as the basis for the Sea Hornet, which was developed to Specification N.5/44 as a carrier-based fighter. The first Sea Hornet (a converted Hornet F.Mk.1) flew on 19 April 1945, and was followed by several more prototypes and some 78 production Sea Hornet F.Mk.20s. A two-seat night fighter variant was also developed for the Royal Navy, the Sea Hornet NF.Mk.21, with an ASH radar 'thimble' installation in its nose. Photo reconnaissance versions of both the Hornet (PR.Mk.2)

The de Havilland Hornet was a very elegant aircraft that was well-liked by its pilots, both in the R.A.F. and those who flew the Royal Navy's Sea Hornets. This Hornet wears the fuselage code letters of No.64 (Fighter) Squadron, R.A.F.

Sea Hornet F.Mk.20s from the naval air station at Hal Far, Malta (Photo: Fleet Air Arm Museum).

and Sea Hornet (PR.Mk.22) were built for the RAF and Royal Navy respectively. A total of 200 Hornets and 181 Sea Hornets (plus seven conversions from Hornets) appear to have been built. Hornets served with several squadrons of the R.A.F.'s Fighter Command between early 1946 and early 1951, and with three squadrons in the Far East from 1951 until early 1955. This represented the R.A.F.'s last piston-engined front-line fighter service, marking the end of a very significant era. Far East Hornet squadrons were used operationally against Communist insurgents in Malaya, making strafing and rocket attacks on their suspected hideouts. Sea Hornets were fully aircraft carrier-compatible, with arrester hooks and folding wings, and they served with several front-line and second-line Fleet Air Arm units between 1946//1947 and 1955, but without seeing combat service.

Specifications – de Havilland Hornet F.Mk.3

Wingspan	45 ft
Length	36 ft 8 in
Maximum speed	472 mph at 22,000 ft
Maximum take-off weight	19,550 lb
Range	3,000 miles with maximum fuel
Service ceiling	35,000 ft
Armament	Four 0.787 in (20 mm) cannons in the nose, two 1,000 lb bombs or eight 60 lb unguided rocket projectiles beneath the wings
Engine	One Rolls-Royce Merlin 130 (left-hand) and one Merlin 131 (right-hand) inline piston engines, of 2,070 hp each
Crew	One

Lockheed Constellation

The Constellation was one of the world's classic civil and military transports. Its history goes back to before America's entry into World War Two, when the famous millionaire Howard Hughes ordered a new high-performance airliner from Lockheed for TWA (Transcontinental and Western Air, later Trans World Airlines). Hughes was an owner of TWA, and the deal was later matched by rival airline Pan Am. The initial flight of the first aircraft was on 9 January 1943. However, the onset of war had by then seen the project taken over by the U.S. Army Air Force as the C-69 Constellation, of which 14 or 15 were built as such of 22 intended. With the end of the war, the civil Constellation program was re-launched, at first with ex-military C-69s then leading to 66 related commercial L-049s. The first of these entered TWA service in November 1945, and commercial operations started in February 1946. The post-war L-649 made its first flight in October 1946 with more powerful examples of the Wright Duplex Cyclone radial engine series used on all production Constellations. Eastern Air Lines ordered 14 before the L-649 was replaced by the L-749, which had increased fuel capacity. The L-749A followed with a larger payload and a strengthened wing, center section and undercarriage, South African Airways becoming the first operator in 1950. Just over 120 L-749/749As were purchased by commercial operators. A fuselage stretch and other modifications created the L-1049 Super Constellation for 71 to 90 plus passengers, in place of the shorter Constellations' 46 to 60 plus. The prototype L-1049 first flew on 13 October 1950, and the type was powered by a turbo-supercharged version of the Wright Duplex Cyclone piston engine. TWA placed the L-1049 into service in late 1951. The L-1049C introduced further up-rated Wright Duplex Cyclones, while the L-1049G (the famous 'Super G') and L-1049H (a cargo or passenger model) used more powerful variants and had wing-tip fuel tanks. The final civil Super Constellation was the L-1649A Starliner, which mated the L-1049G's fuselage with a new long-span wing. Forty-four Starliners (out of a total of 856 Constellations) were built, initially for TWA, Air France and Lufthansa. Most major airline-operated Super Constellations were eventually retired and

The Lockheed Constellation was a major leap forward in civil aviation when it was created, introducing high performance with pressurised comfort. This example is a TWA L-1049 series Constellation, capable of flying the North Atlantic non-stop.

The warning written on the large propeller blades of this preserved military-painted Constellation in the United States says 'Do Not Touch' – something that you would certainly not want to do if the blades were turning! (Photo: John Batchelor).

replaced by jets, but the type continued with some smaller operators or as cargo conversions. The U.S. Air Force ultimately became a major Constellation customer, acquiring L-749A equivalents as C-121As and L-1049 equivalents as C-121Cs, followed by the RC-121C and RC-121D radar-equipped airborne early warning (AEW) aircraft with dorsal and ventral radomes. After testing two PO-1W AEW versions of the L-749, the U.S. Navy acquired the WV-2 (PO-2W) Warning Star (EC-121K post-1962) based on the L-1049 and the R7V-1 transport. Small numbers of numerous other C-121 variants served with the U.S.A.F., U.S. Navy, and even the U.S. Army, including several classified electronic intelligence-gathering examples. Some served in the Vietnam War under various special programs. The final U.S. military Constellation was retired in 1982.

Specifications – Lockheed L-1049G Super Constellation

Wingspan	126 ft 2 in (with wingtip fuel tanks)
Length	116 ft 2 in
Cruising speed	354 mph at 22,600 ft
Maximum take-off weight	137,500 lb
Range	approximately 3,000 miles
Service ceiling	27,300 ft
Engine	Four Wright R-3350-DA-3 Turbo-Compound Duplex Cyclone radial piston engines, of 3,250 hp each
Accommodation	Five flight crew plus stewards/stewardesses, up to 95 passengers

de Havilland D.H.108

The rapid pace of technological development in aviation design and propulsion during the Second World War and post-World War Two periods saw the creation of many impressive aircraft types. Unfortunately, some of these aircraft were perhaps ahead of their time, or simply somewhat dangerous because of the new and unknown frontiers that they were extending towards. In Britain, which as we have seen on other pages in this book was one of the countries that was involved in this type of research, one especially innovative but unfortunately also rather hazardous aircraft was the de Havilland D.H.108. Three examples were built, and all three crashed, killing their pilots. During World War Two in Britain the deliberations of the forward-looking Brabazon Committee had led to proposals for a post-war turbojet-powered airliner, and these developed into the de Havilland Comet civil transport (see pages 104 to 105). In the early stages of its design, the Comet was planned as a radical, tail-less design. This arrangement was comparatively new and unknown, although the Nazi German aircraft industry in World War Two had examined such a concept amongst its many advanced deliberations. The de Havilland company therefore developed to official Specification E.18/45 the de Havilland D.H.108 – sometimes called Swallow – as a research aircraft to explore the tail-less, swept-wing layout for the Comet. Ironically, the Comet was later re-designed into a straightforward and conventional design layout. Nevertheless the D.H.108 went ahead, as a research tool for investigation into the advanced swept-wing tail-less layout possibly for other aircraft types. The first two D.H.108 utilised fuselages taken from the production line of the de Havilland Vampire F.Mk.1 (see pages 36 to 37), mated to a new, swept wing. The first aircraft was intended for low-speed research, and initially flew on 15 May 1946. The second example was intended for high-speed research with a slightly different wing layout, and first flew several weeks

Serial number VW120 was the third de Havilland D.H.108, and it was the first British aircraft to officially break the 'sound barrier,' in September 1948. Unfortunately it crashed in 1950, killing its pilot.

The first de Havilland D.H.108 was serial number TG283, built to research the slow-speed characteristics of the radical tail-less swept-wing design layout and fitted with fixed and prominent wing leading edge slats (Photo: de Havilland).

later – but crashed in September 1946 killing its pilot, Geoffrey de Havilland Junior. It was replaced by a third D.H.108, using the fuselage of a Vampire F.Mk.5, and this initially flew in July 1947. On 9 September 1948 it became the first British aircraft to officially break the 'sound barrier,' but it later crashed in 1950 as did the original aircraft. The three Swallows nonetheless performed useful research, but by that time the Americans were already gaining a big lead over British manufacturers in high-performance swept-wing combat aircraft design. As described on pages 46 to 47, the Americans had been able to successfully fly the Bell X-1 at supersonic speed during October 1947, and from then onwards the American aircraft industry started to gain a considerable advantage over the aircraft designers and builders in other countries.

Specifications – de Havilland D.H.108 (second prototype – some data provisional)

Wingspan	39 ft
Length	24 ft 6 in
Maximum speed	approximately 640 mph
Maximum take-off weight	8,960 lb
Engine	One de Havilland Goblin 3 turbojet engine, of 3,000-3,300 lb st
Crew	One

Douglas AD/A-1 Skyraider

Too late to see action in World War Two, the 'Able Dog' (a name derived from its U.S. Navy AD designation) went on to make a major contribution to the United Nations campaign in the Korean War. It also served with distinction in the American involvement in Southeast Asia, where it was additionally flown by the U.S. Air Force as well as the South Vietnamese Air Force. During the Vietnam War, Skyraiders escorted rescue helicopters to pick-up downed aircrew, occasionally themselves being landed to pick up a fellow pilot. On 20 June 1965 two U.S. Navy Skyraiders from U.S.S. Midway successfully shot down a North Vietnamese MiG-17, another rare example of a piston-engined aircraft shooting down a jet fighter. While the U.S. Navy ceased its Skyraider operations in 1968, U.S. Air Force 'Spads' served until well into the 1970s. Skyraiders were also used in combat by the French in Algeria and probably also by

Chad's forces. Able to fly for up to ten hours with a large load of munitions on up to 15 hardpoints, the Skyraider proved itself to be a versatile and dependable warplane. Having been designed as a rugged attack aircraft, Skyraider variants were also developed for the tactical nuclear bomber, anti-submarine search, airborne early warning, ECM, and target-towing roles, as well as specialized night attack. Created by the famous American designer Ed Heinemann, the prototype Skyraider was the XBT2D-1 which first flew on 18 March 1945. Initial production models were the AD-1 to AD-4 with various detail differences. These were single-seaters, but the AD-5 featured a side-by-side two-seat cockpit arrangement that was designed to combine submarine hunter/killer roles in one airframe. Several kits were also developed to allow the AD-5 (redesignated A-1E from 1962) to be used for transport,

Even in an age that was becoming increasingly dominated by jet aircraft, the piston-engined Douglas AD Skyraider was a potent and very capable warplane. With its arrester hook down, this example attempts a landing aboard its aircraft carrier.

Like most aircraft carrier-based combat aircraft, the AD Skyraider had folding wings. The artist tells us that this example served with U.S. Navy attack squadron VA-194 aboard the aircraft carrier U.S.S. Valley Forge during the Korean War, and was an AD-4 version.

target-towing and photo-reconnaissance tasks as well as attack duties. The night attack-capable AD-5N (later A-1G) followed, but the major production version was the AD-6 (A-1H) equipped for accurate low-level bombing duties. The final version built was the AD-7 (A-1J) with an R-3350-26WB engine and a strengthened airframe. Approximately 50 unarmed radar-equipped three-seat airborne early warning (AEW) Skyraiders equivalent to the U.S. Navy's AD-4W were supplied to Britain's Royal Navy, where they served as Skyraider AEW.Mk.1 from 1951 to the early 1960s. Skyraider production ended in 1957 after 3,180 had been completed. The last Skyraiders in military service were retired by Chad's forces in the early 1980s.

Specifications – Douglas Skyraider AEW.Mk.1

Wingspan	50 ft
Length	38 ft 10 in
Maximum speed	305 mph at 18,500 ft
Maximum take-off weight	25,000 lb
Range	1,250 miles
Service ceiling	27,000 ft
Armament	None in AEW.1; attack models had four wing-mounted 0.787 in (20 mm) cannons, and carried up to 8,000 lb of unguided munitions including bombs and rockets on 15 underside attachments
Engine	One Wright R-3350-26WA Cyclone radial piston engine, of 2,700 hp
Crew	Three

Fairchild C-82 Packet/C-119 Flying Boxcar

Fairchild began design studies for a large freight-carrying aircraft in 1941, and in response to a U.S. Army requirement for such a type a single XC-82 was duly ordered. This made its first flight on 10 September 1944. As a military transport it differed from its contemporaries in having a fuselage pod with rear 'clamshell' loading doors, and tailplanes mounted on twin booms behind the nacelles for its 2,100 hp Pratt & Whitney R-2800-34 Double Wasp engines. This layout allowed easy access for loading cargo, small vehicles or troops. 220 C-82A Packets were produced by Fairchild, while North American built a further three as C-82Ns. The type served with the U.S. Air Force until 1954, with some later having careers with civil cargo airlines. Further development of the Packet's configuration resulted in the C-119 Flying Boxcar, with a re-positioned flight deck, the C-82's ventral fins deleted and two 2,650 hp Pratt & Whitney R-4360-4 Wasp Major radial engines installed. Originally known as the XC-82B, the single prototype was later re-designated XC-119A and was followed by 55 C-119Bs with a slightly wider fuselage, 3,500 hp R-4360-20s with four-blade propellers and a strengthened airframe. Revised tail surfaces resulted in the C-119C (303 built, plus 39 as R4Q-1s for the U.S. Marines), followed by the C-119F (247) and similar C-119G (480), plus 58 R4Q-2s. The final transport versions were the C-119J, K and L, all conversions of existing aircraft. C-119s and R4Qs served in both the Korean War, and the Southeast Asia conflicts. U.S.-flown examples wearing French roundels tried unsuccessfully to resupply besieged French forces at Dien Bien Phu in 1954. During the American involvement in Southeast Asia C-119s served as gunships as the AC-119G Shadow and AC-119K Stinger. The Shadow had four 0.3 in (7.62 mm) Miniguns arranged on its port side, while the Stinger added two 0.787 in (20 mm) cannons, an array of night vision sensors and two podded General Electric J85-GE-17 turbojets under its wings to increase performance. C-119 versions were finally phased out of U.S. Air National Guard service in the mid-1970s, but the type also served with several other air

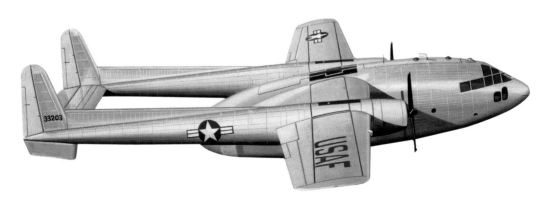

The Fairchild C-119 Flying Boxcar was a direct and more powerful development of the C-82 Packet, seen here in its basic C-119G production form.

The Fairchild C-82 Packet was not an elegant aircraft, but it was capable of taking on-board large loads straight into its rear fuselage through clamshell-opening rear fuselage loading doors. Shown here is the prototype XC-82, serial number 43-13202 (Photo: U.S. Army Air Force).

forces including Belgium, Canada, Ethiopia, India, Italy, South Vietnam and Taiwan. The final military examples in service belonged to Taiwan, being retired in the later 1990s. Some C-119 operators (such as the Indian Air Force) elected to mount a booster turbojet above the main cabin to increase 'hot-and-high' performance. Several former military C-119s were disposed of to the civilian market, but few remained active in 2005.

Specifications – Fairchild C-119G Flying Boxcar

Wingspan	109 ft 3 in
Length	86 ft 6 in
Maximum speed	291 mph at 15,000 ft
Maximum take-off weight	72,700 lb
Range	2,280 miles
Service ceiling	29,670 ft
Engine	Two Wright R-3350-85 Duplex Cyclone radial piston engines, of 3,500 hp each
Crew	Three or four

North American F-86 Sabre

The North American F-86 Sabre was one of the world's classic early jet aircraft. By the latter stages of World War Two, North American Aviation (NAA) already had an excellent reputation in fighter design and manufacture due to its famous P-51 Mustang piston-engined fighter, which is described in the second volume of *The Complete Encyclopedia of Flight*. The F-86 Sabre began life in a 1944 requirement for a future U.S. Army Air Force day fighter primarily for bomber escort work but with ground attack possibilities. These were qualities that had made the P-51 such a formidable warplane, and North American responded with proposals for a straight-wing jet-powered fighter. Two flying prototypes were ordered of the proposed NA-140 as the XP-86, to be powered by the General Electric TG-180 (later J35), an early American axial-flow turbojet engine. In early 1945 the U.S. Navy ordered a planned derivative, the XFJ Fury. However, the increasing realisation that swept-wings were essential for high-speed jet-powered flight convinced NAA that the intended P-86 lay-out should be revised. Although a batch of straight-wing FJ-1 were later built for the U.S. Navy, the whole P-86 design was radically changed to incorporate a new swept-wing design. Rivals Lockheed and Republic did not follow this lead at that time with their respective P-80 and P-84 jet fighter designs, and so North American's re-designed P-86 was somewhat behind these two straight-wing fighters. The prototype P-86 flew on 1 October 1947, and soon proved capable of breaking the 'sound barrier' in a shallow dive. The second prototype introduced the General Electric J47 turbojet, and the Sabre's speed capability was shown when an early example raised the world speed record to 670.84 mph (1,079.61 km/h) in September 1948. Production began with the P-86A (after 1948, F-86A), which entered service with the U.S. Air Force's 1st Fighter Group in 1949. The Korean War began in 1950, and the Sabre came to stand as the symbol of the successful United Nations air power in that war. Initial Sabre deployments were made in November/December 1950, and the

The North American F-86 Sabre will always be chiefly remembered for its exploits against the Communist-operated MiG-15 in the skies over Korea

Sabre was opposed by the famed MiG-15 (see pages 58 to 59). The Sabre and MiG-15 were roughly equal adversaries, but the Sabre's pilots were generally more experienced and eventually claimed a large number of aerial victories. Continuing Sabre development led to the improved F-86E and F-86F, both of which also successfully fought in Korean skies. A separate line of development led to the F-86D 'Sabre Dog' radar-equipped rocket-armed all-weather fighter (also a world speed record holder), and the F-86H fighter-bomber powered by a General Electric J73 turbojet. The Sabre was very popular with foreign buyers, including major service with Britain's Royal Air Force. Large licence-production agreements were made with several countries including Canada, Japan, and Australia. A derivative of the 'Sabre Dog,' the F-86K, was flown by several NATO countries. The U.S. Navy/Marine Corps also used swept-wing navalised Sabres, as the FJ-2, -3, and -4. The amazing total of at least 9,323 Sabres of all types (including the FJ, and foreign production and assembly) were made, and NAA later created the famous F-100 Super Sabre (see pages 148 to 149).

Specifications – North American F-86F Sabre

Wingspan	37 ft 1 in
Length	37 ft 6.5 in
Maximum speed	695 mph at 20,000 ft
Maximum take-off weight	20,357 lb
Range	1,000 miles (with external fuel tanks)
Service ceiling	48,000 ft
Armament	Six forward fuselage-mounted 0.5 in (12.7 mm) machine guns, various combinations of unguided bombs or rockets under the wings
Engine	One General Electric J47-GE-27 turbojet engine, of 5,910 lb st
Crew	One

de Havilland Canada DHC-2 Beaver

Few aircraft can compare to the de Havilland Canada DHC-2 Beaver, one of the world's classic 'bush planes,' for carrying small loads into unprepared landing strips. A high-wing cabin monoplane with a box-like fuselage, the Beaver was the first of a long line of short take-off and landing aircraft from this famous Canadian company, which is related to Britain's de Havilland organisation. The prototype Beaver made its first flight on 16 August 1947, powered by a 450 hp Pratt & Whitney R-985 Wasp Junior radial engine, the powerplant type for the vast majority of the Beavers that were built. A version powered by the ubiquitous Pratt & Whitney Canada PT6A-6A turboprop engine, with a slightly stretched fuselage to carry 10 people and a square-cut tail, was produced in limited numbers as the Turbo-Beaver Mk.III. Although the Turbo-Beaver was a production mod-

el, the basic airframe has also provided the basis for several further and more recent turboprop conversions. The Beaver was seen as such a desirable and capable aircraft by the U.S. Army that the U.S. Congress finally relented with its long-running 'buy-American' policy to allow the Army to procure the type – although it also helped that the Beaver had been compared against several other 'bush-planes' and was judged to be the best. Indeed, the U.S. Army became the largest operator of the aircraft, purchasing the Beaver as the YL-20, L-20A (later U-6A) and L-20B, while some examples used for instruction became TU-6As post-1962. The aircraft formed the backbone of the U.S. Army's aviation elements during the decade before the helicopter came to dominate Army operations, and it was extensively used particularly in Southeast Asia. Beavers were also employed

A de Havilland Canada Beaver wearing the civil registration letters (HK) of Colombia.

by the U.S. Air Force, with many examples being acquired to support ballistic missile units and for use as base and unit 'hacks' (liaison and general 'run-about' aircraft). 980 were eventually acquired by the U.S. military. Many other air arms used the Beaver, including Argentina, Austria, Cambodia, Columbia, Ghana, Kenya, South Korea, Laos, the Netherlands and the Philippines. Britain's Army Air Corps acquired 42 examples as Beaver AL.Mk.1s, four others with British serial numbers passing to the Sultanate of Oman. By 2005 the last operational military examples were in use by the U.S. Navy's Test Pilot School. However, many civilian examples remain active in North America, especially in Canada where some are flown as floatplanes. Approximately 1,657 (possibly 1,692) Beavers were manufactured.

A number of Beavers have operated on floats, such as this Canadian-registered example (Photo: John Batchelor Collection).

Take-off from the snow for a ski-equipped de Havilland Canada Turbo-Beaver (Photo: de Havilland Canada).

Specifications – de Havilland Canada DHC-2 Beaver

Wingspan	48 ft
Length	30 ft 3 in
Maximum speed	163 mph at 5,000 ft
Maximum take-off weight	5,100 lb
Range	733 miles
Service ceiling	18,000 ft
Engine	One Pratt & Whitney R-985-AN-39 or similar Wasp Junior radial piston engine, of 450 hp
Accommodation	One or two crew, normally four to six passengers

Sikorsky S-55 Series

By the time of the appearance of the Sikorsky S-55 series, helicopter design and operation was becoming well established. The Sikorsky S-55 was revolutionary especially in having a nose-located engine, allowing it to be connected to the main rotor on top of the fuselage by an angled driveshaft – thus keeping the area below the rotor free for a large cabin in which ten troops or six stretchers could be accommodated. The YH-19 prototype first flew in November 1949, powered by a 550-600 hp Pratt & Whitney R-1340 Wasp radial engine. Many different powerplants were subsequently used in a wide variety of S-55 versions that were produced for both military and civilian operators. U.S. military versions were the H-19 for the U.S.A.F. and U.S. Army, HO4S for the U.S. Navy and HRS for the U.S. Marines. However, in 1962 all surviving U.S. military variants were re-designated in the H-19

series. H-19s had their baptism of fire in the Korean War, rescuing downed aircrew and flying light transport tasks, and in September 1951 the HRS-1s of U.S. Marine Corps helicopter squadron HMR-161 became the first helicopters to carry U.S. Marines into action. In July 1952 a pair of U.S.A.F. H-19s were the first helicopters to fly in stages across the Atlantic Ocean, a major achievement. U.S. Army UH-19 Chickasaws also fought in Vietnam during the early American involvement in Southeast Asia. Some 1,285 S-55s were built by Sikorsky. The S-55 design was also successfully licence-built in several other countries, including Britain, Japan, and France. In Britain, Westland built and developed the type under the name Whirlwind. Westland produced Whirlwinds in three different series, powered by American piston engines (Series 1, military Mk.1 to Mk.4), British piston engines

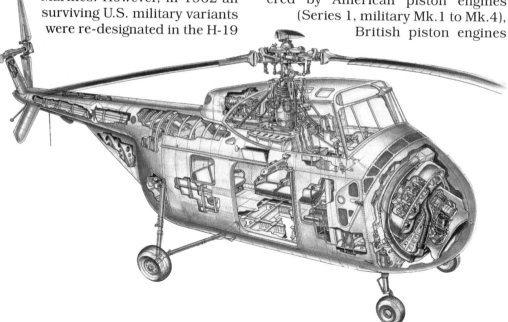

All Sikorsky S-55s and their foreign licence-built counterparts had their engine located in the forward fuselage. This freed the central fuselage area for a cabin of large volume, and had a major influence on future helicopter design layouts.

French-built S-55 derivatives were much-used by the French armed forces in the colonial wars and conflicts of the 1950s onwards (Photo: E.C.P.A.).

(Series 2, Mks.5, 7 and 8) and British shaft turbine engines (Series 3, Mks.9, 10 and 12). However, the first Whirlwinds in British service were the HAR.Mk.21s and HAS.Mk.22s supplied via military assistance agreements to the Royal Navy. Whirlwinds served in British operations in Malaya, Cyprus and in the Suez campaign of 1956. They were also the first anti-submarine helicopters (HAS.Mk.7, from 1957/1958) in Royal Navy service. Many countries (possibly over 40) used military S-55s or licence-built equivalents, sometimes as their first helicopter type. Civil customers also pioneered helicopter operations on the S-55. New York Airways linked New York and district airports with an S-55 service from July 1952, while Sabena started the world's first scheduled international helicopter service between Brussels and other European cities from September 1953. Although long retired by both airlines and military operators, some S-55s have persisted in service in recent times with specialist operators.

Specifications – Westland Whirlwind HAS.Mk.7

Main Rotor Diameter	53 ft
Fuselage Length	41 ft 8.5 in
Maximum speed	109.5 mph at sea level
Maximum take-off weight	7,800 lb
Range	435 miles
Service ceiling	9,400 ft
Armament	One Mk.44 anti-submarine torpedo, or one Mk.11 depth charge
Engine	One Alvis Leonides Major 755/1 radial piston engine, of 750 hp
Crew	Three crew, up to ten troops when required

Boeing Model 377 Stratocruiser

With its characteristic 'double-bubble' fuselage and levels of luxury from a by-gone age of aviation, the Boeing 377 Stratocruiser was a classic civil airliner. However, only 56 were delivered, a figure dwarfed by the 888 related Boeing 367 (C-97) Stratofreighters that were built for the U.S. Air Force. The type was in fact originally designed as a military aircraft. Three prototypes were ordered for the U.S. Army Air Force as XC-97s in early 1942 – the first flying in November 1944 – followed by ten service test//development YC-97/A/Bs. The prototypes mated Boeing B-29 Superfortress bomber flying surfaces and engines to a new passenger/cargo fuselage design, while further development did the same with components from the Boeing B-50 (a developed B-29). The Stratocruiser airliner was a civil development of the YC-97A, intended to seat 100 passengers. The Boeing-owned 377-10-19 prototype made its maiden flight on 8 July 1947. Six airlines ordered Stratocruisers, the main initial customer being the famous American airline Pan American (Pan Am). Deliveries commenced in February/March 1949, and ended in March 1950. A further significant operator was British Overseas Airways Corporation (BOAC). Stratocruisers were much praised for their comfort and long-range, but most of the original airlines had disposed of their Stratocruisers by the late 1950s in favor of jet airliners. The U.S. Air Force continued to order the Stratofreighter following its formation in 1947, as cargo or troop carriers. However, three C-97As were fitted as test aircraft with the Boeing Flying Boom system as KC-97A airborne refuelling tankers, resulting in significant orders for KC-97 series tankers to provide long-range capability to the U.S.A.F.'s Strategic Air Command bomber fleet. The last examples in service soldiered on well into the 1970s. Surplus Stratofreighters were delivered to the air forces of Israel (which also used Stratocruisers) and Spain, while small numbers of ex-U.S.A.F. examples had second careers with civilian owners. Pioneered by Aero Spacelines of the United States, several out-sized cargo-carrying developments of the Stratocruiser/Stratofreighter were developed as conversions. The original 377PG Pregnant Guppy featured an enlarged fuselage to carry spacecraft assemblies, making its first flight in September 1962. It was followed by the 377MG Mini Guppy, and two versions with even larger fuselages. These were the 377SG

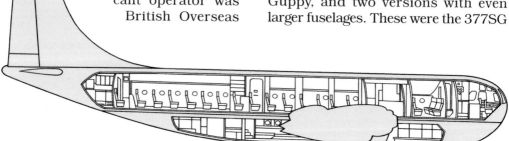

The Boeing Model 377 Stratocruiser had a spacious fuselage, giving a very comfortable journey experience to its passengers and crew. Some examples even carried a 'sleeper' internal arrangement for overnight flights.

Several dramatic but practical out-sized cargo-carrying conversions were made of Stratocruisers/ /Stratofreighters, a practice pioneered as shown here by Aero Spacelines in the United States (Photo: Boeing).

Super Guppy and the Guppy 201, four of which spent much of their time in Europe flying Airbus airliner components between various Airbus Industries factories.

The launch customer for the Boeing Model 377 Stratocruiser was the famous American carrier Pan Am, which eventually operated 27 examples.

Specifications – Boeing Model 377-10-28 Stratocruiser

Wingspan	141 ft 3 in
Length	110 ft 4 in
Maximum speed	375 mph at 25,000 ft
Maximum take-off weight	148,000 lb
Range	2,750 miles plus
Service ceiling	33,000 ft
Engine	Four Pratt & Whitney R-4360-TSB-6 Wasp Major radial piston engines, of 3,500 hp each
Accommodation	Five crew, various seating arrangements including 89 or 112 passengers

Vickers Viscount

The VC2 Viscount was designed to the wartime Brabazon Committee's IIB requirement for a turboprop-powered 24-seat short/medium-range airliner. The prototype eventually flew as the Type 630 32-seat transport powered by four Rolls-Royce Dart RDa.1 Mk.502 turboprops on 16 July 1948. However, no interest was shown in the aircraft by British European Airways (BEA) so Vickers stretched the fuselage adding pressurisation for between 40 and 59 passengers and replaced the RDa.1 engines with more powerful RDa.3s, producing the Type 700. Certified in April 1953, the type's speed and level of passenger comfort resulted in orders for Type 700 derivatives being placed by BEA, which used the original prototype to inaugurate the world's first scheduled turbine (turboprop-powered) passenger service (between London and Paris) in July 1952. The first Type 701 for BEA flew on 20 August 1952, entering revenue-earning service on 18 April 1953. Other airlines, including Air France, Aer Lingus, TAA, TCA and Capital Airlines, also ordered Type 700 variants. The sales to TCA and Capital Airlines represented a breakthrough into the important North American market. Further development including a slightly lengthened and revised fuselage led to the 800-Series Viscount. An important early customer for the Type 802 was BEA (24 delivered), together with other airlines. 1,700 shp RDa.7 Dart Mk.520s were used on the Type 806, and 1,800 shp RDa.7/1 Dart Mk.525s on the revised Type 810 series, which

The Vickers Viscount is one of the most famous of Britain's post-World War Two airliners. Part of its success was due to its popularity in the American market, as exemplified here by a Viscount in the colors of American airline Capital Airlines.

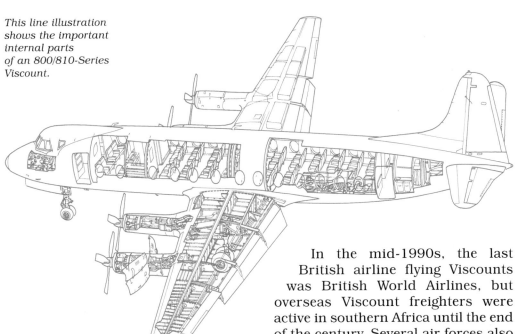

This line illustration shows the important internal parts of an 800/810-Series Viscount.

also had an airframe re-stressed for greater weights and higher airspeeds. The first Viscount 810 flew on 23 December 1957. A total of 444 Viscounts were built, with the last making its maiden flight on 2 January 1964. Following service with major airlines, Viscounts became a mainstay of many charter and second-line airlines in the late-1960s and 1970s.

In the mid-1990s, the last British airline flying Viscounts was British World Airlines, but overseas Viscount freighters were active in southern Africa until the end of the century. Several air forces also used Viscounts for transport duties, including those of South Africa and Turkey, and some were flown by British military test establishments. These included the second prototype, completed as the Type 663 and used to pioneer fly-by-wire controls during the 1950s. However, it is as Britain's most successful post-war airliner in terms of numbers produced that the Viscount will be justifiably remembered.

Specifications – Vickers V.810 Viscount

Wingspan	93 ft 8.5 in
Length	85 ft 8 in
Maximum speed	350 mph at 20,000 ft
Maximum take-off weight	72,500 lb
Range	1,725 miles with maximum payload
Service ceiling	25,000 ft
Engine	Four Rolls-Royce Dart Mk.525 (R.Da.7) turboprop engines, of 2,100 ehp each
Accommodation	Three or four crew plus cabin attendants, up to 70 passengers in tourist class layout

Convair B-36 Peacemaker

With World War Two in progress, the U.S. Army Air Corps' need for a transatlantic bomber crystallised into a requirement released in April 1941 which eventually produced the giant Convair B-36 Peacemaker. A twin-tailed design powered by six pusher engines with a flush canopy, Consolidated's original design studies were ordered as the XB-36, the layout being refined to have a single fin before flying. Rolled out at Fort Worth, Texas, in September 1945, the XB-36 first lumbered into the air on 8 August 1946. Poor pilot visibility resulted in a cockpit canopy redesign and other changes incorporated on the YB-36. The first of 22 B-36A flew in August 1947, these being mainly used for air and ground crew training and familiarisation. They were followed by 73 B-37Bs, the first truly operational version, and the B-36D which introduced four General Electric J47 turbojets in pods of two under the outer wings to improve performance. A total of 22 were built, and 64 B-models were upgraded to B-36D standard, while production switched to the more powerful B-36F and B-36H. The last production bomber version was the B-36J (33 built), featuring several improvements including increased fuel capacity and a strengthened undercarriage. The huge size of the Peacemaker allowed it to carry bulky nuclear weapons over vast distances, with bomber crews regularly staying aloft for over 24 hours. To provide the type with a fighter escort on long-range missions, the curious Fighter Conveyor (FICON) program was initiated, whereby fighters were carried beneath the bomb bay of the B-36. Small numbers of FICON B-36s were used by SAC in the mid-1950s, the B-36s involved carrying Republic RF-84K Thunderflash fighter/reconnaissance aircraft (see pages 86 to 87) to provide a long-range reconnais-

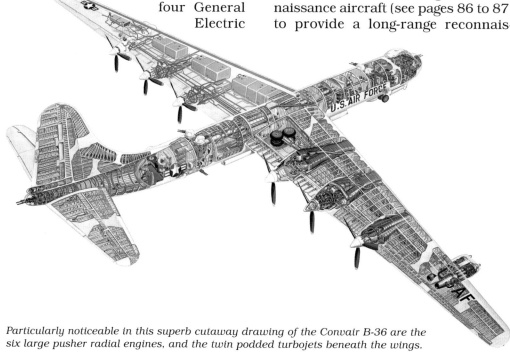

Particularly noticeable in this superb cutaway drawing of the Convair B-36 are the six large pusher radial engines, and the twin podded turbojets beneath the wings.

82

A true Cold War warrior, the Convair B-36 gave the U.S. Air Force its first real intercontinental strike capability. Pictured is a preserved B-36J (Photo: U.S. Air Force).

sance capability. Indeed, strategic reconnaissance was an important B-36 mission, with three versions produced for the task. The RB-36D (17 built), RB-36E (22 conversions), RB-36F (24 built) and RB-36H (73 built) carried a larger crew (up to 22) than the bombers' normal 15-man crew, to work their on-board reconnaissance equipment. They occasionally violated Communist airspace to take illicit photographs, relatively safe above the operating height of Communist-operated MiG fighters in those pre-surface-to-air missile (SAM) days. A singe NB-36H test-bed carried a nuclear reactor aloft to test radiation shielding, the reactor not supplying power to the aircraft. Two YB-36G swept wing jet-powered derivatives were flown as YB-60s, as possible follow-on strategic bombers. The type, however, lost out to the Boeing B-52 Stratofortress (see pages 176 to 177), the B-36's eventual successor in SAC. The final active B-36s were phased out of service in early 1959, but Convair's innovative designers also created the equally impressive B-58 Hustler bomber described on pages 144 to 145.

Specifications – Convair B-36J Peacemaker

Wingspan	230 ft
Length	162 ft 1 in
Maximum speed	411 mph at 36,400 ft
Maximum take-off weight	410,000 lb
Range	6,800 miles with a 10,000 lb bomb load
Service ceiling	39,900 ft
Armament	Sixteen 0.787 in (20 mm) cannons in nose, tail and six fuselage turrets (some examples flew with all but the tail guns deleted) bomb load of up to 46,000 lb possible, although normal load was usually some 10,000 lb
Engine	Six Pratt & Whitney R-4360-53 radial piston engines, of 3,800 hp each, and four General Electric J47-GE-19 turbojets, of 5,200 lb st each
Crew	Fifteen (some with reduced armament had fewer crew)

Supermarine Attacker

Britain was at the forefront of jet engine design and development in the 1930s and into the 1940s (in addition to Nazi Germany), but Britain's lead in jet aircraft design in the immediate post-World War Two years was lost in several important areas. One of these was in the development of naval jet aircraft for operation from aircraft carriers, and this was one of the areas in which the United States successfully forged ahead while Britain's military only slowly moved forward with jet combat aircraft acquisition. This situation was characterised by the Supermarine Attacker, an aircraft whose development took so long due partly to a lack of direction in official procurement that it was virtually obsolete before it entered front-line service. The Supermarine company was already world-famous for its legendary Spitfire series of fighters (see

pages 38 to 39), and a development of the Spitfire was the Spiteful. This fighter had a laminar flow wing of special section (much different to the Spitfire's elliptical wing), and a planned naval derivative of it was the Seafang. Unfortunately neither of these proved successful, the laminar flow wing in particular causing handling problems at low speeds. However, Supermarine had decided late in World War Two to create a future jet fighter, and a quick way of doing this was thought to be to use the Spiteful/Seafang wing mated to a new fuselage containing a jet engine and new tail surfaces. Originally developed to Specification E.10/44, the new jet aircraft had a cigar-shaped fuselage containing the new Rolls-Royce Nene centrifugal-flow turbojet. The first aircraft (Type 392) flew on 27 July 1946. Two further prototypes were built, and these (plus later the

The Supermarine Attacker was a neat and attractive jet fighter, that unfortunately came too late for meaningful service after a long development and procurement process.
Its tailwheel-type undercarriage was additionally out-dated as a jet aircraft configuration.
It was, however, the Royal Navy's first jet fighter for aircraft carrier operation. The example illustrated, serial number WA493, was an Attacker F.Mk.1, assigned to No.800 Naval Air Squadron of the Fleet Air Arm aboard the aircraft carrier H.M.S. Eagle
(hence the code 'J' on its tail).

original aircraft, after the second prototype crashed) were flown to naval development standard as Supermarine Type 398. In the immediate post-Second World War years the value of having a swept-back wing for jet-powered high-speed flight was being increasingly understood, but Supermarine nevertheless continued with the 'straight' laminar flow wing for the Type 398. Named Attacker, the type was eventually ordered into production in the late 1940s following a number of delays. The first production aircraft flew in the spring of 1950, the initial production-standard version being the F.Mk.1 with a Nene 3 turbojet and four wing cannons only, although some were finished as FB.Mk.1 with fighter-bomber capability. The main production model was the FB.2, of which 84 or 85 were built. These had full air-to-ground capability with provision for underwing bombs or rockets. Wing folding was included as standard for aircraft carrier operation, and the pilot had an early ejection seat to sit on. The type's front-line service career was brief. The first unit to equip was No.800 Naval Air Squadron in the summer of 1951, but in mid-1954 the Attacker was retired by the Royal Navy from front-line service. By then it was already outclassed by other types, with jet fighter design being dominated by swept-back wings and tricycle undercarriage layouts. An export customer for the Attacker was Pakistan, which bought 36 of a de-navalised version called the Type 538 in the early 1950s.

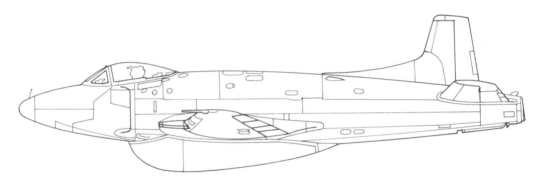

A side view of the Supermarine Attacker FB.Mk.1.

Specifications – Supermarine Attacker FB.Mk.2

Wingspan	36 ft 11 in
Length	37 ft 6 in
Maximum speed	590 mph at sea level
Maximum take-off weight	17,350 lb
Range	590 miles
Service ceiling	45,000 ft
Armament	Four wing-mounted 0.787 in (20 mm) cannons, two 1,000 lb bombs or up to 12 unguided rockets
Engine	One Rolls-Royce Nene 102 turbojet engine, of 5,100 lb st
Crew	One

Republic F-84 Series

The United States lagged behind both Britain and Germany in jet engine and airframe research and development during the 1930s and early 1940s, and near to the end of World War Two a major effort was made to redress this balance. Several American companies were officially encouraged to work on future jet fighter projects, these including Lockheed with the P-80/F-80 Shooting Star (see pages 52 to 53) and North American with the F-86 Sabre (pages 72 to 73). A third company, Republic, also became involved. Like Lockheed and North American, it too had a very important piston engine fighter in widespread and successful service during the war. This was the P-47 Thunderbolt, and Republic's initial thoughts were to upgrade the P-47's layout by installing a jet engine into the Thunderbolt's fuselage. This idea was eventually abandoned, and Republic began a completely new design for jet power. This became the F-84, appropriately named Thunderjet, which was a conventional straight-wing early-generation jet fighter with a simple straight-through air supply for the axial flow turbojet within the fuselage. The powerplant chosen was a turbojet design which grew into the Allison J35, and the prototype XP-84 first flew on 28 February 1946. A second prototype was followed by 15 pre-production/development YP-84 aircraft, and the first main production version was the P-84B (F-84B after 1948). An early jet fighter in many senses of the word, the F-84B had an unsophisticated ejection seat, machine gun armament, air-conditioned cockpit and a performance that was hardly sparkling. However, further development included the provision of more powerful versions of the J35 turbojet, and jet-assisted take-off (JATO) equipment. Several production models culminated in the much more capable F-84G, 3,024 or 3,025 of which were built. In addition to service with the U.S. Air Force, many examples operated with NATO air arms in Europe. Thunderjets served extensively in the Korean War of 1950 to 1953 as fighter-bombers for United Nations forces. By the time of the appearance of the F-84G, however, the importance of swept-back wings for high-speed jet-powered flight was fully recognised, and further development led to a completely revised derivative of the Thunderjet called the Thunderstreak. This had swept wings, greater weapons capability, and a completely revised fuselage with a different engine, the British-derived Wright J65 turbojet. The main production model was the F-84F Thunderstreak, which first flew in prototype/development form (as the YF-96A) in June 1950. Some 2,349 F-84F were built, and they

The Republic F-84F was the swept-wing development of the basic F-84 layout, and was bulky and comparatively underpowered although it served widely with U.S. and NATO forces.

A rare photograph of an RF-84K FICON 'parasite' aircraft. Note the angled-down tailplane unique to this Thunderflash derivative, and the large hook on the upper nose which was a part of the equipment to hang the aircraft beneath a Convair GRB-36D 'mother ship' for air-launching and retrieval (Photo: John Batchelor).

served extensively with U.S. and NATO forces, plus other export customers. A direct derivative was the RF-84F Thunderflash. This variant featured a revised 'solid' nose with cameras for photo-reconnaissance, and so moved the F-84F's fuselage nose engine air intake to its wing roots. 715 RF-84F were built, and served with the U.S.A.F. and some export customers. Several with revised tail surfaces and other alterations served as RF-84K in the curious Fighter Conveyer (FICON) 'parasite' fighter program, carried beneath converted Convair B-36 bombers (see pages 82 to 83) to increase their range.

Specifications – Republic F-84F Thunderstreak

Wingspan	33 ft 7 in
Length	43 ft 3 in
Maximum speed	691 mph at sea level
Maximum take-off weight	27,000 lb
Radius of action	750 miles
Service ceiling	47,500 ft
Armament	Four fuselage-mounted and two wing-mounted 0.5 in (12.7 mm) machine guns, up to 6,000 lb of bombs or other unguided munitions
Engine	One Wright (or Buick) J65-W-3 (or -B-3) turbojet engine, of 7,200 lb st
Crew	One

de Havilland D.H.104 Dove/D.H.114 Heron

British post-World War Two civil aviation development was largely influenced by the deliberations of the wartime Brabazon Committee, as explained on pages 122 to 123. Amongst many considerations, its Type 5B Specification called for a replacement for the de Havilland D.H.89 Dragon Rapide series pre-war biplane civil transport, which is described in the first Volume of *The Complete Encyclopedia of Flight*. This requirement eventually resulted in the D.H.104 Dove all-metal construction low-wing tricycle undercarriage light transport, with accommodation for two crew and eight passengers. The prototype made its maiden flight on 25 September 1945, and was initially offered in two versions. The Mk.1 was a feeder-liner and the Mk.2 was an executive transport, both powered by two 330-340 hp Gipsy Queen 70-3 inline engines (or 340 hp 70-4s in the Mk.1B/2B versions). Continuing development lead to service with Britain's Royal Air Force, 39 or 40 examples being delivered as Devon C.Mk.1s from 1947. Some were later re-engined with 400 hp Gipsy Queen 70 Mk.3s as the Devon C.Mk.2. In the mid-1950s the Royal Navy purchased 13 examples as Sea Devon C.Mk.20s. India, New Zealand and South Africa amongst others also ordered Devons. Slightly more powerful versions of the Dove Mk.1 and Mk.2 were the Mk.5 and Mk.6 or – with a domed cockpit roof and slightly more power – the Mk.7 or Mk.8s. Production of the Dove continued until 1967, apparently with 544 built including two prototypes. Design of a larger four-engined unso-

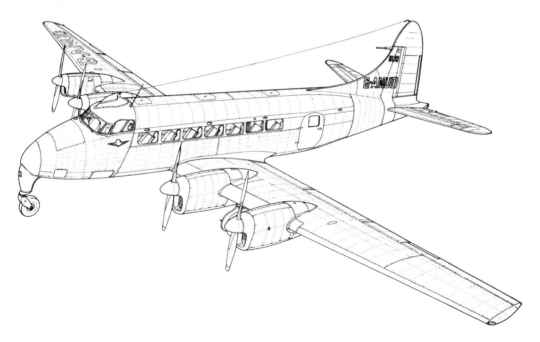

The de Havilland Heron was basically a scaled-up, enlarged de Havilland Dove development with four small piston engines. It could seat up to 17 passengers in some seating layouts. The example shown here has a fixed undercarriage.

phisticated airliner derivative of the Dove, the D.H.114 Heron, began in 1949. In its Mk.1 version it featured a fixed undercarriage and four 250 hp Gipsy Queen 30-series inline engines, entering service first with New Zealand National Airways in 1952. From the seventh production aircraft (the last built at Hatfield before the production line transferred to Hawarden) a retractable undercarriage was fitted as standard to produce the Mk.2 series. Small numbers served with the R.A.F., including The Queen's Flight, while five ex-Jersey Airlines and West African Airways Corpo-

ration Herons flew with the Royal Navy as Sea Heron C.Mk.20s, plus a sixth (ex-R.A.F.) as a VIP transport. The manufacture of 149 examples including the prototype was completed in 1964. Both the Dove and the Heron formed the basis of several conversions, mainly for the American market. These included the Lycoming inline engine-powered Riley Dove and the stretched Carstedt CJ-600A Jet Liner, the Riley Heron and the Canadian turboprop-powered longer-fuselage Saunders ST-27. Small numbers of Doves and Herons remain airworthy in 2005.

This de Havilland Heron with the British civil registration G-ALZL was actually the prototype Heron, built from some Dove and some new components. It first flew on 10 May 1950. Note its fixed undercarriage, replaced with retractable units from the seventh production aircraft onwards.

Specifications – de Havilland D.H.114 Sea Heron C.Mk.20

Wingspan	71 ft 6 in
Length	48 ft 6 in
Maximum speed	183 mph at 8,000 ft
Maximum take-off weight	13,000 lb
Range	approximately 805 miles
Service ceiling	18,500 ft
Engine	Four de Havilland Gipsy Queen 30 inline piston engines, of 250 hp each
Crew	Two crew, up to 14/17 passengers (often less)

Gloster Meteor Late Series

Britain's Gloster Meteor holds a particularly important aviation record, having been the first-ever jet aircraft to reach regular front-line squadron service. This was achieved in July 1944, and the Meteor was thus the first – and only – Allied jet aircraft to enter service during World War Two. The early story of this significant warplane is covered in the second Volume of *The Complete Encyclopedia of Flight*. Development of the Meteor continued during and after the war, and the type went on to serve into the 1950s in several key roles. The first major post-war production version was the Meteor Mk.IV, powered by two Rolls-Royce Derwent 5 turbojet engines. This was a single-seat day fighter model, and well over four hundred were ordered for Royal Air Force service, plus many others for export. Also called Meteor Mk.IV, but actually converted from a Mk.III airframe, was a Meteor that broke the world speed record in November 1945, followed in September 1946 by a real Meteor Mk.IV at an average speed of 616 mph. Developed from the Mk.IV was an unarmed

two-seat trainer, which was ordered for the R.A.F. as the Meteor T.Mk.7. This version featured a lengthened fuselage to allow tandem-seating for its crew of two. The best-known post-war single-seat Meteor was the F.Mk.8, even though this was theoretically a stop-gap until more advanced jet fighter designs became available. The F.8 had an aerodynamically cleaner airframe, ejection seat, and slightly wider engine air intakes that helped to marginally increase the type's maximum speed. Some 1,079 (possibly 1,090) were built for the R.A.F., but Meteor F.8s also served widely with various export customers including assembly by Fokker in the Netherlands. Australian-operated Meteor F.8s flew in the Korean War, firstly as fighters but later for ground attack. Several Communist-operated MiG-15 fighters were shot down, but generally the Meteor was outclassed as a fighter by the MiG. Two specific reconnaissance marks of the Meteor were also built, the FR.Mk.9 and the PR.Mk.10, and in addition four dedicated radar-equipped two-seat night fighter versions were also manufac-

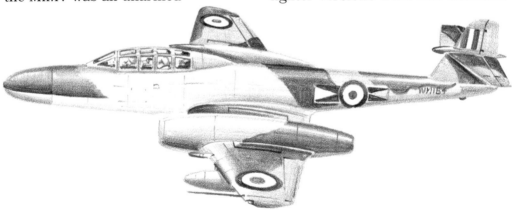

The Meteor NF.Mk.11 was one of four Meteor Night Fighter marks that were built, responsibility for these lying with Armstrong Whitworth rather than Gloster. This aircraft is in the markings of the R.A.F.'s No.141 Squadron.

Airworthy examples of some of the early jet-powered aircraft are nowadays very rare. This Gloster/Armstrong Whitworth Meteor NF.Mk.11 night fighter serial number WM167 is still fully airworthy, and is flown in Britain from Coventry Airport with the British civil registration G-LOSM (Photo: Malcolm V. Lowe).

tured. These were Britain's first jet-powered night fighters, and were an interim until the all-weather Gloster Javelin (see pages 124 to 125) became available. Four versions were developed from the original Specification F.24/48, as a replacement for the piston-engined de Havilland Mosquito NF.Mk.36 night fighter. The first true Meteor NF.Mk.11 prototype flew in May 1950, well over three hundred of this mark being built and serving with the R.A.F. and several export customers. Following the further developed NF.12 and NF.13 versions, the NF.Mk.14 was a revised model with a teardrop-like cockpit canopy. Some of the two-seat Meteors were later converted into target-towers, and served (shore-based) with Britain's Royal Navy. In addition to all this important service, several Meteors were used for various test purposes. One of these was the Trent Meteor, which was powered by two Rolls-Royce Trent turboprop engines in place of its jets, and was the world's first turboprop-powered aircraft to fly.

Specifications – Gloster Meteor F.Mk.8

Wingspan	37 ft 2 in
Length	44 ft 7 in
Maximum speed	592 mph at sea level
Maximum take-off weight	15,700 lb
Range	690 miles
Service ceiling	44,000 ft
Armament	Four nose-mounted 0.787 in (20 mm) cannons
Engine	Two Rolls-Royce Derwent 8 turbojet engines, of 3,500 lb st each
Crew	One

Dassault Mystère Series

Considerable experimental work into aviation developments was carried out in France during the post-Second World War years (see pages 48 to 49), but French aircraft designers eventually discovered like their contemporaries in other countries that conservative and conventional aviation designs were the most likely to succeed. The first production post-war jet fighter in France was the Dassault M.D.450 Ouragan, a very conventional straight-wing fighter and fighter-bomber powered by a Hispano-Suiza licence-built British Rolls-Royce Nene turbojet, which first flew on 28 February 1949. The Ouragan proved successful in French, Indian and Israeli service, and continuing development with the addition of the growing science of swept-wings for high-speed jet-powered flight

resulted in the swept-wing Mystère series of fighters and fighter-bombers. The first, swept-wing M.D.452 Mystère I flew on 23 February 1951. A series of prototypes and pre-production aircraft followed, the Hispano-Suiza licence-built British Rolls-Royce Tay turbojet engine being introduced, plus experimentation with the SNECMA Atar. The first major series version for the French air force was the Mystère IIC, which first flew in production form in mid-1954. Further development had meanwhile led on to the Mystère IV, which had flown in prototype form in September 1952 and subsequently entered production as the Mystère IVA. The type served with France, India and Israel. Initially powered with the French-built Tay engine, later production Mystère IVA received

A quartet of French air force (Armée de l'Air) Dassault Mystère IVA operated by the 8th Escadre de Chasse (Photo: Armée de l'Air).

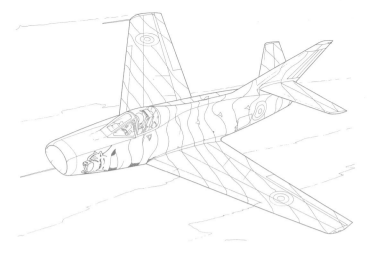

The Dassault Super Mystère B2 was the fastest of the Mystère family of fighters and fighter-bombers, and was a contemporary of the North American F-100 Super Sabre described separately in this book.

the Hispano-Suiza Verdon turbojet developed from the Tay. A two-seat night-fighter version was also proposed but not proceeded with. Mystère IVA were used by French forces in combat during the Suez operations in late 1956. The world-famous 'Patrouille de France' aerobatic demonstration team of the French air force also operated the type. Continuing development led to the Super Mystère B2, first flown in prototype form as the Super Mystère B1 on 2 March 1955. With a modified wing featuring more sweepback, many other changes and the addition of an afterburning SNECMA Atar 101-series turbojet, the production Super Mystère B2 was capable of supersonic speed in level flight – the first production European frontline fighter to achieve this. The initial production aircraft flew in February 1957, and 180 production examples were manufactured. In addition to French service, Israel made good use of this type during conflict with her neighbors, and also re-engined some examples with American turbojet engines. By then, the Dassault company was already involved with the next famous type from its drawing boards, the Mirage series as described on pages 182 to 183.

Specifications – Dassault Mystère IVA

Wingspan	36 ft 5.75 in
Length	42 ft 2 in
Maximum speed	696 mph at sea level
Maximum take-off weight	20,944 lb
Range	569 miles
Service ceiling	49,213 ft
Armament	Two lower nose-mounted 1.18 in (30 mm) cannons, various unguided bombs or rockets on underwing pylons
Engine	One Hispano-Suiza Verdon 350-series turbojet engine, of 7,716 lb st
Crew	One

de Havilland D.H.112 Venom and D.H.110 Sea Vixen

The de Havilland Vampire that is described on pages 36 to 37 proved to be a successful early jet fighter and fighter-bomber. An early development Vampire had even been the first solely jet-powered aircraft ever to land on an aircraft carrier. In their fighter-bomber roles Vampires could carry a variety of underwing bombs or unguided rockets, and it was in that role that the type particularly excelled. Further development by de Havilland to extend the potential and the comparatively modest performance of the Vampire and its basic and unique twin-boom/fuselage pod layout led to the more powerful and capable D.H.112 Venom fighter-bomber series. The Venom grew out of the Vampire FB.Mk.8 proposals, and featured several significant differences compared to the Vampire including a new wing, and the adoption of the de Havilland Ghost turbojet engine. Development was covered under Specification F.15/49, and the Venom prototype/ /development aircraft flew on 2 September 1949. The type entered Royal Air Force service in its initial FB.Mk.1 version in 1952. Continuing development led to several succeeding models, including (as had also been the case with the Vampire line) a two-seat radar-equipped night fighter with side-by-side seating. Britain's Royal Navy was also a major customer, for the two-seat folding-wing carrier-borne night fighter derivatives (a role then being increasingly called 'all-weather'). Several overseas buyers purchased Venoms, and licence-production was performed in Switzerland, Sweden, and France (some French aircraft being called Aquilon). Venoms carried out significant combat operations, for example with the R.A.F. during the Malayan Emergency, but most noticeably during the Suez crisis in late 1956. Totally new, although retaining the twin-boom/central fuselage layout of the Vampire and Venom series, was the de Havilland D.H.110 Sea Vixen. This was a completely different aircraft to the Venom, being a big, powerful twin-engined two-seat high-performance all-weather naval fighter and strike aircraft with folding-wings. It had originally been intended

A de Havilland Sea Vixen FAW.Mk.1 in Royal Navy markings. The type represented the ultimate development of the Vampire/Venom's twin-boom/fuselage pod design layout.

The long protrusion extending from the wing of this Sea Vixen is an in-flight refuelling probe, which considerably extended the type's range and endurance (Photo: Royal Navy).

for land-based all-weather fighter operations for the R.A.F., but that role was later taken up by the Gloster Javelin (see pages 124 to 125). Instead the D.H.110 was developed exclusively for the Royal Navy, and the first of two prototypes initially flew on 26 September 1951. Famously and tragically, this aircraft crashed at the 1952 Farnborough air show, killing its crew and 29 spectators on the ground. Despite this setback the type was developed for Royal Navy service. The first production version was the Sea Vixen FAW.Mk.1, and this entered front-line service in 1959/1960. A somewhat more capable version with more fuel capacity and other changes was the FAW.Mk.2, and total Sea Vixen production appears to have been 148. Some 67 Mk.1s were later brought up to Mk.2 standard, and the last front-line aircraft were retired in 1972. None were ever used in action, although some flew on the 'Beira Patrol' off southeast Africa.

Specifications – de Havilland D.H.110 Sea Vixen FAW.Mk.2

Wingspan	50 ft
Length	55 ft 7 in
Maximum speed	640 mph at sea level
Maximum take-off weight	37,000 lb
Range	1,200 miles
Service ceiling	48,200 ft
Armament	Four guided air-to-air missiles, two 1,000 lb bombs or other underwing weapons including unguided rocket pods
Engine	Two Rolls-Royce Avon 208 turbojet engines, of 10,000 lb st each
Crew	Two

Early American Jet Bombers

During the latter stages of World War Two, the U.S. Army Air Force began to recognise that future combat aircraft would need to embrace the developing technology and performance capabilities of jet propulsion. A number of specifications and operational requirements were therefore formulated that included future needs for jet-powered fighter and bomber aircraft. In the case of fighter development, initial American designs such as the Bell P-59 Airacomet were soon superseded by successful early jet fighters like the Lockheed P-80 Shooting Star and – a little later – by the excellent North American F-86 Sabre (all of these aircraft are covered elsewhere in this book). However, in the field of jet bomber and attack aircraft, the United States was not initially as successful. Indeed, the American company Martin eventually licence-built and developed a British design, the English Electric/BAC Canberra bomber (see pages 112 to 113) as the B-57, an unusual case of an American company building an aircraft designed in another country. The earliest jet bomber of American design and manufacture to reach the U.S. Air Force was the North American B-45 Tor-

nado, a straight-wing four-jet bomber of comparatively limited performance that is better known as a reconnaissance aircraft particularly during the Korean War. In late 1944 the U.S. Army Air Force produced a requirement for a future jet bomber that would carry a large bombload over a range of 3,500 miles (5,633 km) at a speed of 500 mph (805 km/h). The three main contenders for this requirement were the six-jet Martin XB-48, the sleek four-jet Convair XB-46, and a number of Boeing design studies. Both the XB-46 and the Martin Model 223 XB-48 combined a straight-wing format with several comparatively low-powered early jet engines. The first of two XB-48 prototypes flew in June 1947, but the aircraft's straight-wing design layout was already obsolete due to advances in the understanding of swept-wing technology for jet aircraft. Eventually, Boeing incorporated a swept-wing into its own revised design, and thus was born the excellent B-47 Stratojet (see pages 110 to 111) which was much better than the XB-46 and the XB-48. Another early straight-wing American jet bomber design that did not survive was the Douglas XB-43. This was

The Douglas XB-43 – sometimes called Jetmaster – was the United States' first jet-powered bomber to fly, and was based on the unusual idea of having the aircraft's jet engines buried within the fuselage.

The impressive-looking Martin XB-48 had its six General Electric (Allison) J35 turbojet engines mounted in unorthodox cowlings beneath its wings. The type's wingspan was 108 ft 4 in (33.02 m), but it was not put into production.

based on an earlier design, the wartime Douglas XB-42. The first of two XB-42s first flew in May 1944 and was powered by two Allison piston engines buried within its fuselage and driving two sets of 'pusher' propellers at the tail. At first called the XA-42, this design was later revised to mount two small Westinghouse turbojets beneath its wings as a 'mixed power plant' bomber (and sometimes called Mixmaster). Further revised, the design grew into the all-jet XB-43, with a pair of General Electric J35 turbojets within its fuselage. The XB-43 prototype flew on 17 May 1946, followed by a YB-43, but the type's arrangement was soon outdated, and the design did not enter production.

Specifications – Douglas XB-43 Jetmaster

Wingspan	71 ft 2 in
Length	51 ft 5 in
Maximum speed	503 mph at sea level
Maximum take-off weight	40,100 lb
Range	1,100 miles
Service ceiling	38,200 ft
Armament	Up to 8,000 lb of bombs
Engine	Two General Electric J35-GE-3 turbojet engines, of 3,750 lb st each
Crew	Three

Northrop Flying Wing Bombers

One of the pioneers and exponents of the flying wing design layout for military aircraft was American John K. Northrop. As explained on pages 40 to 41, Northrop's company has been responsible over the years for many of the flying wings that have so far been built. These include the innovative but ultimately unsuccessful XP-56 Black Bullet flying wing fighter prototypes of the World War Two period. In the field of bomber design, Northrop has also been very active on a number of occasions. In the early 1940s Northrop began to experiment with flying wing designs that investigated the concept of a feasible bomber layout. This process commenced with the low-powered twin-engine N-1M, and progressed to four N-9M twin-engined proof-of-concept aircraft. These were built in response to official U.S. Army Air Force interest in Northrop's work, which led to a rather ambitious order in late 1941 for two XB-35 flying wing bombers. The four N-9M were in effect manned scale models of the planned XB-35 layout, and they proved the basic ideas of the proposed design. The XB-35 was intended to be powered by four Pratt & Whitney Wasp Major piston engines, driving contra-rotating propeller units in a 'pusher' arrangement. Eventually thirteen development/service test YB-35 (five as YB-35A) were additionally ordered, but the development of the bomber was protracted and difficult. The first flight was finally made on 25 June 1946, well after World War Two had ended. The usefulness of the design was therefore lost, and the advent of jet propulsion for bombers and the selection of the Convair B-36 Peacemaker (see pages 82 to 83) as the Air Force's major new post-war bomber ended the XB-35 project. However, Northrop had anticipated these problems, and two of the YB-35 were converted to jet power. Re-designated YB-49, they emerged as very impressive all-jet bombers, the first being powered by eight Allison J35 turbojets of 4,000 lb st each. The initial example flew in October 1947, but sadly the second aircraft crashed the following year. A YRB-49A was also made with a different jet engine arrangement, but 30 planned production RB-49 series aircraft were eventually cancelled. This was by no means the end of the story, however, because many years later the flying wing design returned, this time with considerable success, in the form of

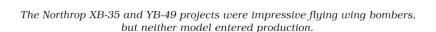

The Northrop XB-35 and YB-49 projects were impressive flying wing bombers, but neither model entered production.

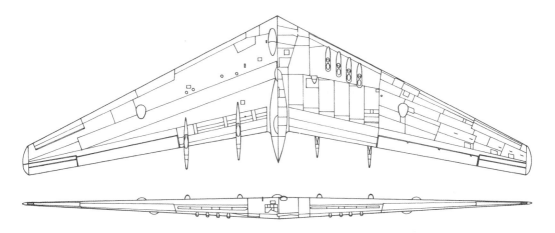

The unconventional flying wing tail-less design layout of the XB-35 and YB-49 is shown here. The YB-49 in particular was an outstanding achievement, and was the largest all-jet flying wing up to that time.

Four reduced-scale twin-engined Northrop N-9M flying wings were built to test the feasibility of the planned flying wing bomber program. This photograph illustrates one of the four N-9M in flight (Photo: Northrop).

the Northrop Grumman B-2 Spirit – see pages 296 to 297.

Specifications – Northrop XB-35

Wingspan	172 ft
Length	53 ft 1 in
Maximum speed	391 mph at 35,000 ft
Maximum take-off weight	209,000 lb
Range	720 miles fully loaded
Service ceiling	40,000 ft
Armament	None installed, intended armament was 20 0.5 in (12.7 mm) machine guns in various gun turrets, up to 10,000 lb of bombs
Engine	Four Pratt & Whitney R-4360-series Wasp Major radial piston engines, of 3,000 hp each
Crew	Seven

Handley Page Hastings

Designed to Specification C.3/44 as a replacement for the Avro York (see pages 26 to 27), the Hastings formed the backbone of the Royal Air Force's Transport Command (later Air Support Command) from the early post-war period to the mid-1960s. R.A.F. transport versions were the H.P.67 Hastings C.Mk.1, C.Mk.2 (with increased fuel, wider tailplane and more powerful Bristol Hercules engines) and the C.Mk.1A, a modification of the Mk.1 with many features of the Mk.2. In addition, four H.P.94 Hastings C.Mk.4 VIP transports were delivered to the R.A.F. Two further versions were produced by modification, consisting of the Hastings Met.Mk.1 used on long-range meteorological flights over the Atlantic, and eight Hastings T.Mk.5 bomb-aimer trainers. The prototype Hastings first flew on 7 May 1946. From the autumn of 1948 No.47 Squadron, R.A.F. became the first operational unit, employing its new C.Mk.1 aircraft on the Berlin Airlift, in which it was later joined by

fellow Hastings unit No.297 Squadron. 147 Hastings were eventually allocated British military serial numbers. In service Hastings were mostly used on long-range 'truck-routes,' flying between outposts of the diminishing former British Empire, allowing the smaller Vickers Valetta transport to tackle the tactical tasks. However, with the delivery of the R.A.F.'s Bristol Britannia transport aircraft from 1959, the Hastings was switched to tactical (shorter-range) missions only. Hastings supported the logistics supply mission during all of the conflicts British forces were involved in during its service life with the R.A.F. It also undertook more tactical roles in some of those campaigns, for example dropping 3 Para at El Gamil, Egypt, during the Suez campaign of 1956. Other operations included support during the anti-Mau Mau campaign in Kenya during the 1950s, reinforcing Kuwait against threatened Iraqi invasion in 1961, and dropping supplies to British troops during the conflict with

Hardly an elegant aircraft, the Handley Page Hastings was a powerful and functional transport which gave valuable service to the Royal Air Force the post-war period.

An historic photograph showing the Handley Page Hastings prototype, serial number TE580, at the 1946 British aviation trade show at Radlett, Hertfordshire. Nowadays this exhibition is held at Farnborough and is one of the world's premier aviation trade fairs. Note the side loading doors of the Hastings, shown here trying to embark a small vehicle (Photo: Handley Page).

Indonesia in the early 1960s. The last Hastings in service were four R.A.F. T.Mk.5s. Serial number TG511 made the type's last flight when it was delivered to the R.A.F. Museum at Cosford during 1977. The only export customer for the Hastings was the Royal New Zealand Air Force, which used a small number of H.P.95 Hastings C.Mk.3s between the early 1950s and mid-1960s. A civil transport version of the Hastings was the Handley Page Hermes. The initial Hermes flew (and crashed) in December 1945, but 25 production Hermes Mk.IV were eventually built with some serving into the 1960s.

Specifications – Handley Page Hastings C.Mk.2

Wingspan	113 ft
Length	82 ft 8 in
Maximum speed	348 mph at 22,000 ft
Maximum take-off weight	80,000 lb
Range	1,690 miles
Service ceiling	26,500 ft
Engine	Four Bristol Hercules 106 radial piston engines, of 1,675 hp each
Crew	Six, plus 30 paratroops or 50 troops

North American AJ/A-2 Savage

The AJ Savage was developed as a three-seat aircraft carrier-based nuclear attack aircraft, and was a 'mixed power plant' aircraft similar to the Ryan Fireball (see pages 56 to 57). The U.S. Navy was determined to have a strategic role for its aircraft carriers, and the Savage was its first attempt to operate an aircraft capable of carrying the bulky nuclear weapons of the late-1940s from their decks. The Savage used a pair of Pratt & Whitney R-2800 Double Wasp radial engines as its primary powerplant, but also featured a single Allison J33-A-10/19 turbojet in the rear fuselage to provide a 'dash' capability. At the time of its first flight in July 1948 the Savage was the largest carrier-borne aircraft designed as such, although Lockheed P2V-2 Neptunes (see pages 188 to 189) had flown from an aircraft carrier earlier in 1948 as a stop-gap carrier-borne nuclear bomber. Three XAJ-1 prototypes were followed by 40 AJ-1s, the first flying in May 1949, with deliveries to U.S. Navy squadron VC-5 taking

place four months later with the unit becoming operational on the type the following year. By the end of 1951 four Composite Squadrons (VC) equipped with AJ-1s and Neptune variants had been established, with other units forming later. The revised AJ-2P photo-reconnaissance version, of which 30 examples were produced, was equipped with up to 18 cameras and an increased fuel load. The AJ-2P in fact preceded the AJ-2, which made its maiden flight early in 1953. The AJ-2 had a revised tailplane with no dihedral, a taller vertical tail and increased fuel capacity. Production ended after 70 AJ-2s were built, bringing total Savage manufacture to 143. A turboprop development powered by two 5,100 shp Allison T40-A-6 turboprops and no jet engine was built as the XA2J-1, but failed to enter production. Service use of the Savage was shortened because of the development of a jet successor, the Douglas A3D (A-3) Skywarrior (see pages 136 to 137), which reached U.S. Navy Heavy Attack

A North American AJ-2 Savage, Bureau Number 134061, shows off the bulky lines of this early nuclear-armed naval bomber.

The photo-reconnaissance derivative of the AJ Savage was the AJ-2P, which could carry up to 18 cameras and had a revised nose profile amongst other alterations from the standard Savage layout (Photo: North American Aviation).

Squadrons by mid-1956. As they were replaced in the nuclear strike role a number of Savages were equipped as airborne refuelling tankers, retaining the AJ-1 and –2 designations until the introduction of the tri-service scheme in 1962, when they became A-2As and A-2Bs respectively. While the AJ-2P had been retired by the end of 1960, the Navy had to wait until sufficient Skywarriors were converted for the airborne tanking role in the early-1960s before it could completely retire the Savage.

Specifications – North American AJ-2 (A-2B) Savage

Wingspan	75 ft 2 in
Length	63 ft 1 in
Maximum speed	471 mph at 15,000 ft
Maximum take-off weight	52,862 lb
Range	1,727 miles carrying a Mk 15 bomb
Service ceiling	27,000 ft
Armament	One Mk 4, Mk 6 or Mk 15 nuclear bomb, or a nominal load of 9,600 lb (4,355 kg) of conventional munitions
Engine	Two Pratt & Whitney R-2800-48 Double Wasp radial piston engines, of 2,400 hp each, and one Allison J33-A-10 turbojet, of 4,600 lb st
Crew	Three

de Havilland D.H.106 Comet

In one of its more far-sighted deliberations, Britain's wartime Brabazon Committee produced its Type IV requirement for the development of a jet-powered airliner for post-war civil operations. A beautiful aircraft, the Comet nonetheless suffered a series of terrible crashes that resulted in a massive accident investigation program. Eventually the problem was traced to metal fatigue around the windows, caused by repeated pressurisation of the fuselage – at that time a new and unknown phenomenon. Unfortunately, the Comet never regained its reputation in the market after the accidents and Britain watched its lead in jet airliners slip away to the Americans. The prototype first flew on 27 July 1949 powered by four 4,450 lb st de Havilland Ghost 50 Mk 1 turbojets, and differed from the subsequent production Mk.1s by having a single wheel main undercarriage. Only BOAC ever used Comet 1s to carry fare-paying passengers, initially on its London-

Johannesburg service. This started on 2 May 1952 and was an important moment in civil aviation – the world's first-ever jet-powered fare-paying civil transport flight. The Mk.1 was followed by the Mk.1A with more powerful Ghost turbojets, deliveries going to three airlines and the Canadian military. Mk.2s powered by 7,300 lb st Rolls-Royce Avon Mk 503s were rejected by BOAC and so were transferred to Britain's Royal Air Force, No.216 Squadron becoming its first-ever jet transport unit. Attempting to recapture the airline market, the prototype Comet 3 later became the first jet to complete an around the world flight. However, it was superseded by the Comet 4 with 11,500 lb st Avon Mk 524s, 19 of which successfully entered BOAC service together with a small number of other airlines. BOAC launched transatlantic services with a Comet 4 in October 1958, just before the American Boeing 707. The Mk.4B had a stretched fuse-

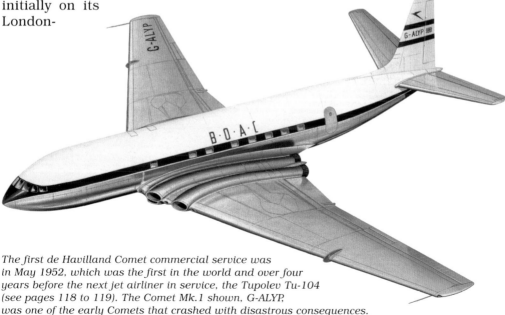

The first de Havilland Comet commercial service was in May 1952, which was the first in the world and over four years before the next jet airliner in service, the Tupolev Tu-104 (see pages 118 to 119). The Comet Mk.1 shown, G-ALYP, was one of the early Comets that crashed with disastrous consequences.

The de Havilland Comet was a beautiful but flawed airliner, the type never gaining the success that it deserved following dreadful early crashes. This is a Comet 4 of BOAC (Photo: British Overseas Airways Corporation).

lage for 99 passengers and a shorter wingspan, entering BEA service in 1960. The final version developed was the Mk.4C, using the longer wings of the Mk.4 and fuselage of the Mk.4B, which was flown by the R.A.F. and several civil operators. Total Comet production was 115, including the two original prototypes and the last two which were converted as prototypes for the Nimrod maritime reconnaissance aircraft. Most of the surviving Comet 4 variants were eventually acquired by the British airline Dan-Air, which ultimately flew the last passenger service of the design in November 1980. Several Comets were used by Britain's Ministry of Defence for test duties until well into the 1990s. However, the Nimrod still serves with the R.A.F., and in 2005 was being subjected to a re-manufacturing program that will allow the basic Comet airframe in upgraded Nimrod form to remain flying for another 30 plus years.

Specifications – de Havilland D.H.106 Comet Mk.4B

Wingspan	107 ft 10
Length	118 ft
Maximum speed	532 mph at 20,000 ft
Maximum take-off weight	156,000 lb
Range	up to 3,350 miles
Service ceiling	23,500 ft
Engine	Four Rolls-Royce Avon 524 turbojet engines, of 10,500 lb st each
Accommodation	Five flight crew plus stewards/stewardesses, up to some 99 passengers

'Parasite' Fighters

One of the more curious post-Second World War military programs was that of the 'parasite' fighter. In fact the idea was not new even then. During the inter-war period, both the Russians and Americans in particular had experimented with fighter aircraft based on or underneath other aircraft or airships. The U.S. Navy initiated a comparatively successful program in which biplane Curtiss F9C fighters were hung from a 'trapeze' beneath the envelope (fuselage) of airships such as the U.S.S. Akron. Each fighter was fitted with a special frame above its fuselage that, in simplest terms, hooked onto the 'trapeze' extended from the underside of the airship. The fighter could 'take-off' from this precarious position, fly its mission to defend the airship against attack or perform other duties, and then land back on earth or return to the airship for a 'hook-on.' In the Soviet Union, small fighters were hung in this way from the fuselages or wings of large

bombers, or even based above the wings of the giant aircraft that they were intended to defend. In World War Two, it was expected that bombers would have increasing range possibilities greater than those of their escort fighters, thus making it perhaps sensible for them to carry their own defending fighters along for protection. It was also feared in the United States that if Britain was defeated by Nazi Germany, bombing missions would need to be flown against Germany from bases in America. Large strategic bombers were likely to have the range or endurance to achieve this, but not their escort fighters. The parasite fighter concept was therefore re-evaluated in a program launched in 1942. The McDonnell company (which later became one of America's aviation giants) responded by designing a tiny, jet-powered fighter intended to fit into the bomb-bay of a Convair B-36

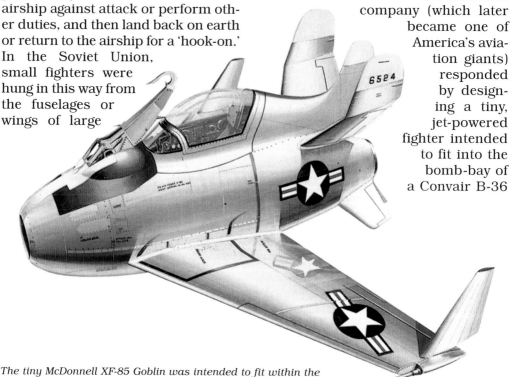

The tiny McDonnell XF-85 Goblin was intended to fit within the bomb-bay of a Convair B-36 bomber, the large retractable hook in front of its windscreen designed to attach to the bomber's 'trapeze' structure.

*A sequence of photographs showing an XF-85 attempting
a 'hook-on' to the trials EB-29B's extended 'trapeze'
(Photos: U.S. Air Force).*

bomber (see pages 82 to 83). An elaborate retractable trapeze was devised to allow the little fighter to be extended below the bomber's fuselage in flight, 'take-off' and fly its defensive mission and then return to the bomber (or land on earth with a skid undercarriage). In reality all this was somewhat fanciful, and the whole idea never reached operational status. Nevertheless, two prototype McDonnell XF-85 Goblin fighters were ordered. No B-36 was ever made available to test out the program and so a Boeing B-29 Superfortress bomber was converted instead to act as the test EB-29B 'mother ship.' In a very risky operation with a completely untried aircraft, the XF-85's first flight was made from the B-29 on 23 August 1948. The XF-85 was found to need some modification to aid handling, and in total seven actual flights including three 'hook-ons' were achieved by the two XF-85 prototypes, plus others in which they simply hung from the bomber's 'trapeze.' Eventually, the successful widespread deployment of in-flight refuelling systems rendered the whole idea obsolete, by allowing in-flight refuelled fighters similar range capabilities to the bombers that they might need to defend. However, the 'parasite' concept did find one comparatively useful post-war application for the FICON reconnaissance aircraft system (see pages 86 to 87).

Specifications – McDonnell XF-85 Goblin (some data provisional)

Wingspan	21 ft 1.5 in
Length	16 ft 3.25 in
Maximum speed	648 mph at sea level
Maximum take-off weight	5,600 lb
Endurance	77 minutes (maximum)
Service ceiling	48,200 ft
Armament	Four nose-mounted 0.5 in (12.7 mm) machine guns (planned for production examples)
Engine	One Westinghouse J34-WE-22 turbojet engine, of 3,000 lb st
Crew	One

Boulton Paul P.111 and P.120

The development of jet propulsion and the new advances in design and aerodynamics during the World War Two period opened the way towards some spectacular warplanes in the post-Second World War era. In reality, however, much research had to be carried out to verify new concepts and to try out new ideas, and the post-war period saw many research aircraft and odd 'one-offs' created for these purposes. Some of these trials aircraft are covered elsewhere in this book, but as noted on pages 66 to 67, some of them proved to be less than safe. One design layout that gained much interest after the war was the tail-less delta design for bombers and fighter aircraft. This idea had already existed for some time and much research had been made in Nazi Germany into the delta-wing concept. Nevertheless a large amount of investigation still needed to be done, especially as Britain's aircraft industry

was viewing this type of design layout with interest for several new warplanes. In response to a need by Britain's Royal Aircraft Establishment (RAE) for a transonic-capable (i.e. able to fly in the range of velocities just below and above the speed of sound) delta-shaped research aircraft, Specification E.27/46 was drafted. The Boulton Paul company was able to gain the contract for this work, and the new research aircraft was given the company designation P.111. It was designed specifically to examine the characteristics of the delta wing and so its wingspan and shape could be altered by the addition or deletion of two extra wingtip sections. The height of its vertical tail could also be altered. The single prototype first flew in October 1950, but its handling qualities were quite difficult to master. Damaged in a landing accident in late 1951 or early 1952, the P.111 was repaired and slightly altered, and was

The sole Boulton Paul P.111, serial number VT935, was a delta-wing research aircraft. It is seen here after re-build into P.111a configuration with its smart yellow and black paint scheme.

After retirement from its research programs, the Boulton Paul P.111a was based at Cranfield in England for instructional and training purposes, and this photograph shows it on display at that airfield. It is now displayed in the Midland Air Museum at Coventry Airport (Photo: John Batchelor).

re-designated P.111a. In this form, and painted yellow, it flew again in July 1953. In early 1954 it was assigned to the RAE, and performed various tests and trials until mid-1958. A second delta-wing research aircraft was also built by Boulton Paul. Designated P.120, this machine differed from the P.111 in having small horizontal tailplane surfaces set high on its vertical tail, plus other differences including moveable wingtips. It first flew in August 1952, but was destroyed later that month due to a fatigue failure of the hinges for the left-hand elevon surfaces. Other important development work into delta-wing concepts was carried out by the Avro 707 and Fairey F.D.2 research aircraft, and types such as the Gloster Javelin, Avro Vulcan and Dassault Mirage series (all described later in this book) were successful front-line delta-winged aircraft.

Specifications – Boulton Paul P.111

Wingspan	33 ft 6 in (with wingtips installed)
Length	26 ft 1 in
Maximum speed	Mach 0.95-0.98, theoretically supersonic in dive
Maximum take-off weight	9,600 lb
Service ceiling	(not specified)
Engine	One Rolls-Royce Nene 3-series turbojet engine, of some 5,100 lb st
Crew	One

Boeing B-47 Stratojet

A total of just over 2,000 B-47 Stratojets helped form the backbone of the U.S. Air Force's Strategic Air Command (SAC) bomber fleet – poised to unleash nuclear Armageddon on the Soviet Union – during the darkest days of the Cold War. While it was produced in greater numbers than most other post-war bomber aircraft, the Boeing B-47 had a relatively short career in its primary role and was – thankfully – destined never to be used in anger. However, the various RB-47 reconnaissance versions produced were active around the borders of the Iron and Bamboo Curtains for many years, ferreting out vital intelligence data, and attacks by Communist fighters resulted in two being shot down. The B-47 was designed as America's first swept-wing bomber, with a fighter-type cockpit and an unusual tandem wheel undercarriage layout. The prototype XB-47 made its first flight on 17 December 1947, powered by six J35 turbojet engines. These were replaced by J47 turbojets

in the second prototype, and these powerplants in successive marks powered all later B-47 versions. Ten B-47A were followed by 399 B-47Bs with a higher all-up weight and eventually J47-GE-23s, the Korean conflict and Cold War adding great speed to the whole program. The definitive Stratojet bomber was the B-47E with –25/25A engines and up to 33 jettisonable JATO bottles, built-in provision for air-refuelling and heavier calibre tail guns than the B-model. The B-47E was produced in four distinctive versions (B-47E-I to –IV) by Boeing (931 examples), Douglas (274) and Lockheed (385 or 386). Many of the B-47Bs were later upgraded with E-model improvements as B-47B-IIs. In SAC service bomber B-47 units were rotated on overseas deployments, as the aircraft did not have the range to strike all of the targets within the Soviet Union from bases in the United States. Reconnaissance versions consist of the eight-camera carrying RB-47B that were used to train

A Boeing B-47E Stratojet in flight. The U.S. Air Force was the only operational user of the type.

A nice head-on air-to-air photograph of an early Boeing B-47 Stratojet, possibly a B-47A, which shows the engine arrangement of this highly-capable early jet bomber (Photo: Boeing).

crews for the definitive longer-nosed RB-47E, and the RB-47K combat weather reconnaissance version. The RB-47E had a short service life, as photo-reconnaissance was soon overtaken in SAC by electronic reconnaissance. The main electronic reconnaissance Stratojet was the RB-47H, used alongside small numbers of ERB-47Hs in Classified electronic surveillance roles. Other versions were converted for weather reconnaissance (WB-47B and E), communications relay (EB-47L), target drone (QB-47E), conversion training (TB-47B) and as engine test-beds (XB-47D with Wright turboprops, and the Canadair CL-52 with a large Canadian-derived Orenda Iroquois jet engine). The last Stratojet in SAC service was an RB-47H, retired in December 1967, although a pair of EB-47Es were used by the U.S. Navy in the ECM 'aggressor' role until late 1977.

Specifications – Boeing B-47E-II Stratojet

Wingspan	116 ft
Length	107 ft 1 in
Maximum speed	606 mph at 16,300 ft
Maximum take-off weight	198,180 lb
Range	4,035 miles
Service ceiling	40,500 ft
Armament	Two rearward-firing 0.787 in (20 mm) cannons, up to 20,000 lb of bombs in the bomb-bay
Engine	Six General Electric J47-GE-25 or 25A turbojet engines, of 7,200 lb st each with water injection
Crew	Three

English Electric/BAC Canberra

The English Electric/BAC Canberra is one of the classic British military jet aircraft, and was the Royal Air Force's first operational jet bomber. Combining a pair of Rolls-Royce Avon axial flow turbojets within mid-set engine nacelles in a broad wing with a sleek fuselage, the Canberra was a great success, and was even built under licence in the United States. The prototype English Electric A.1 first flew on 13 May 1949, with three other Canberra A.1/B.Mk.1 examples following to specification B.3/45, the second powered by Rolls-Royce Nene turbojets, although Avons powered all subsequent examples. Delayed development of an advanced radar-bombing system resulted in the adoption for the Canberra of an optical system, and thus a clear-glazed nose for a bombardier. The resulting aircraft was the Canberra B.Mk.2, over four hundred examples of which were built with the first joining No.101 Squadron, Royal Air Force, in May 1951. The subsequent B.Mk.6 was a longer-range version

with Avon Mk.109 engines, some being modified as B.Mk.15s with underwing pylons. The good high-altitude performance of the basic Canberra layout resulted in two revised specialist photo-reconnaissance versions, the PR.Mk.3 and PR.Mk.7. A larger wing and a redesigned nose section were combined in the reconnaissance PR.Mk.9, allowing it to climb to some 58,000 ft (17,678 m) – 23 production examples were delivered for the R.A.F. by Short Brothers. R.A.F. reconnaissance Canberras were frequently involved in penetrating Soviet airspace during the Cold War. Low-level interdiction versions were also produced, including the interim B(I).Mk.6, the dedicated B(I).Mk.8 with a new off-set tandem-seating cockpit layout, and several export versions. B(I).Mk.8s based in West Germany were the R.A.F.'s last operational bomber Canberras. Conversion training for Canberra aircrew was undertaken using the Canber-

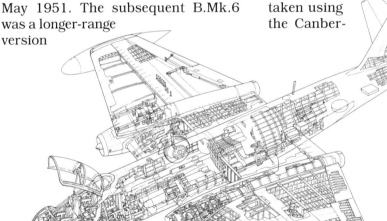

The English Electric/BAC Canberra was one of the classic early jet-powered combat aircraft. The type represented here is a bomber-interdiction model, the B(I).Mk.8, with tandem seating for its two crew members.

Training aircraft are often painted in high-visibility color schemes. This BAC Canberra with black and yellow undersides is a land-based Royal Navy target-towing Canberra TT.Mk.18, serial number WJ614 (Photo: Flight Refuelling Ltd.)

ra T.Mk.4 training derivative. Target-towing, electronic warfare, radar training, and target drone versions of the Canberra were produced by converting existing airframes, including some specialized versions that served (shore-based) with Britain's Royal Navy. Many former R.A.F. Canberras were refurbished for export in a multitude of versions, joining others that were sold directly to overseas customers. Canberras served with the air arms of Argentina, Australia, Chile, Ecuador, Ethiopia, France, India, New Zealand, Peru, South Africa, Sweden, Venezuela, West Germany and Rhodesia/Zimbabwe, while the Commonwealth Aircraft Corporation appropriately built Canberra B.Mk.20s in Australia. Very unusually, the Canberra was licence-built in the United States as the Martin B-57, this being one of America's first jet-powered bombers and included specially-developed high-level reconnaissance derivatives. Canberras or B-57s fought in many wars including the Falklands conflict of 1982, southern African bush wars, India-Pakistan confrontations, the Suez crisis in 1956, and during the long American involvement in Southeast Asia during the Vietnam War. In 2005, India and the R.A.F. still operated Canberras, the latter with several irreplaceable PR.Mk.9 for specialized reconnaissance duties on strength. Some 1,352 of all Canberras, including overseas licence-production, were built.

Specifications – English Electric Canberra B.Mk.2

Wingspan	63 ft 11.5 in
Length	65 ft 6 in
Maximum speed	570 mph at 40,000 ft
Maximum take-off weight	46,000 lb
Range	2,656 miles
Service ceiling	48,000 ft
Armament	Up to 6,000 lb of bombs in the fuselage bomb-bay
Engine	Two Rolls-Royce Avon RA.3 Mk.101 turbojet engines, of 6,500 lb st each
Crew	Two or three

Northrop F-89 Scorpion

One of the great advances in warplane capability that arose during World War Two was the appearance of the radar-equipped night fighter. Hitherto, fighters were equipped principally to fight by day. The rise of the night fighter extended the capabilities of what fighter aircraft could achieve, and after World War Two this capacity started to be extended further. Thus, in our own time, most combat aircraft can now fight equally well at night or in all weather conditions as well as during clear daytime conditions. In the 1950s the 'all-weather' fighter came to the fore, sometimes armed with air-to-air rockets – this was the period in which guided air-to-air missiles were in their infancy, and the traditional gun or cannon armament of previous fighters was regularly being abandoned for rocket-only or eventually missile-only armament. One of the most famous of the 1950s all-weather fighters was the Northrop F-89 Scorpion, which was also arguably the first nuclear-armed

fighter in service. The F-89 was the winner of a U.S. Army Air Force design requirement late in World War Two for a future night fighter. Northrop had already created the only purpose-built Allied night fighter of the war – the twin piston-engined P-61 Black Widow – but the F-89 was intended from the start for jet propulsion. The first XP-89 (later called XF-89), powered by two Allison (General Electric) J35 turbojets, flew on 16 August 1948. Unfortunately the development of this type proved to be lengthy, the first of the two prototypes built being lost in February 1950 due to horizontal tail problems. The delays in the whole F-89 program were worsened by fears over the Soviet Union's growing capability to attack the Continental United States with nuclear-armed bombers, the F-89 by then having been identified as the main future all-weather interceptor to defend the U.S. against such attack. The initial production model was the cannon-armed F-89A, followed very soon by the F-89B, and the F-89C with a revised horizontal tail. A

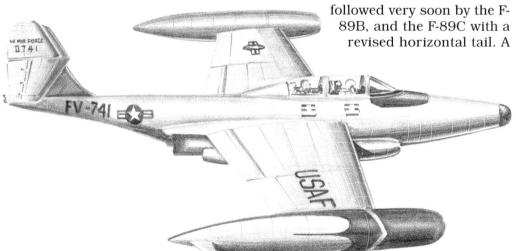

Serial number 50-741 was the first production Northrop F-89C Scorpion, officially an F-89C-1-NO. The F-89C was the last of the cannon-armed Scorpions before an all-rocket or missile armament took over.

The Northrop F-89 Scorpion was a heavily-armed and very capable all-weather fighter. Unlike the fighters of the Second World War era, it relied principally on unguided rockets or (later) guided missiles to attack opposing aircraft. This development YF-89D is firing a salvo of unguided rockets from its wing-tip pods (Photo: Northrop).

significant change came about with the F-89D. This version was the first Scorpion to be rocket-armed, it being thought that firing salvoes of unguided rockets into bomber formations might be the best way to defend America if a Soviet attack ever came. The F-89D was fitted with two huge wingtip pods mounting up to 104 FFARs (Free Flight or Folding Fin Aerial Rockets). 682 F-89D were built as the most numerous Scorpion version, some 350 later being converted to F-89J standard from 1956 and equipped with GAR-1 (later AIM-4) Falcon early-generation guided air-to-air missiles or the AIR-2 Genie nuclear-armed rocket. The F-89H was the first (and last) new-build Scorpion to use the Falcon guided missiles from the start. Scorpions eventually played a large part in the extensive defence system that the Americans built during the 1950s to defend the United States from possible Soviet attack during the Cold War. After retirement from regular U.S.A.F. service, many Scorpions were used by the second-line Air National Guard until 1969.

Specifications – Northrop F-89D Scorpion (early production)

Wingspan	59 ft 8 in
Length	53 ft 10 in
Maximum speed	638 mph at 11,000 ft
Maximum take-off weight	46,614 lb
Radius of action	approximately 382 miles
Service ceiling	48,900 ft
Armament	104 2.75 in (70 mm) unguided FFARs in wingtip pods
Engine	Two Allison J35-A-33A turbojet engines, of 7,200 lb st each with afterburning
Crew	Two

Bristol Freighter and Wayfarer

Air transport is very different in our time compared to the post-Second World War period. Fast, comfortable passenger jet aircraft with long-range performance are commonplace nowadays, and shorter air transport routes are covered by efficient and smart turboprop-powered aircraft or jet-powered regional airliners. Today, however, air travellers the world over are unable to take with them on their airline flights one essential part of everyday life – their car. How different in the 1950s! During the 1950s and 1960s it was not thought out of place to take your car along for the ride, and a particular British transport aircraft was able to achieve just that. The Bristol Type 170 Freighter is almost unique in the annals of air transport by being able to carry passengers AND their cars. Design of what became the Bristol Freighter began during World War Two, one of the roles envisaged for the proposed design being as a transport for military vehicles up to lorry size under Specification C.9/45. Another specification, 22/44, related to

a passenger-carrying role and eventually the Freighter was designed by the Bristol company with the possibility of a variety of military and civil transport utility applications. Four prototypes were initially intended to test out these diverse roles, the first being a Type 170 Freighter Mk.I cargo aircraft with front fuselage clamshell-loading doors. It first flew on 2 December 1945. The initial passenger-carrying Type 170 Mk.II Wayfarer flew in April 1946. There were therefore two separate but related developments of the Type 170 configuration, and the Freighter cargo-carrier eventually evolved into a car-carrier rather than a military vehicle transport. After a number of changes to the prototype configuration, production was initiated of a number of specific versions, the most important early production standard being the Mk.21. This version could be configured as either a freight carrier, or with a mixed freight/passenger layout, or simply as a 32-passenger airliner depending on interior configuration and customer require-

The Bristol Type 170 Freighter was a unique air transport aircraft that in some of its possible internal configurations could carry cars as well as their drivers and passengers. Particularly noticeable on this drawing of a Mk.31 Freighter are the clamshell-opening front fuselage loading doors.

A famous operator of the Bristol Freighter on car-carrying flights across the English Channel was Silver City Airways. Pictured is a long-nose Type 170 Mk.32, often called a Super Freighter (Photo: Silver City Airways).

ment. The Mk.31 introduced a prominent dorsal fin, and the Mk.32 Super Freighter added more capacity to the Freighter's already spacious fuselage with a lengthened nose. One of the best-known uses for the Type 170 was on the Channel air bridge, in which Freighters plied across the English Channel between south-eastern England and northern France carrying cars and their owners. This was a virtually unique air transport operation that sadly ceased many years ago with the development of sea-going car-carrying passenger ferries. Freighters also served relatively widely as military transports, military export customers including Pakistan, Australia, Canada, New Zealand, Argentina, Iraq, and Burma. In total, 214 Type 170 were built, production ceasing in the late 1950s.

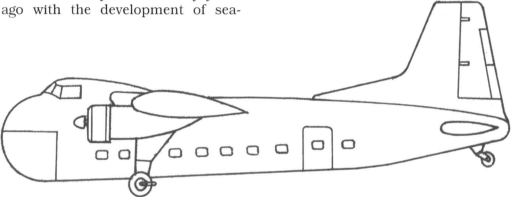

The Type 170 Freighter (this is a Mk.31 version) was a bulky but practical transport that saw widespread use despite being built in comparatively small numbers.

Specifications – Bristol Type 170 Freighter Mk.21E

Wingspan	108 ft
Length	68 ft 4 in
Maximum speed	224 mph at 6,500 ft
Maximum take-off weight	40,000 lb
Range	up to 970 miles
Service ceiling	24,850 ft
Engine	Two Bristol Hercules 672 radial piston engines, of 1,700 hp
Accommodation	Three or four crew, up to 32 passengers in passenger configuration

Tupolev Tu-104

The increasing use of jet propulsion for civil as well as military aircraft was one of the great steps forward in civil aviation during the post-World War Two era. A relative of Britain's de Havilland Comet airliner as described on pages 104–105, jet propulsion at last gave civil aircraft the performance capabilities to fly a viable number of passengers non-stop over increasingly long distances. Although Britain gained the great accolade of having the first civil jet transport in passenger-carrying service with the Comet, this aircraft suffered some catastrophic early crashes in the 1950s. At that time a second country, the Soviet Union, was also developing a historically-significant production civil jet transport. This was the Tupolev Tu-104, which was a product of the Tupolev design bureau within the Soviet Union's unwieldy centralised aircraft industry. Unlike Britain's Comet airliner, however, the Tu-104 was not wholly an original design, because it drew on the general layout of an existing military production aircraft. This was the Tu-16 bomber, known to NATO as the 'Badger.' The first Tu-16 flew in April 1952, and the type was a successful bomber design for Soviet forces. Design of the Tu-104 airliner began in 1954, as a response to the growing need for a modernisation of the fleet of the Soviet State airline Aeroflot, whose traffic volume was rapidly growing. For short-range routes several designs resulted, including eventually the turboprop-powered Antonov An-24 series (see pages 174 to 175). For longer routes, requiring higher performance, the Tupolev design team adapted the Tu-16 bomber layout with a new passenger-carrying pressurised fuselage to create the Tu-104. The prototype first flew on 17 June 1955, built with some Tu-16 components. After successful trials and performance-proving flights to Western Europe by prototype and development examples, the Tu-104 entered scheduled airline service in September 1956 on Aeroflot's internal

This 1960s photograph gives a good idea of the size of the Tupolev Tu-104 series jet civil transport (note the two men standing near the right-hand wing). The Tu-104 was a true pioneer, and was in service before the famous American Boeing 707 airliner (Photo: via Hans Meier).

The Tupolev Tu-104 was an elegant aircraft in flight, quite in addition to its being an important step forward in civil aviation. This example, registration CCCP-L5413, was flown by Aeroflot (the Soviet Union's State airline) with the fleet number 27. It is recorded as being a Tu-104G, and was probably built as a conversion from a Tu-16 bomber.

Moscow-Omsk-Irkutsk (Siberia) route. Thus the Tu-104 was the second-ever jet-powered airliner to enter regular scheduled airline service, approximately two years before the American Boeing 707. The initial major production model was the Tu-104, with seating for 50 passengers – some are believed to have been converted from Tu-16 airframes. Further development led to the 70-passenger Tu-104A with increased power and revised passenger seating. Used by Aeroflot, six of this version were also operated by the Czechoslovak State airline CSA. A slightly lengthened version, the 100-passenger Tu-104B, was later devel-

oped, and several changes in seating arrangement were later made to aircraft already in service. Total production of the Tu-104 is believed to have been just over 200 (possibly 207), with service continuing until 1981. A small number were used by the Soviet military, in addition to one employed for cosmonaut (Soviet astronaut) training. Some Tu-104G were re-built from Tu-16 airframes, and a single Tu-107 (a transport Tu-16) was built. A related aircraft was the Tu-124 (first flight 1960, the first turbofan-engined production airliner), a smaller, shorter-range derivative, of which at least 112 were built.

Specifications – Tupolev Tu-104B

Wingspan	113 ft 4 in
Length	131 ft 4.75 in
Maximum speed	590.5 mph at 32,808 ft
Maximum take-off weight	167,550 lb
Range	1,647 miles
Service ceiling	37,730 ft
Engine	Two Mikulin AM-3M-500 turbojet engines, of 21,385 lb st each
Accommodation	Five flight crew plus stewards/stewardesses, 100 passengers

Grumman Albatross

Although flying-boats and seaplanes were popular during the pre-World War Two period, and proved very useful in various military roles during the war, the general popularity of water-based aircraft has not been as great in the post-war world. As pointed out on the following two pages, attempts to continue the pre-Second War Two tradition of water-borne airliner flying-boats did not meet with long-term success. However, a number of amphibians (conventional undercarriage-equipped flying-boats) have persisted in the post-war era, and one of the best-known is the Grumman Albatross. In fact even this design was originally born during World War Two, when the Grumman company commenced in 1944 development work to produce a follow-on to the successful Grumman Goose amphibian already in widespread service. Utility roles such as transport, casualty evacuation, search and rescue (SAR) and related roles were envisaged for the new aircraft. Two Model G-64 prototypes designated XJR2F-1 under the U.S. Navy's eccentrically cumbersome designation system were built, the first flying in October 1947. The Albatross was a bigger, more aerodynamically refined aircraft compared to the

Goose. Both the U.S. Navy and U.S.A.F. duly ordered the Albatross, the latter receiving the first examples in 1949 under the designation SA-16A. Early U.S. Navy examples were UF-1s, but the type also entered U.S. Coast Guard service as the UF-1G in the early 1950s. U.S.A.F. SA-16As served on SAR duties during the Korean War, carrying out several perilous missions to rescue downed Allied airmen. A major change subsequently arose with the Model G-111, which introduced an increased span wing with revised configuration, a taller vertical tail and other alterations. This was built for the U.S.A.F. as the SA-16B, with some earlier SA-16A being upgraded to this standard. In 1962 the designations for U.S. military aircraft were rationalised, the Air Force Albatrosses becoming HU-16A and HU-16B, U.S. Navy machines becoming HU-16C and HU-16D, and the U.S. Coast Guard's improved Albatrosses being HU-16E. An anti-submarine version of the SA-16B (UF-2) was developed, fitted with a retractable tail-mounted magnetic anomaly detector (MAD) boom, nose radar and provision to carry weapons

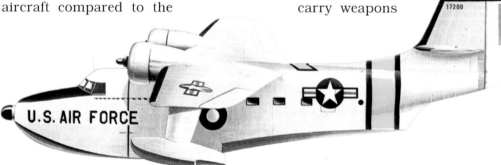

Even though it usually operated from water, the Grumman Albatross was widely used by the U.S. Air Force in addition to the U.S. Navy. This example is a tall-tail SA-16B (HU-16B) in U.S.A.F. search and rescue (SAR) markings.

Take-offs from, and landings onto water, are potentially dangerous operations. This is an anti-submarine SA-16B (UF-2) derivative with nose-mounted radar, and (in the rear fuselage) a retracted MAD (magnetic anomaly detector) boom for detecting submerged submarines (Photo: Grumman History Center).

beneath its wings. Some were exported to Norway, which was one of many foreign operators of various Albatross versions. In total, 464 Albatrosses plus two prototypes are thought to have been built. U.S.A.F. Albatrosses served on SAR duties during the Vietnam War, several being destroyed in this dangerous work, while a small number were temporarily used as flying command and control directors for SAR operations. The second-line Air National Guard in the U.S. employed Albatrosses until 1971, and the type has also been used for civil airline work. The best-known civil-operated Albatrosses were those flown by Chalk's in Florida, for operations in the Caribbean.

Specifications – Grumman HU-16B Albatross (SAR configuration)

Wingspan	96 ft 8 in
Length	62 ft 9 in
Maximum speed	236 mph at 20,000 ft
Maximum take-off weight	29,000 lb
Range	2,850 miles
Service ceiling	25,000 ft
Engine	Two Wright R-1820-76 radial piston engines, of 1,425 hp each
Crew	Six

Saro SR.45 Princess

During the later stages of World War Two, when it became increasingly obvious that Britain and her Allies were going to be victorious in the war, attempts were made in Britain to foresee and plan for the development of civil aviation after the conflict. This planning included the Brabazon Committee, which set out to plan and shape civil aircraft design and requirements for the coming peace. Several important designs drew their inspiration from this Committee's deliberations, including for example the Vickers Viscount airliner (see pages 80 to 81). However, the Brabazon Committee's examinations were focused on landplanes, with little or no regard to flying-boats. This was perhaps unusual because in the 1930s, the far-flung reaches of the former British Empire were being visited by successful Short 'C' Class flying-boats. Indeed, post-war some success was achieved by Short with the Sandringham and Solent civil conversions and derivatives of R.A.F. flying-boats (see pages 60 to 61). One British company that was thinking really big at that time was Saunders-Roe (Saro) on the Isle of Wight in southern England. Saro planned an enormous, turboprop-engined airliner flying-boat with intercontinental range that found expression in the SR.45 Princess design. Three prototypes were ordered by Britain's Ministry of Supply in May 1946 at a cost of £2.8 million. The Princess was an incredible technical achievement. Its large size presented considerable challenges in construction, and its design also included fuselage pressurization which was still being developed and perfected, together with power-operated controls of the type that were innovative at that time. The Princess was designed for ten turboprop engines, and the Bristol company met many difficulties in developing the Proteus turboprop for the Princess and also the Brabazon landplane airliner. Eight of the engines were paired

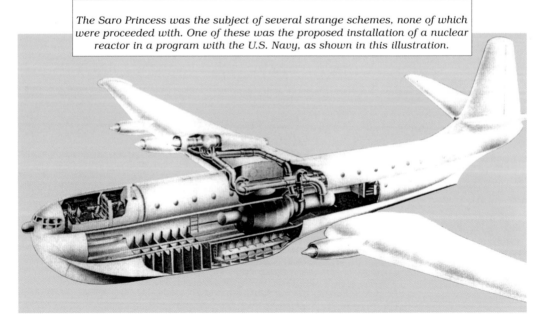

The Saro Princess was the subject of several strange schemes, none of which were proceeded with. One of these was the proposed installation of a nuclear reactor in a program with the U.S. Navy, as shown in this illustration.

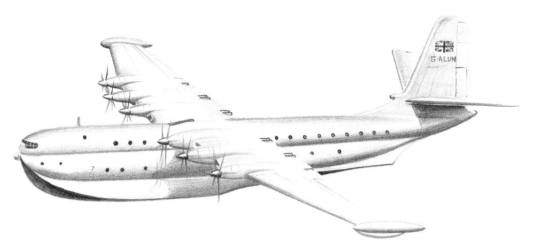

The Saro SR.45 Princess was a fine achievement, and would have been a veritable cruise liner of the skies. Unfortunately it was not a practical proposition in a post-war civil airliner market that was increasingly dominated by long-range landplanes.

and mounted in the inner four sets of engine nacelles. Eventually the costs and technical problems of the project soared out of control, and there were many delays. The first Princess, registration G-ALUN, eventually flew on 22 August 1952, but persistent problems especially with the engines resulted in the abandoning of the completion of the second and third aircraft. There was in fact no customer for these aircraft, Britain's British Overseas Airways Corporation (BOAC) never committing to operate them. It was rumoured that Britain's Aquila

Airways was a potential buyer, and at one time the Royal Air Force was the intended recipient to use the Princesses as troop-carriers or even as radar-equipped airborne early-warning aircraft. All work on the project ended in 1954, but several incredible schemes were later rumoured for the stored airframes. These included the installation of a nuclear reactor in a U.S. Navy program, and employment to air-lift sections of the Saturn V Moon rocket system. None came to fruition and the three airframes were eventually scrapped.

Specifications – Saro SR.45 Princess (some data estimated)

Wingspan	219 ft 6 in
Length	148 ft
Cruising speed	380 mph at 37,000 ft
Maximum take-off weight	315,530 lb
Range	5,270 miles
Endurance	15 hours
Engine	Ten Bristol Proteus Series 600 turboprop engines, of 3,200-3,500 shp each
Accommodation	Six flight crew, 105 passengers

Gloster Javelin

The unique Gloster GA.5 Javelin was the first front-line twin-engined delta-wing aircraft in the world. It was designed to Specification F.4/48 as a high-performance all-weather long-range fighter able to intercept fast bombers at high altitude. Development was a long process, resulting in nine basic variants. The first prototype made its maiden flight on 26 November 1951, and was followed by several further prototypes. The first production Javelin FAW.Mk.1 flew in July 1954, but service entry was delayed until early 1956 when No.46 Squadron at R.A.F. Odiham received its first examples. After 40 Mk.1s the FAW.Mk.2 entered production, with a shorter nose containing an American AI.Mk.22 (APQ-43) airborne interception radar in place of the standard British AI.Mk.17. For conversion training on this rather demanding aircraft, a batch of radar-less Javelin T.Mk.3 dual-control trainers was additionally built. The next fighter versions were the FAW.Mk.4 with an all-moving tailplane, the similar FAW.Mk.5 with additional fuel in the wings and the FAW.Mk.6, with the AI.22 radar again installed. Up to the Mk.6 standard, the Javelin's armament had normally comprised wing-mounted cannons, but the FAW.Mk.7 introduced

Firestreak guided air-to-air missiles as well as many airframe improvements, including wing-mounted vortex generators and a lengthened rear fuselage. Armstrong Siddeley Sapphire Sa.6 turbojets were replaced by more powerful Sa.7s from the FAW.Mk.7, the most numerous version built. The FAW.Mk.8 added a rudimentary reheat system to the Sapphires and was the final version equipped with the AI.22 radar, entering service in late 1959/early 1960. A Javelin FAW.Mk.8 was the last of 428 production examples of Gloster's 'flat iron' produced, the ultimate FAW.Mk.9 being a conversion of the Mk.7 with a modified leading edge, an autopilot and variable-area jet nozzles. Around 40 of these upgraded aircraft also had a large air refuelling probe, showing the gradual acceptance of this essential range and endurance-increasing equipment. Javelins served with some fourteen R.A.F. Fighter Command squadrons, but were replaced by the English Electric Lightning (see pages 172 to 173) by late 1963. However, No.11 Squadron in West Germany retained Javelins

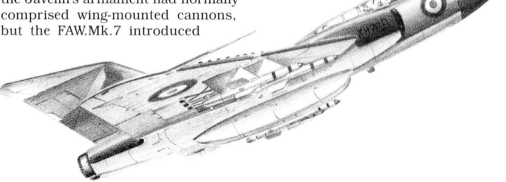

The Gloster Javelin's delta-wing layout appeared to be the best solution to the demanding Specification F.4/48. The type was only just subsonic, and is often attributed the accolade of being the R.A.F.'s first guided-missile armed fighter.

The artist tells us that this colorful Javelin FAW.Mk.9, serial number XH897, was involved in trials work at the A&AEE Boscombe Down for many years, including service with the Calibration Unit there. It is now in the aviation museum at Duxford.

until the mid-1960s, and the last R.A.F. squadron, in Singapore, flew them until 1968. While never firing a shot in anger, Javelins did fly patrols during the Confrontation with Indonesia in the early 1960s, escorting Tupolev Tu-16s and Ilyushin Il-28s away from the friendly territory of Malaysia. The last airworthy Javelin flew on trials duties from Boscombe Down in southern England until it was delivered to the aviation museum at Duxford in the mid-1970s. A proposed supersonic-capable Olympus-powered Javelin derivative was never built.

Specifications – Gloster Javelin FAW.Mk.9

Wingspan	52 ft
Length	56 ft 4 in
Maximum speed	620 mph at 40,000 ft
Maximum take-off weight	44,700 lb
Range	930 miles
Service ceiling	52,000 ft
Armament	Four wing-mounted 1.18 in (30 mm) cannons, up to four air-to-air guided missiles, or four packs of unguided air-to-air rockets beneath the wings
Engine	One Armstrong Siddeley Sapphire Sa.7R Mk.205 (left-hand) and one Mk.206 (right-hand), of 11,000 lb st each (12,300 lb st each with afterburning)
Crew	Two

Mikoyan-Gurevich MiG-17 and MiG-19

Warplane development is often a continuing form of evolution, and the line of jet-powered fighter aircraft designed by Mikoyan-Gurevich in the Soviet Union is a good illustration of this process. MiG was one of the pioneers of jet-powered combat aircraft in the Soviet Union with its MiG-9, as explained on pages 28 to 29. Subsequent design work led to the MiG-15 described on pages 58 to 59, which was one of the classic early front-line jet fighters. Nevertheless, although the MiG-15 was a successful design, it had some drawbacks including marked instability at high subsonic speeds. Continuing studies based on the MiG-15's basic design layout led to an improved derivative which first appeared under the 'SI' or I-330 designation. A new wing design with an altered vertical tail shape were the most obvious amongst several important alterations. The first of three SI prototypes flew on 1 February 1950. Unfortunately one of these three aircraft crashed during testing, but the new design was eventually found to be faster than the MiG-15 and much better to handle at high

speeds. Testing was completed in the summer of 1951 and the new type under the designation MiG-17 was ordered into production in August 1951. Initial deliveries followed soon after but it was later in 1952 before full production-standard aircraft were available in numbers. The basic MiG-17 was intended as a fighter with ground attack capability, and was followed by slightly upgraded models including the radar-equipped MiG-17P for rudimentary all-weather interception. A major change came with the MiG-17F, which was powered by a derivative of the MiG-17's standard British-derived VK-1 turbojet fitted with an afterburner as the VK-1F. The MiG-17F was the major MiG-17 production model, joined by the MiG-17PF radar-equipped derivative and the guided air-to-air missile-armed MiG-17PFU. MiG-17s served widely with Soviet forces and a large number of export customers. Licence production was additionally undertaken in Poland as the Lim-5 (MiG-17F) and Lim-5P (MiG-17PF), and in China as the J-5/F-5 and J-5A/F-5A. A two-seat derivative was also developed in

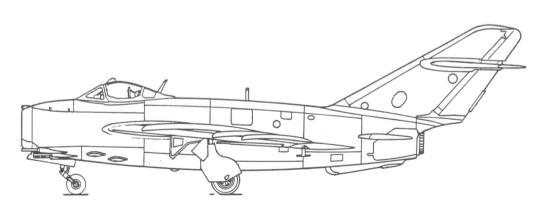

Although resembling the earlier MiG-15, the Mikoyan-Gurevich MiG-17 incorporated many new features including a re-designed wing of revised sweep-back and three wing 'fences' rather than the MiG-15's two, and the addition in some versions of an afterburning turbojet engine.

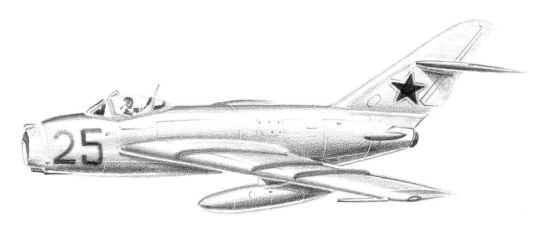

The MiG-17F was the most important production model of the MiG-17 line. This is a MiG-17F which was known to NATO as the 'Fresco-C.' MiG-17s saw a lot of combat during the Vietnam War, operated by the North Vietnamese.

China as the JJ-5/FT-5. Total production of all MiG-17 versions appears to be near to 9,000, and the type was known to NATO as 'Fresco.' MiG continued its evolutionary design work to create a fighter that would fly at supersonic speed in level flight. A long development process finally led to the twin-engined SM-9 which first flew in January 1954. From this was derived the production twin-engined MiG-19.

Fully supersonic in level flight, the MiG-19 was built in several versions which included licence production in Czechoslovakia and China. At least 2,500 (probably many more) were built of all marks, and the type was a contemporary of the North American F-100 Super Sabre (see pages 148 to 149) as one of the two initial supersonic fighter designs to enter service.

Specifications – Mikoyan-Gurevich MiG-17F

Wingspan	31 ft 7 in
Length	36 ft 11.5 in
Maximum speed	702 mph at 16,405 ft
Maximum take-off weight	13,382 lb
Range	1,038 miles with external fuel tanks
Service ceiling	54,462 ft
Armament	Three lower forward fuselage-mounted 0.9 in (23 mm) cannons, up to 2,205 lb of bombs or other ordnance on four underwing pylons
Engine	One Klimov VK-1F turbojet engine, of 7,452 lb st with afterburning
Crew	One

Vickers Valiant

The Vickers Valiant was the first of the famous trio of 'V-Bombers' that provided Britain's Royal Air Force with its long-range nuclear deterrent force from the late-1950s until nuclear missile-equipped submarines became operational with the Royal Navy. A total of 104 production Valiants was built, plus two prototypes and one B.Mk.2 prototype, a version optimized for the lower operating levels that many Valiants eventually flew at rather than the higher levels originally envisaged. Designed in response to Specification B.9/48 for a nuclear bomber capable of carrying a 10,000 lb bomb over 3,600 miles, the Valiant prototype made its first flight on 18 May 1951, and was followed by a developed second prototype. Five pre-production Valiants were also built, and 31 production Valiant B.Mk.1s. These started replacing English Electric/BAC Canberras (see pages 112 to 113) in R.A.F. service from early 1955. Three further Valiant versions were produced. Originally ordered as Valiant B.Mk.1s, ten were delivered as B(PR).Mk.1s plus a B.Mk.1 converted as this sub-type's prototype. The Valiant B(PR).Mk.1 was capable of carrying three different camera sets in its bomb bay for survey, or day- and night-photography. As the Valiant's bomber role was increasingly assumed by Handley Page Victors and Avro Vulcans (the other two British 'V-Bombers'), the Valiant had its primary role changed to that of single-point air-refuelling tanker aircraft, resulting in the BK.Mk.1, 44 of which were delivered. In addition, 14 B(PR)K.Mk.1s were built, combining the capabilities of the B(PR).Mk.1 and BK.Mk.1 into a single airframe. The Valiant went to war in 1956 when important numbers of these aircraft were used to attack Egyptian airfields during the abortive Suez campaign, flying from bases in Malta. Valiants were also used in British atomic bomb tests, with No.49 Squadron dropping the first nuclear weapon from a British aircraft on 11 October 1956 over Maralinga, southern Australia, and the first British hydrogen bomb on 15 May 1957 over Malden Island in the South Pacific. Valiants additionally served in the development program for Blue Steel, but did not carry this nuclear missile in squadron service. The switch to low-level operational flight profiles in the early 1960s

The Vickers Valiant was the first of the trio of 'V-Bombers' for Britain's nuclear deterrent, but the type was used as a conventional bomber during the Suez operations in late 1956.

Vickers Valiant BK.Mk.1 serial number XD823 was built as an in-flight refuelling tanker aircraft (Photo: Vickers Ltd.).

resulted in increased metal fatigue in the overall Valiant fleet. Cracks were discovered in the wing spars of several aircraft, forcing the fleet to be grounded in late 1964/early 1965. The majority of Valiants were scrapped soon after, although one continued to fly until 1968 for various duties.

Vickers Valiant at Farnborough in 1955 (Photo: Vickers Ltd.).

Specifications – Vickers Valiant B.Mk.1

Wingspan	114 ft 4 in
Length	108 ft 3 in
Maximum speed	567 mph at 30,000 ft
Maximum take-off weight	138,000 lb
Range	4,500 miles
Service ceiling	54,000 ft
Armament	One 10,000 lb nuclear or conventional bomb, or 21 1,000 lb bombs
Engine	Four Rolls-Royce Avon 204 or 205 turbojet engines, of 10,050 lb st each
Crew	Five

Handley Page Victor

Britain's Royal Air Force was not slow to see that the combination of the atomic bomb and jet propulsion would revolutionise strategic bombing after World War Two. In Operational Requirement (OR) 229 it outlined the need for a jet bomber capable of carrying the bulky first generation atomic weapons over a radius of 1,725 miles (2,776 km). This led to Specification B.35/46, to which Handley Page responded with its H.P.80 design, eventually building 86 examples as the unique, crescent-wing Victor. The Victor thus became the third of the famous trio of R.A.F. 'V-Bombers,' which also comprised the Avro Vulcan and Vickers Valiant described elsewhere in this book. Two prototype H.P.80s were ordered in April 1948, the first flying on Christmas Eve 1952, and the second in September 1954. The first production aircraft flew in February 1956 following an initial order for 25 Victor B.Mk.1s. No.232 OCU (Operational Conversion Unit) of the R.A.F. became the first service unit in November 1957, training crews for the first operational squadron, No.10, based at R.A.F. Cottesmore. A further

order that eventually included 25 B.Mk.1s followed, many of which later had an in-flight refuelling probe, new electronic countermeasures (ECM) equipment, drooping leading edges and tail warning radar added to become B.Mk.1As. Development continued to produce the B.Mk.2, 34 of which were built. The Mk.2 had a greater wingspan, increased maximum take-off weight and Rolls-Royce Conway turbofan engines in a redesigned wing root, in place of the Armstrong Siddeley Sapphire turbojets of the Mk.1. From late 1963 the B.Mk.2s were modified with fairings bearing chaff dispensers on the wing trailing edges as B.Mk.2Rs. Between 1963 and 1968 B.Mk.2Rs carried the Blue Steel nuclear stand-off weapon as their primary armament, although conventional and nuclear free-fall munitions could also be carried. Other Mk.2s were converted for the strategic reconnaissance role as B(SR).Mk.2s. As they were retired from the bomber role, Victor B.Mk.1s and Mk.1As were modified as one of several different air-refuelling tanker configuration standards. These includ-

Handley Page Victor SR2 of 543 Squadron R.A.F.

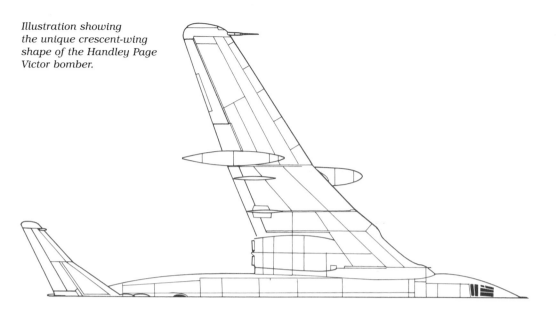

Illustration showing the unique crescent-wing shape of the Handley Page Victor bomber.

ed three-point layouts with refuelling equipment in pods under the wings, and a hose drum unit in the bomb-bay, and a separate configuration with just the wing-mounted units. Replaced as a bomber after 1968, many of the B.Mk.2Rs and (when they were retired in the 1970s) B(SR).Mk.2s were converted to three-point K.Mk.2 tankers.

Some of these Victor K.Mk.2s flew air-refuelling missions during the Falklands conflict of 1982, and in support of operations against Iraq in 1991. No.55 Squadron, the last Victor unit, disbanded in October 1993, finally bringing the R.A.F.'s 'V-Bomber' era to an end.

Specifications – Handley Page Victor B.Mk.2R

Wingspan	120 ft
Length	114 ft 11 in
Maximum speed	610 mph at 25,000 ft
Maximum take-off weight	approximately 238,000 lb
Range	approximately 4,900 miles
Service ceiling	52,500 ft
Armament	Up to six free-fall nuclear bombs or 35 1,000 lb conventional bombs carried internally, or one Blue Steel air-to-surface stand-off nuclear weapon
Engine	Four Rolls-Royce Conway RCo.17 Mk.201 turbofan engines, of 20,600 lb st each
Crew	Five

Boeing 707, 717 and 720

The disasters that befell Britain's pioneering de Havilland Comet airliner (see pages 104 to 105) opened the way for American domination of the jetliner market. The aircraft that initially contributed most to this dominance was the Boeing 707, the first in the highly-successful range of jet airliners from this American manufacturer. The type was developed initially as the Boeing Model 367-80, and was aimed at both the airlines and as an aerial tanker/transport for the U.S. Air Force. The Dash 80 was the forerunner of not only the civil Boeing Model 707 and 720 line, but also the Model 717, produced for the U.S.A.F. as the C-135 in a variety of versions. It made its first flight on 15 July 1954. Structurally the Dash 80 was very different from the first production 707-100 Series airliners, which had longer wings and a wider, longer fuselage. Pan Am was the launch customer, initially operating its Model 707s on the New York to Paris and London services from October 1958. The Boeing 707 therefore became the third jet-powered airliner, behind the Comet and Tupolev Tu-104, to enter airline service. Several airlines including American Airlines, Continental,

and TWA also ordered 707–100s, while Qantas of Australia acquired a shorter, long-range version for its Sydney to London service. Five 'hot-and-high' 707-200s were followed by the larger 707–300 designed for transoceanic flights, and the 707–300B with an even longer wing, increased maximum take-off weight and JT3D-3 turbofan engines. The 707-300C was a passenger/cargo convertible variant, but was also built as a windowless freighter. Rolls-Royce Conway 505/508 turbofans powered the 37 707-400s acquired by BOAC, Air India, El Al, Lufthansa and VARIG. On 23 November 1959 the prototype Boeing 720, developed for short/medium haul routes, made its maiden flight. A total of 154 were built. The last of the commercial 707s was the one-off 707-700, powered by CFM56 turbofan engines. 707s and 720s had long lives with the major airlines before being sold on for further service with second-tier operators, many eventually ending up as freighters in Africa or the Middle East. Several air arms used 707s as tankers or head-of-state VIP transports with, for example, specially-configured VC-137 aircraft serving as

The Boeing 707 is one of the world's classic jet airliners. The launch customer for this famous aircraft was the American airline Pan American (Pan Am), which put the type into service in October 1958.

Detail photographs of a Boeing 707, showing the flight deck and the engine installations (Photos: John Batchelor).

the U.S. President's 'Air Force One.' The military Model 717 program resulted in some 820 C-135s, 724 being KC-135A Stratotanker flight-refuelling tankers to complement the bomber force of the U.S.A.F.'s Strategic Air Command, although C-135A/B Stratolifters provided the Military Air Transport Service with its first jet transport. Numerous versions of the C-135 were produced by conversion for reconnaissance, air command post, test-bed, range telemetry and weather research tasks, while the tankers were subject to two separate re-engining efforts. Approximately 970 transport Model 707 were sold, although with the number of derivatives and civil/military operators this figure is open to some debate. While civil Boeing 707s were rare by 2005, more than half the C-135s built remain in service. A related development is the Boeing E-3 Sentry (see pages 276 to 277).

Specifications – Boeing 707-320B Intercontinental

Wingspan	145 ft 9 in
Length	152 ft 11 in
Maximum speed	627 mph at 25,000 ft
Maximum take-off weight	333,600 lb
Range	4,300 miles
Service ceiling	39,000 ft
Engine	Four Pratt & Whitney JT3D-7 turbofan engines, of 19,000 lb st each
Accommodation	Four flight crew plus stewards/stewardesses, up to 189 passengers

Sukhoi Su-7

The Soviet Union, as pointed out earlier in this book, was one of several major countries that considered it very important to develop jet-powered combat aircraft after World War Two. The MiG-15, MiG-17 and later, the MiG-19, became highly important early jet fighter aircraft that were produced by the Soviet Union's aircraft industry. However, development in the Soviet Union was not just limited to jet fighters. In the early 1950s the Sukhoi design bureau was re-established after several years of official disfavor under the repression of the Soviet Union's dictator Josef Stalin. Sukhoi at once began design work on a new ground attack jet-powered design. This early work was the start of what became one of the most important lines of combat aircraft in the post-war period, and the Sukhoi organisation continues to exist to this day as Russia's premier combat aircraft designer. Development work commenced in 1953, and the new type utilised swept-wing technology

from the start. Designated S-1, the new aircraft first flew on 7 September 1955. Powered by a Lyulka AL-7-series turbojet of comparatively modest performance, the S-1 was nevertheless fast and comparatively agile, but further development led to the revised S-2 second prototype which was developed as the initial production standard for the tactical Su-7B and later series. Therefore two main prototypes were built, and the type was represented in the flypast during the June 1956 aviation day celebration at Tushino near Moscow. The new warplane entered production late in 1957/early 1958 as the Sukhoi Su-7, and it received the NATO reporting name 'Fitter.' The later, two-seat Su-7U trainer series was subsequently called 'Moujik.' Very early Su-7s were basically fighters, but all subsequent single-seat models were dedicated attack aircraft. The first major production version of this configuration was the Su-7B (later called 'Fitter-A') strike fighter. The type was officially

The Sukhoi Su-7 was the principal Soviet tactical ground attack combat aircraft of the 1960s. Despite its limited weapons-carrying capabilities it served very widely.

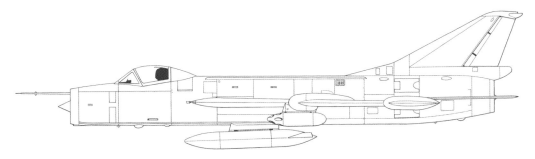

The Sukhoi Su-7 could only carry a modest amount of weaponry, as shown by the small unguided rocket pod beneath the wing of this example, and it suffered like many other early jet combat aircraft from limited endurance.

accepted for operational service with the Soviet air force in January 1961, and was eventually superseded by the improved Su-7BM. This version introduced various upgrades including more internal fuel to increase range and endurance. Continuing development led to a number of subsequent marks, significant amongst which was the Su-7BKL. This version was intended for operations from unpaved and relatively unprepared runways near to the front-line, and featured a modified undercarriage with additional skids for operations on grass. Production of the Su-7 line finally ended in 1971, after well over two thousand Su-7s of all types had been built. The main user was the Soviet air force, but the type was also exported. Eastern Bloc countries such as Czechoslovakia and Poland flew the type, as did countries around the world which claimed the Soviets as their friends such as Algeria, Egypt, North Korea, and India. Egyptian and Indian Su-7s saw considerable combat, and were generally successful if not outstandingly so. Continuing development of the Su-7 line resulted in the 'swing-wing' Su-17 and Su-22 family – see pages 238 to 239.

Specifications – Sukhoi Su-7BM

Wingspan	30 ft 6.5 in
Length	54 ft 5.75 in
Maximum speed	approximately Mach 1.6 at 42,651 ft
Maximum take-off weight	30,490 lb
Radius of action	199 miles
Service ceiling	60,696 ft
Armament	Two 1.18 in (30 mm) cannons, one in each wing root, normal load 2,205 lb of bombs or rocket pods with two auxiliary fuel tanks
Engine	One Lyulka AL-7F-series turbojet engine, of 21,164 lb st with afterburning
Crew	One

Douglas B-66 Destroyer

Development of the B-66 Destroyer was initiated as a minimum change version for the U.S.A.F. of the U.S. Navy's existing aircraft carrier-based Douglas A3D Skywarrior attack aircraft. It was intended as a replacement for the Douglas B-26 Invader and Martin B-57 Canberra in the interdiction, light bombing and reconnaissance roles. However, it emerged as a completely different aircraft compared to the Skywarrior, with a similar outline but with redesigned wings, a new powerplant (the problematic Allison J71 jet engine) and a fuselage structurally different from its Navy ancestor. The first of five pre-series RB-66As made the type's maiden flight on 28 June 1954, but the RB-66B night photo-reconnaissance version was the first production and most widely produced model, first flying several months later. It carried a selection of cameras and photo-flash bombs, and entered U.S.A.F. service in the United States during January 1956. Some examples served at R.A.F. Sculthorpe in Britain, and at Sembach and Spangdahlem in West Germany. An RB-66B was shot down in March 1964 after penetrating East German airspace. Only the B-66B was built solely for the bombing role, carrying nuclear or conventional bombs. The type were based in England for most of its service life, being withdrawn in mid-1962. However, 13 were converted with electronic countermeasures equipment as 'Brown Cradle' aircraft, taking part in operations in Southeast Asia from June 1966. The related RB-66C electronic reconnaissance and jammer variant first flew in October 1958, with many of the 36 built used extensively over Vietnam to provide electronic escort for strike aircraft and – from 1967 – stand-off jamming. These aircraft were redesignated as EB-66Cs in 1966, while the 'Brown Cradle' aircraft became EB-66Bs. Such was the need for electronic jammers over Vietnam that redundant RB-66Bs were converted as EB-66Es, becoming the most capable electronic warfare Destroyer variant produced. Destroyers continued flying operations until the end of the U.S. involvement in Southeast Asia, five being shot down by surface-to-air missiles and one falling victim to a North Vietnamese MiG-21 jet fighter. The final production version was the WB-66D combat

A Douglas RB-66B Destroyer.
Although the B-66 was intended as a bomber, it found most use as a reconnaissance aircraft and for electronic warfare tasks.

In the upper photograph is a U.S. Navy Douglas A3D (later A-3) Skywarrior, showing the general similarity of the design with the B-66 Destroyer. In the lower picture is an RB-66C (Photos: McDonnell Douglas).

weather reconnaissance aircraft, retaining a central crew compartment in place of the bomb bay, a feature introduced in the RB-66C. The 36 built brought Destroyer production to 293 examples. Two were later converted as Northrop X-21A test-beds with special laminar flow surfaces, powered by two XJ79 turbojets attached to the rear fuselage to keep the special new wing surfaces free of pylons. Destroyers finally left U.S.A.F. service in March 1973.

Specifications – Douglas B-66B Destroyer

Wingspan	72 ft 6 in
Length	75 ft 2 in
Maximum speed	594 mph at 36,000 ft
Maximum take-off weight	83,000 lb
Range	1,500 miles
Service ceiling	38,900 ft
Armament	Two 0.787 (20 mm) cannons in a remotely-controlled rear turret, up to 15,000 lb of bombs in an internal weapons bay
Engine	Two Allison J71-A-13 turbojet engines, of 10,200 lb st each
Crew	Three

Hawker Hunter

One of the classic military jets of all time, the Hawker Hunter rates alongside the equally important North American F-86 Sabre (see pages 72 to 73) as one of the West's most important early swept-wing jet fighters. The Hunter is one of the icons of Britain's post-Second World War aircraft industry, a real success story amongst a large number of cancelled projects and small-scale production. The Hawker company was already well established as a supplier of fighter aircraft to Britain's Royal Air Force when the company's designers began to look at the possibility of jet-powered fighters in the middle years of the Second World War A large number of projects and ideas ensued, none of which at that time came to fruition. However, the appearance of the F-86 Sabre made it clear that Britain's aircraft industry was suddenly and very seriously lagging behind American developments. Specification F.3/48 was created for a swept-wing day fighter with secondary ground attack capabilities, partly to replace the first-generation jet-powered Gloster Meteor (see pages 90 to 91). Hawker's response was the P.1067. Three prototypes were ordered in

November 1948, and the first of these flew on 20 July 1951. Two of the prototypes were Rolls-Royce Avon-powered, the third was Armstrong Siddeley Sapphire-engined. There were some lengthy development problems before the type entered service, despite the project being given high priority due to the Korean War. The initial production model for the R.A.F. was the F.Mk.1. This entered service in 1954, and was Avon-powered. Unfortunately, engine cut-outs ('flame-outs') occurred amid other problems, and it was not until the Avon-powered Mk.4 and Sapphire-engined Mk.5 entered front-line service that the Hunter began to mature into a fully-competent combat type. In particular the F.Mk.4 introduced underwing fuel tanks, which considerably improved the type's endurance, and the first were delivered in March 1955. The Mk.4 was also the first version that was widely exported, the qualities of the Hunter having by then become obvious. In addition, the type was licence-manufactured in the Netherlands by Fokker, and in Belgium. January 1954 marked the first flight of the improved and more powerful Mk.6, which later saw wide-

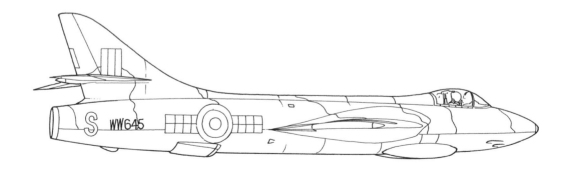

A simple drawing of a Hawker Hunter F.Mk.1 in Royal Air Force markings. The Hunter gave many years of front-line service to the R.A.F., from 1954 to the early 1970s.

The Hawker Hunter is probably the most famous of Britain's post-Second World War jets, and is much sought-after by private collectors. This privately-owned example in a non-standard overall red color scheme and registered in Britain as G-HUNT, was photographed at Hurn (now Bournemouth) Airport in southern England during the 1980s (Photo: John Batchelor).

spread R.A.F. service, and again was significantly exported, to India and Switzerland among others. In addition to these single-seat day fighter versions, there were T.Mk.7 two-seat trainer models which were also widely exported under a variety of designations. The Royal Navy additionally used both single- and two-seat Hunters as shore-based trainers. Further development led to the FGA.9 dedicated ground attack Hunter based on the F.Mk.6. In addition to initial export successes, many ex-R.A.F. aircraft were later refurbished and exported to new operators. Over 1,952 Hunters were built, and some remained in service until comparatively recently. Others such as those of India have seen important combat operations, Indian Hunters actually having met Pakistani-operated F-86 Sabres in action.

Specifications – Hawker Hunter FGA.Mk.9

Wingspan	33 ft 8 in
Length	45 ft 10.5 in
Maximum speed	Mach 0.95 at 36,000 ft
Maximum take-off weight	18,000 lb
Radius of action	544 miles with underwing fuel tanks and rockets
Service ceiling	48,900 ft
Armament	Four 1.18 in (30 mm) cannons in the lower forward fuselage, various underwing weapons including two 1,000 lb or two 500 lb bombs, unguided rockets
Engine	One Rolls-Royce Avon 207 turbojet engine, of 10,000-10,150 lb st
Crew	One

Nord Noratlas

The post-World War Two French air force was re-born alongside the rebirth of the French nation itself following several years of German occupation during the war. Initially, the newly re-established French air force had to use a 'mixed bag' of miscellaneous aircraft, some of which were ex-German machines or aircraft that had been built in France under the German occupation. By the late 1940s the need for a brand-new transport aircraft was becoming obvious, to replace wartime-vintage transports such as French-built Junkers Ju 52/3m tri-motors. Design work was duly commenced on a new transport design by Nord Aviation, part of the wartime nationalised French aircraft industry which persisted after the war. The resulting prototype N.2500

first flew on 10 September 1949. It was a rather unconventional aircraft, with a large box-like fuselage. Its rear fuselage clamshell-opening loading doors were unobstructed by a tail-plane structure because the tail was held out of the way by two booms extending back from the high-set wings. This layout was similar to the American Fairchild C-82 transport (see pages 70 to 71). The original N.2500 prototype was powered by two Gnome-Rhone radial piston engines, but the subsequent N.2501 proto-type/development aircraft introduced the French-built Bristol Hercules radial engine from Britain as the production Noratlas power layout. Having gained considerable interest from the French air force, this combination duly entered production. There was an initial batch of 40 production N.2501, which were delivered up to mid-1954. The French-manufactured Hercules radials of the French-built Noratlas were available in a number of versions with different propeller combina-

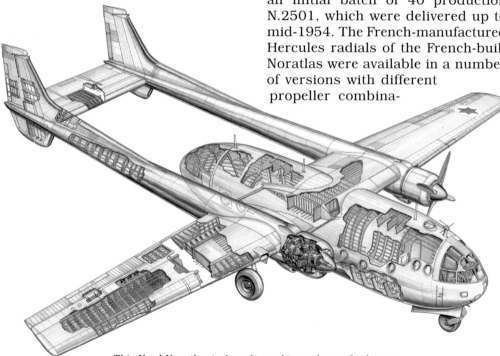

This Nord Noratlas in Israeli markings shows the large box-like fuselage of the type and the prominent twin-boom and tailplane arrangement.

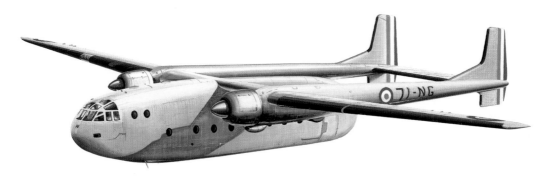

The largest user of the Nord Noratlas was the French air force (the Armée de l'Air), as exemplified by this example.

tions. Eventually, the French received over two hundred Noratlas, and some of these served well into the 1980s. In their normal transport/cargo configurations the N.2501 could carry up to 45 troops, or 36 paratroops (the Noratlas being quite capable of dropping paratroops), or equipment including small vehicles. However, a number of French examples were specially equipped with considerable on-board electronic equipment for secret electronic intelligence missions. There was also useful export interest in the Noratlas, resulting in the emergent air force of West Germany also operating the type from the late 1950s. Except for an initial batch of 25 examples that were supplied from France, all West German Noratlas were built by a combination of West German aircraft companies called Flugzeugbau Nord (Nordflug), following a 1956 licence agreement. The West German Luftwaffe eventually received 185 or 186 Noratlas. Other users of this versatile and reliable transport included Israel, and a variety of additional countries received second-hand examples including Greece, Niger, and Djibouti. A number of variations of the basic Noratlas also existed, one version being fitted with small wing-tip turbojet engines for better performance. A total of 425 Noratlas are believed to have been built from the French and German production lines.

Specifications – Nord N.2501 Noratlas

Wingspan	106 ft 7.5 in
Length	72 ft
Maximum speed	273 mph at 10,000 ft
Maximum take-off weight	46,297 lb
Range	1,553 miles
Service ceiling	24,606 ft
Engine	Two SNECMA-built Bristol Hercules 739 radial piston engines, of 2,040 hp each
Crew	Four or five crew, up to 45 troops

Avro Vulcan

The Avro Vulcan was ordered alongside the Handley Page Victor (see pages 130 to 131) as a nuclear bomber, to fulfil Specification B.35/46, and became one of the trio of famous British 'V-Bombers.' The Vulcan's planned delta wing shape was tested on the reduced scale research Avro 707 series, before the prototype Type 698 (later christened Vulcan) made its first flight on 30 August 1952. It was powered by four Rolls-Royce Avon turbojets, although all subsequent Mk.1s were powered by Olympus Mk.101/102/104 turbojets. At high altitude the Vulcan's pure delta wing was found to be prone to compressibility buffet and stall problems when pulling 'g,' so the 45 production Vulcan B.Mk.1s featured a redesigned wing leading edge incorporating three different sweep angles. The first production Vulcan B.Mk.1 made its maiden flight in February 1955, this variant serving with five front-line Royal Air Force squadrons from 1957 onwards. Many had electronic countermeasures (ECM) equipment subsequently added in an extended tailcone, becoming B.Mk.1As. The second prototype Vulcan was used to develop a wing of increased dimensions and area with improved aerodynamic properties. This new wing, more powerful Olympus Mk.201 or 301 engines and the improved ECM equipment later used on the B.Mk.1As became the distinguishing features of the B.Mk.2, 88 of which were built (plus a static test airframe). All five B.Mk.1/1A R.A.F. squadrons later converted to the B.Mk.2, and four more Vulcan bomber units were also established. Vulcans were based at R.A.F. Coningsby, Cottesmore, Finningley, Scampton and Waddington in Britain, and at Akrotiri in Cyprus. Many of the Mk.2s had bomb-bay modifications and engine upgrades as B.Mk.2As to allow them to carry the Blue Steel stand-off nuclear weapon, while others carried free-fall nuclear bombs. However, when Polaris-armed nuclear missile submarines entered service with Britain's Royal Navy, the Vulcan fleet was progressively switched to the tactical bombing role. Some became maritime reconnaissance aircraft, while in the twilight of the Vulcan's service life several were re-configured as K.Mk.2 airborne-refuelling tankers. The tanker conversions were a direct result of the drain on air-refuelling

The Avro Vulcan was a large and extremely powerful bomber – the ground would literally shake when one of these four-engined aircraft took off.

The Avro Vulcan was the world's only delta-wing jet bomber to enter service (Photo: John Batchelor).

assets caused by the 1982 Falklands conflict, during which bomber Vulcans had flown their only sorties in anger. Known as 'Black Buck' missions, the attacks were flown from Ascension Island against Argentine targets on the Falkland Islands. In 2005 they remained the longest bombing raids ever undertaken by the R.A.F., requiring multiple Handley Page Victor air-refuelling tankers to support each sortie. The last Vulcan squadron was the K.Mk.2-equipped No.50 – it disbanded in 1984 – but one aircraft remained airworthy for display appearances until 1993, and has since been the focus of fund-raising attempts by enthusiasts in Britain to restore it to flying condition.

Specifications – Avro Vulcan B.Mk.2

Wingspan	111 ft
Length	105 ft 6 in including refuelling probe
Maximum speed	645 mph at 36,000 ft
Maximum take-off weight	225,000 lb
Range	4,604 miles
Service ceiling	60,000 ft
Armament	One Blue Steel stand-off nuclear missile (B.Mk.2A), or one Yellow Sun or WE177 free-fall nuclear bomb, or up to 21 1,000 lb conventional bombs
Engine	Four Bristol Siddeley Olympus Mk.201 turbojet engines, of 17,000 lb st each, or four Olympus Mk.301s, of 20,000 lb st each
Crew	Five

Convair B-58 Hustler

The great achievement of creating sustained and safe supersonic flight in the years following World War Two was a very hard – won accomplishment. In the years after the success of the Bell X-1 (see pages 46 to 47), the possible performance capabilities of warplanes moved ever onwards and upwards. Several countries, including France, Britain, the Soviet Union, and the United States, eventually developed supersonic combat aircraft as described elsewhere in this book. Most of these were fighters, but the United States was the first to develop a supersonic delta-winged bomber. This was the impressive Convair B-58 Hustler. Arising out of design studies initiated by the U.S. Army Air Force and its successor the U.S. Air Force from 1947, and eventually embodied in operational requirements issued in the early 1950s, the B-58 was designed to be a high-level long-range strategic bomber and reconnaissance aircraft. Convair (previously known as Consolidated) had a long tradition of producing combat aircraft

for the U.S. military (including the famous B-24 Liberator bomber during the Second World War, and the B-36 described on pages 82 to 83), and had carried out design studies post-war into delta-wing designs with the prototype XF-92A fighter project. The B-58 was a major design challenge, the delta wing layout being a revolutionary concept based to an extent on German World War Two design studies. Powered by four General Electric J79 afterburning turbojet engines, the B-58 was designed with an 'area-ruled' fuselage planform. This resulted in a distinctive 'coke-bottle' waisted appearance where the large wing was attached to the fuselage, to allow better high-speed performance. The prototype XB-58 first flew on 11 November 1956, and was followed by a second development prototype plus 28 pre-production/development YB-58A aircraft. The Hustler was one of the first aircraft designs in which all the necessary high-technology avionics and other complicated systems (including the

The Convair B-58 Hustler was one of the most visually-impressive warplanes ever created, and had a dazzling performance to match.

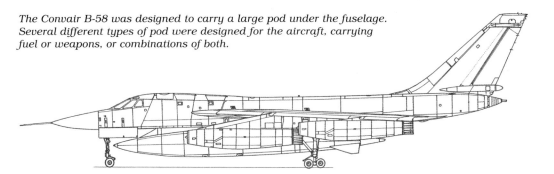

The Convair B-58 was designed to carry a large pod under the fuselage. Several different types of pod were designed for the aircraft, carrying fuel or weapons, or combinations of both.

engines) were integrated into the type as a complete weapons system program. A unique feature was the B-58's under-fuselage pod, which carried fuel and a variety of munitions including nuclear bombs. In production aircraft the three-man crew sat in tandem in unique separate capsules which could be ejected in an emergency. Only 86 B-58A production Hustlers were built, although several of the pre-production aircraft were brought up to production standard and eight were converted into dual-control TB-58A trainers. The Hustler was a very expensive aircraft (some $30 million each at mid-1960s prices), and the first production B-58A flew in 1959. Problems with this advanced aircraft resulted in the first operational unit, the 43rd Bomb Wing of the U.S. Air Force's Strategic Air Command, only becoming fully operational in 1962. The type served until early 1970, and never saw combat even though the Vietnam War was at its height during that time. Demonstrating its excellent performance capabilities, the Hustler achieved several world records in specific classes during the early 1960s.

Specifications – Convair B-58A Hustler

Wingspan	56 ft 10 in
Length	96 ft 9.3 in
Maximum speed	Mach 2.1 at 40,000 ft
Maximum take-off weight	163,000 lb
Range	approximately 2,000 miles
Service ceiling	approximately 63,000 ft
Armament	One rearward-firing tail-mounted 0.787 in (20 mm) cannon, various underfuselage weapons pods for nuclear or conventional free-fall weapons, or up to four free-fall nuclear bombs on underwing pylons
Engine	Four General Electric J79-GE-5A turbojet engines, of 15,600 lb st each with afterburning
Crew	Three

Tupolev Tu-95

As far as longevity of service matched with potency are concerned, two military aircraft continued to reign supreme in the early years of the 21st Century. Both are strategic bombers and both first flew in 1952, yet they both remain in important front-line service in 2005. One of these is the American jet-powered Boeing B-52 Stratofortress strategic bomber (see pages 176 to 177). The other is the equally impressive Russian Tupolev Tu-95 strategic bomber, known to NATO as 'Bear,' and powered by four large and powerful turboprop engines. Although it might look like an aircraft from an earlier age, the Tu-95 at the start of the 21st Century represented the main nuclear strike weapon of Russia's strategic air assets. Development of what became the Tu-95 began in the later 1940s, and used the then comparatively new technology of turboprop powerplants.
The proto-

type Tu-95/1 first flew on 12 November 1952, with four Kuznetsov 2TV-2F 12,000 shp turboprops (making it the most significant aircraft up to that time to fly on turboprop power), and initial operational deployment of the first production version (known to NATO as 'Bear-A,'

probably designated Tu-95M), took place in 1956. Continuing development led to the Tu-95K-20 ('Bear-B') of 1959 which featured a guided air-to-surface missile armament, while the Tu-95KD of the early 1960s added in-flight refuelling which gave the 'Bear' truly intercontinental range. A separate but related line of development led to the Tu-114 airliner (see pages 164 to 165) and the Tu-126 (NATO reporting name 'Moss') airborne early warning aircraft. The Tu-95 'Bear' series served throughout the Cold War in the stand-off between the Soviet Union and the West, and while doing so proved the effectiveness of the turboprop powerplant for military operations in long-range long loiter-time operations. Continuing development led to the Tu-142 line with slightly revised dimensions and thoroughly altered equipment mainly for shore-based long-range naval aviation reconnaissance and anti-submarine patrol, plus a special version for long-range airborne communications relay with submerged Soviet-operated nuclear submarines. The most important later 'Bear' versions for the Soviet air force included the Tu-95MS (Tu-96M-55

The Tupolev Tu-95 'Bear' is a big, impressive warplane, a propeller-driven bomber in a world dominated by jet-powered front-line military aircraft. The example illustrated made a goodwill visit to Britain in 1993, at the time when the Cold War was ending and the relations between East and West were steadily improving (Photo: Malcolm V. Lowe).

'Bear-H') series, based on the Tu-142 airframe. These included the Tu-96MS-6 ('Bear-H6') able to carry six Kh-55 series (AS-15 'Kent' to NATO) ALCM (Air-Launched Cruise Missiles), and the Tu-96MS-16 ('Bear-H16') able to carry no less than 16 ALCMs – a very potent flying arsenal in its own right. The Tu-95MS entered operational service in 1984, and a variety of models from this line are now the Russian air force's principal strike force alongside Tu-22M supersonic bombers (see pages 214 to 215) and the impressive but small in number Tu-160. However, as a result of various arms reduction treaties between the former Soviet Union (now Russia) and the West, the capabilities of these Cold War warriors are now somewhat diminished, although they remain today a significant strike force. The Tu-142 is also operated in small numbers by India, and the break-up of the Soviet Union resulted in the Ukraine and Kazakhstan also flying small numbers of 'Bears.'

Specifications – Tupolev Tu-95MS ('Bear-H')

Wingspan	164 ft 2 in
Length	161 ft 2.25 in
Maximum speed	575 mph at 25,000 ft
Maximum take-off weight	407,850 lb
Radius of action	3,977 miles
Service ceiling	39,370 ft
Armament	One rearward-firing tail-mounted 0.9 in (23 mm) twin-barrel cannon, six Kh-55 (AS-15A 'Kent') long-range nuclear ALCM cruise missiles (on Tu-95MS-6 'Bear-H6') SALT/START Treaty configuration
Engine	Four Samara Kuznetsov NK-12MP turboprop engines, of 14,795 eshp each
Crew	Seven

North American F-100 Super Sabre

The North American F-86 Sabre (see pages 72 to 73) was one of the classic early jet-powered warplanes. Official go-ahead for a greatly improved F-86 Sabre derivative was given in January 1951, although the resulting F-100 Super Sabre emerged as a totally new design. Mating a 45° swept wing, all-moving tailplanes and a thin-lipped nose inlet for a J57 afterburning turbojet created the YF-100. Before it was built the YF-100 was further refined as the YF-100A, test pilot George Welch breaking the sound barrier during its maiden flight on 25 May 1953. Highlighting the type's high speed, a YF-100A was used to establish a new world speed record of just over 755 mph in October 1953. The F-100A entered service with the U.S. Air Force in 1954, making it one of the first supersonic-capable aircraft to become operational. Unfortunately the type was grounded in November 1954 after a series of crashes. Increasing the tail area and extending the wings cured the problem that had caused the crashes, but the simple day fighter F-100As were quickly replaced in serv-

ice. Production instead switched to the fighter-bomber F-100C, which amongst other changes had six underwing hardpoints (pylons for munitions) and provision for in-flight refuelling. A total of 476 were built, one being used to raise the world speed record to just over 822 mph in August 1955. The major production version was the F-100D, with a taller tail, increased wing area, a weapon control system and provision for Sidewinder air-to-air guided missiles for self-defence. First flown on 24 January 1956, 1,274 F-100Ds were built and they bore the brunt of U.S.A.F. operations over Vietnam during the Vietnam War. A two-seat F-100 derivative was developed as the TF-100C (later re-designated F-100F) omitting two of the four standard cannons in the nose of the single-seaters. Two-seat Super Sabres acted as fast Forward Air Control (air strike directors) over Vietnam, while seven were modified to become the first U.S.A.F. 'Wild Weasel' anti-ground-based radar aircraft. In Vietnam, F-100s flew more sorties than all of the North American P-51 Mustang

The North American F-100 Super Sabre is a classic warplane from the jet age. It was one of the first supersonic-capable jet fighters to enter service, sharing this accolade with the Soviet Union's MiG-19 described on pages 126 to 127. This is a Super Sabre of the 'Thunderbirds' aerobatic team.

The F-100 Super Sabre was the first of the famous 'Century Series' of classic American warplanes, and the type served with distinction in the long and hard fighting in Southeast Asia during the 1960s.

fighters in World War Two, flying more combat sorties during the war than any other type in the conflict, before being retired from the theatre in 1971. 193 are believed to have been lost to enemy action. The U.S.A.F. aerobatic demonstration team the 'Thunderbirds' also flew the F-100. The U.S. Air National Guard retired the F-100 in 1979, but some 290 were converted as unmanned drones and were still being shot down for target practice or weapon development work into the 1990s. Denmark, France, Taiwan, and Turkey flew F-100s, supplied via various military assistance programs. Most of these export examples had been retired by 1989, but a handful of F-100Fs were used as target-towers for NATO training work until comparatively recently.

Specifications – North American F-100D Super Sabre

Wingspan	38 ft 9.5 in
Length	47 ft 4.5 in (excluding nose probe)
Maximum speed	Mach 1.3 at 36,500 ft
Maximum take-off weight	38,048 lb
Radius of action	approximately 600 miles
Service ceiling	46,900 ft
Armament	Four lower fuselage-mounted 0.787 in (20 mm) cannons, up to approximately 7,500 lb of external ordnance including unguided bombs, rocket pods, Bullpup air-to-surface guided missiles and Sidewinder air-to-air guided missiles
Engine	One Pratt & Whitney J57-P-21A turbojet engine, of 16,000 lb st with afterburning
Crew	One

Sud-Aviation/Aérospatiale Caravelle

The Sud-Aviation/Aérospatiale Car-avelle was another of the world's impor-tant early jet airliners. During the 1950s the de Havilland Comet, Tupolev Tu-104, and Boeing 707 (all covered elsewhere in this book) pioneered and introduced jet-powered medium to long-haul commercial services. The Caravelle was also an important if less well-known member of this exclusive club, in being the first to introduce short to medium-haul jet-powered passenger services. Design studies began in 1951 in response to a French government requirement to create a jet airliner to ensure France's involve-ment in the new field of jet-powered commercial transports. Several French manufacturers responded to this far-sighted requirement, and in January 1953 SNCASE (later Sud-Aviation) won the design competition with its SE 210 proposal. This was a radical design, mounting its two turbojet engines in pods at the rear fuselage instead

of below or within the wings – this lay-out was later much used for other designs. Two prototypes were ordered, and the first flew on 27 May 1955. Early Caravelles were powered by the Rolls-Royce Avon turbojet engines from Britain, and the first production version was the Caravelle I. The launch customer was France's nation-al airline Air France, which signed for twelve examples. The world's first-ever jet-powered short/medium-dis-tance commercial services started with SAS and Air France in April and May 1959. These early production Caravelles were slightly longer than the original prototypes, and could seat 64 passengers in a standard seating layout. The Caravelle I was followed by the Mk.IA with slightly more powerful Avon engines, after which the Car-avelle III introduced even more power, with many of the earlier examples subsequently up-rated to this stan-dard. The increasing

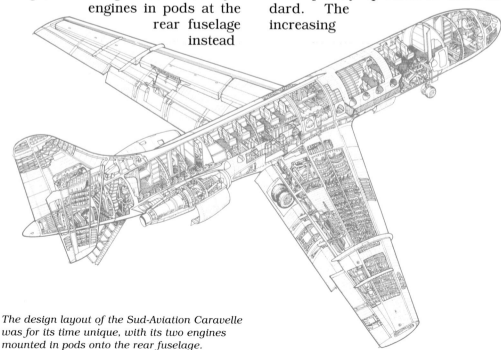

The design layout of the Sud-Aviation Caravelle was for its time unique, with its two engines mounted in pods onto the rear fuselage.

A principal user of the Sud-Aviation/Aérospatiale Caravelle was the French national airline Air France. The first Caravelle for this airline was delivered in the first half of 1959.

power available allowed higher operating weights and better overall performance. A subsequent model, the Caravelle VI series, attracted a major order from the United States by United Air Lines. These examples were delivered from mid-1961 and featured thrust reversers (as VIR) for their Avon engines to allow for shorter landing runs. The lengthened Caravelle 10B (or Super B, or Super Caravelle) was a re-engined derivative with Pratt & Whitney JT8D turbofan engines, and could seat up to 104/105 passengers. The initial example flew in March 1964, with Finnair being the first to put the type into service. More powerful versions of this engine led to the Caravelle 11R with a lengthened fuselage and capable of cargo or passenger operations. Production ended in 1973 with the Caravelle 12, a further lengthened version which had the highest operating weights of all Caravelles and could seat up to 139/140 passengers. By that time Sud-Aviation had become a part of the French aviation giant Aérospatiale, and 282 Caravelles of all types and prototypes had been built. Following service with major airlines, many Caravelles had second careers with smaller carriers elsewhere in the world, with several remaining in service until comparatively recently. Caravelles also saw military service with several countries, France operating the type from 1963 and Sweden flying two including one configured for secret electronic operations.

Specifications – Sud-Aviation/Aérospatiale Caravelle 12 Series

Wingspan	112 ft 6.5 in
Length	118 ft 10.75 in
Maximum cruising speed	513 mph at 25,000 ft
Maximum take-off weight	127,868 lb
Range	2,153 miles
Service ceiling	39,370 ft
Engine	Two Pratt & Whitney JT8D-9 turbofan engines, of 14,500 lb st each
Accommodation	Two or three crew plus stewards/stewardesses, normally 128 passengers

McDonnell F-101 Voodoo

The McDonnell F-101 Voodoo fighter and reconnaissance aircraft was a development of a failed design, the McDonnell XF-88 penetration fighter, that had been designed to escort bombers of the U.S. Air Force's Strategic Air Command (SAC) and itself drop small nuclear weapons. First flown on 29 September 1954, the initial F-101A suffered from instability problems. In addition, its J57-P-13 turbojets had compressibility problems, and other design requirements could not initially be met. By the time these problems had been solved, SAC had decided to dispose of its fighter force and the first F-101A unit, the 27th Strategic Fighter Wing, was transferred instead the U.S.A.F.'s Tactical Air Command (TAC) in July 1957, shortly after receiving the aircraft. TAC then passed its F-101As to U.S.A.F. forces in Western Europe in 1958/59. The F-101C with an improved structure followed the A-models, most later joining the earlier version in service with U.S. Air Force squadrons based in Western Europe. While the Voodoo unfortunately proved to be of limited use as a tactical fighter, it was to be of greater utility as a reconnaissance aircraft. The first reconnais-

sance-configured YRF-101A flew on 10 May 1956, and initial production RF-101As were delivered in May 1957, with examples later going to the Nationalist Chinese on Taiwan. The definitive production reconnaissance version was the RF-101C, flying first in July 1957. With the slow build-up in Southeast Asia by American forces at the start of what became the Vietnam War, Voodoos started flying reconnaissance missions over the war zone from late 1961. The first was lost to enemy action in 1964 and attrition increased as North Vietnamese defences improved until the type was withdrawn from the theatre in 1970, having been replaced by the RF-4C Phantom. RF-101Cs were also active during the Cuban missile crisis in October 1962. After U.S.A.F. service, RF-101Cs flew with the second-line Air National Guard (ANG) until January 1979, operating alongside F-101As and C-models converted as reconnaissance aircraft (as RF-101G and RF-101H respectively). In a different but related line of development, 480 Voodoos were built as two-seat F-101B interceptor fighters for the U.S.A.F.'s Continental-U.S. based Air Defence Command (ADC), with a

One of the McDonnell Voodoo's most important roles was that of reconnaissance, and several dedicated reconnaissance RF-101 versions were employed by the U.S. Air Force. This reconnaissance Voodoo wears the 'RG' tail code of the 165th Tactical Reconnaissance Squadron of the Kentucky Air National Guard, which spent some time on active duty alongside the regular U.S.A.F. in the late 1960s.

Nice detail view of the nose of a two-seat ex-U.S. Air Force Voodoo. Note the profusion of stencils on the aircraft's light grey paintwork (Photo: John Batchelor).

radar intercept officer in the rear seat. First flying in March 1957, the F-101B entered service with ADC squadrons in 1959. F-101Bs served with ADC until 1971, although many were later passed on to the ANG, being withdrawn in 1981/1982. Some F-101B were fitted with dual-controls as F-101Fs, while others were converted for reconnaissance work. Some were supplied to the Canadian Armed Forces as CF-101Bs. Canada also flew an EF-101B – an electronic-warfare configured aircraft and the last active Voodoo – until 1987. Altogether 807 Voodoos were built.

Specifications – McDonnell F-101B Voodoo

Wingspan	39 ft 8 in
Length	67 ft 4.75 in (or slightly longer)
Maximum speed	1,094 mph (c. Mach 1.65) at 35,000 ft
Maximum take-off weight	52,400 lb
Range	1,519 miles on internal fuel only
Service ceiling	52,000 ft
Armament	Four AIM-4 Falcon air-to-air missiles under the fuselage, or two AIM-2A Genie unguided nuclear-armed air-to-air missiles
Engine	Two Pratt & Whitney J57-P-53 or -55 turbojet engines, of 14,990 lb st each with afterburning
Crew	Two

North American X-15

The remarkable and record-breaking X-15 program produced the fastest and highest-flying aircraft ever built. Originally designed in a very forward-looking project as a hypersonic research aircraft, the X-15 was jointly sponsored by the National Advisory Committee for Aeronautics (NACA, nowadays NASA), the U.S.A.F. and the U.S. Navy. The radical North American NA-240 design was ordered in September 1955, as the X-15 (later X-15A). As the originally-intended liquid oxygen and anhydrous ammonia-burning Thiokol (Reaction Motors) XLR99-RM-1 rocket motor was delayed, the first two X-15s initially flew with a pair of Thiokol XLR11s. Although only producing 16,000 lb st – some 28% of the XLR99's thrust – the XLR11 installation was still expected to propel the X-15 beyond Mach 3. Carried aloft by one of NASA's specially-converted Boeing NB-52 Stratofortress 'mother ships,' the second X-15 made its first (un-powered) flight on 8 June 1959 with A. Scott Crossfield in the cockpit. He also made the first powered flight on 17 September 1959, reaching just over Mach 2 which was truly remarkable

for an initial powered flight. On 5 November 1959 an engine fire forced an emergency landing to be made, breaking the fuselage of the second aircraft but luckily not injuring Crossfield. It was later rebuilt. The first Mach 3 flight was completed on 12 May 1960 by NASA's Joe Walker. A total of 29 flights were powered by XLR11s, with a top speed being reached of Mach 3.5 on 7 February 1961. By then, the first X-15A had been re-engined with an XLR99. Joe Walker used the similarly powered third aircraft to set an unofficial speed record of 4,104 mph (6,605 km/h) on 27 June 1962 and an altitude record of 354,200 ft (107,960 m) on 22 August 1963. Following another crash landing on 9 November 1962, the second X-15A was rebuilt as the X-15A-2 with a modified windscreen, a lengthened fuselage and the ability to carry two

The North American X-15 was one of the most remarkable aircraft programs ever created. This illustration shows some of the main features of the type, including the very powerful liquid-fuel rocket motor.

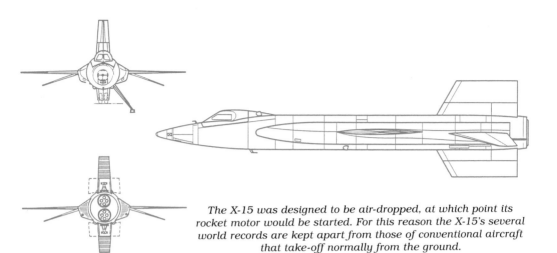

The X-15 was designed to be air-dropped, at which point its rocket motor would be started. For this reason the X-15's several world records are kept apart from those of conventional aircraft that take-off normally from the ground.

external fuel tanks. The modifications were designed to take the aircraft to higher speeds, and these required a special coating to protect the airframe from thermal (heat) damage. This X-15 was therefore eventually colored white, in marked contrast to the usual black color scheme of the X-15s. On 3 October 1967, William J. Knight took the X-15A-2 to Mach 6.72 (4,534 mph, 7,297 km/h). This is, and probably always will be, the fastest flight ever recorded by a manned aircraft. However, a pylon holding a dummy ramjet burnt through, forcing Knight to land above the maximum landing weight, writing off the aircraft. On 15 November 1967 the third X-15A disintegrated in flight, killing Major Michael Adams. This left the first aircraft to make the final X-15 flight, dropped as always from the Boeing NB-52 Stratofortress 'mother ship,' on 24 October 1968. Thus ended a truly breathtaking program that had pushed aviation to its furthest limits. All records that have subsequently bettered the achievements of the X-15s were achieved by spacecraft.

Specifications – North American X-15A

Wingspan	22 ft 4 in
Length	50 ft 9 in
Maximum speed	4,104 mph at 100,000 ft
Maximum launch weight	33,300 lb
Range	typically 275 miles horizontally under its own power
Service ceiling	354,200 ft maximum altitude
Engine	One Thiokol (Reaction Motors) XLR99-RM-2 single-chamber liquid-fuel rocket motor, of 57,000 lb st
Crew	One

British Experimental Jets

Whilst the American aircraft industry forged ahead with ground-breaking aviation programs like the X-15 described on the previous two pages, unfortunately Britain's aircraft industry found itself seriously lagging behind foreign competition such as this in several important fields by the mid- to late 1950s. Although there was much innovation and skill available in Britain, it was sadly sometimes compromised by a lack of vision from some politicians, and a lack of clear objectives from procurement bodies within the military. In 1957 the then British defence minister, Duncan Sandys, pronounced that in future all combat would be performed by unmanned missiles and not aircraft. This strange and incorrect appraisal led to several major British projects being cancelled. One development series that in particular was damaged by this pronouncement was the Avro 730 project, for an advanced supersonic reconnaissance/ /bomber aircraft. It had been pro-

posed to build this aircraft from stainless steel, a material that is not usually employed in the major components of aircraft. Therefore to test the effects of long periods of heating and friction on such an aircraft at supersonic speeds, the Bristol company was contracted to build a Mach 2-capable research aircraft to Specification ER.134 made from stainless steel to perform these investigations. Thus was born the Bristol 188, a large stainless steel aircraft equipped with two powerful turbojets. However, the engines chosen to power the type were not the engines originally intended (they too had been cancelled). The first of two Bristol 188s first flew on 14 April 1962, and the second in April 1963. Unfortunately, the type had a number of development problems and its heavy fuel consumption did not allow it to fly at high speed for long enough for meaningful measurements into heating at high speeds to be made. Near to Mach 2, the aircraft is said to have become almost uncon-

The Short S.C.1 was a test aircraft, intended to develop and prove VTOL capabilities for aircraft. The lift engines to achieve this type of flight were buried within the fuselage, beneath the intakes in the aircraft's spine.

The Bristol 188 was a very impressive-looking experimental aircraft. This example is XF923, one of the two examples built, photographed by Artist John Batchelor returning to its home airfield at Filton near Bristol after a test sortie (Photo: John Batchelor).

trollable. Somewhat more successful was a totally different experimental project, intended to pioneer and prove vertical take-off and landing (VTOL) for aircraft. This capability was well-established for helicopters by the 1950s, but achieving it for aircraft was a very different procedure. The challenge of getting an aircraft to take-off vertically, and then transition into normal horizontal flight, was a very difficult puzzle. French, British and American engineers examined this problem in the 1950s and 1960s. In Britain, Short Brothers built two S.C.1 research aircraft to Specification ER.143, powered by five small turbojet engines. Four of these were vertically-mounted in the fuselage for vertical take-off, the fifth was in the tail for horizontal flight. The first S.C.1 made (after many tethered 'hops') the first true flight in which a vertical take-off was followed by successful transition to horizontal flight on 6 April 1960. The S.C.1's engine layout was eventually thought, however, to be unsatisfactory. The ultimately successful Hawker Siddeley Harrier V/STOL aircraft (see pages 210 to 211) instead later used swivelling nozzles to direct the blast from a single jet engine in the directions needed for take-off and transition into normal horizontal flight.

Specifications – Bristol Type 188

Wingspan	35 ft 1 in
Length	71 ft
Maximum speed	Mach 1.88 at unspecified altitude
Maximum take-off weight	37,527 lb
Engine	Two de Havilland Gyron Junior DGJ.10 turbojet engines, of 14,000 lb st each
Crew	One

Cessna A-37 Dragonfly

The compact Cessna T-37, sometimes called 'Tweet,' was selected by the U.S.A.F. as its first jet primary trainer in December 1952. A total of 534 T-37As and 552 T-37s were delivered to that service, while Cessna built 273 T-37Cs for export via various military aid programs. A large number of T-37s continue to serve with the U.S. Air Force. In 1963 the U.S.A.F. contracted to have the prototype T-37C and a T-37B evaluated as counter-insurgency (COIN) aircraft for limited ground attack missions, resulting in the modification of the two as YAT-37Ds. The conversion involved replacing the original J69-T-25 turbojets with J82-GE-2/5s nearly doubling the available power, increasing the maximum take-off weight to 10,500 lb (4,763 kg), adding cockpit armour and a Minigun in the forward fuselage, six pylons and wingtip fuel tanks. The first flight of a YAT-37D was made on 22 October 1963. The YAT-37Ds were evaluated by the U.S. Air Force, but a need for them at that time was not recognised. However, the war in Southeast Asia renewed U.S.A.F. interest in the type. A fourth pylon was added to each wing and operating weights were again increased. The U.S.A.F. ordered 37 AT-37Ds, later redesignated A-37D Dragonfly, for combat evaluation at Bien Hoa, South Vietnam, between August and December 1967 under the code name 'Combat Dragon.' In May 1968, 127 upgraded A-37Bs were ordered, with once more an increased maximum take-off weight and more powerful J85-GE-17A engines. In flight, pilots regularly shut down one engine to conserve fuel. Well over five hundred A-37Bs were eventually built, including the A-37As that were upgraded to B-standard. Of these, 254 went to the South Vietnamese Air Force, becoming operational in March 1969. Initially effective in combat, the aircraft became vulnerable to shoulder-launched surface-to-air missiles and so were fitted with an infra-red countermeasures system. With the fall of South Vietnam in 1975, some 95 A-37Bs were captured by North Vietnamese forces, some later being used in the invasion of Cambodia. Other South Vietnamese A-37Bs escaped, and were subsequently passed on to the air forces of Cambodia, South Korea and

The Cessna A-37 and T-37 line of light attack and training aircraft have served for many years in a variety of guises. Currently the U.S. Air Force's fleet of T-37 trainers is intended to serve for several more years. Illustrated is a South Vietnamese A-37.

An interesting view of a Cessna A-37 Dragonfly as it banks away from the camera to show its underwing stores-carrying capacity (Photo: U.S. Air Force).

Thailand. Other operators included Chile, Colombia, Ecuador, El Salvador, Guatemala, Honduras, Peru and Uruguay. In the U.S., OA-37B forward air control versions flew with second-line Air National Guard until October 1992, although one NOA-37B was used for at least a decade afterwards on test duties.

Specifications – Cessna A-37B Dragonfly

Wingspan	38 ft 4 in including wing-tip fuel tanks
Length	31 ft 10 in with refuelling probe
Maximum speed	415 mph at 7,000 ft
Maximum take-off weight	14,000 lb
Range	465 miles with maximum weapon load
Service ceiling	41,765 ft, but limited to 25,000 ft by U.S.A.F. restrictions as an unpressurised aircraft
Armament	One 0.3 in (7.62 mm) Minigun in the forward fuselage, up to 5,680 lb of weapons on eight underwing pylons
Engine	Two General Electric J85-GE-17A turbojet engines, of 2,850 lb st each
Crew	One usually, but room for two

Westland Wasp and Scout

Proving that it is not just the headline-stealing high-performance warplanes that are important to any military organisation, the small but effective Westland Wasp and Scout family of light helicopters gave many years of quiet but efficient service usually well away from the headlines. The greatest moment for the Wasp naval anti-ship and anti-submarine helicopter came in 1982 during the Argentine occupation of Britain's Falkland Islands and other territories in the South Atlantic. Operating in poor weather conditions, a British Royal Navy Westland Wasp successfully helped to disable an Argentine submarine at the start of what became Britain's ultimately successful operations to win back the Falklands and other islands from Argentine occupation. The Wasp and Scout series date originally to the 1950s, in a program that was initiated by the British Saunders-Roe company. In July 1958 the prototype of the Saunders-Roe P.531 light helicopter was flown. Continuing development led to the P.531-2 powered by a Blackburn/Turboméca turboshaft engine, which was later developed into the Bristol Siddeley Nimbus turboshaft. However, the Saunders-Roe helicopter operation was subsequently taken over in 1959 by Westland, which was by then growing into Britain's premier helicopter maker (a position that Westland still holds to this day). Development of the P-531-2 continued under Westland control, interest already having been shown in the design from the British military. A specific pre-production batch of P.531-2 examples was subsequently evaluated for service with Britain's Army Air Corps, and a production order followed in the latter half of 1960. Known as the Scout AH.Mk.1, eventually 148/150 of these skid-undercarriage helicopters were delivered for Army Air Corps use. Some were armed with anti-tank guided missiles or machine gun/cannon installations, and a number served in the Falkland Islands conflict in addition to Royal Navy Wasps. Scouts were also supplied to Jordan, Australia, Bahrain, and Uganda. Alongside the development of the Scout, Westland additionally pursued the creation of a ship-based naval derivative for anti-ship and anti-submarine

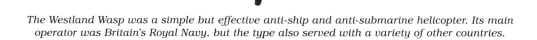

The Westland Wasp was a simple but effective anti-ship and anti-submarine helicopter. Its main operator was Britain's Royal Navy, but the type also served with a variety of other countries.

The Westland Wasp HAS.Mk.1 was typical of the comparatively austere warplanes that rarely steal the limelight, as it had a limited endurance and similarly limited electronics to perform its anti-ship and anti-submarine operations (Photo: Westland Helicopters).

work. Fitted with a quadricycle wheeled undercarriage, and with folding rotor blades and tail boom for easier shipboard stowage, the type was originally called Sea Scout until the name Wasp was adopted. After evaluation of prototype/development examples, the first Sea Scout/Wasp HAS.Mk.1 flew in October 1962. Royal Navy Wasp service commenced from 1963 onwards, and subsequently Wasps operated from small helicopter decks on a variety of Royal Navy ships, armed with anti-submarine or anti-ship weapons but without their own detection equipment. 98 Wasps were built for the Royal Navy, and the type also served with Brazil, the Netherlands, South Africa, New Zealand, Malaysia, and Indonesia. The final British Wasps were retired in the late 1980s, but New Zealand-operated examples flew well into the 1990s.

Specifications – Westland Wasp HAS.Mk.1

Main Rotor Diameter	32 ft 3 in
Fuselage Length	30 ft 4 in
Maximum speed	120 mph at sea level
Maximum take-off weight	5,500 lb
Range	303 miles
Service ceiling	12,500 ft
Armament	Two Mk.44 torpedoes, or depth charges, or two AS-12 anti-ship guided missiles
Engine	One Rolls-Royce (Bristol Siddeley) Nimbus 503 turboshaft engine, of 710 shp
Crew	Two crew, seats for (normally) three other occupants

Lockheed F-104 Starfighter

Conceived by the famous aircraft designer Clarence 'Kelly' Johnson as a simple high-performance fighter, the F-104 Starfighter was christened the 'missile with a man in it' because of its long fuselage and short, thin wings. The first of two XF-104s, powered by a 7,800 lb st Wright XJ65-W-6 Sapphire turbojet, made its first flight on 28 February 1954. The service test YF-104As that followed were powered by 14,800 lb st afterburning General Electric YJ79-GE-3s, the engine that was to power all subsequent Starfighters in various guises. Entering U.S. Air Force service in January 1958 as the F-104A and two-seat F-104B, the Starfighter was the U.S.A.F.'s first Mach 2 aircraft. After brief U.S.A.F. service many of the 153 F-104As built were supplied to Taiwan, Jordan or Pakistan. The F-104C followed, 77 of which were built for the U.S.A.F.'s Tactical Air Command. They also served briefly in Southeast Asia during the Vietnam conflict. The F-104D was a conversion trainer version of the C-model, both models last serving with the Puerto Rico Air National Guard in 1975. While U.S.A.F. service was limited, the aircraft formed the backbone of many European air forces from the 1960s to the early-1980s. The F-104G (and two-seat TF-104G conversion trainer) was a multi-role version designed for the newly recreated West German Luftwaffe, making its maiden flight on 7 June 1960. A reconnaissance version – the RF-104G – was also produced. Lockheed highlighted during its sales campaigns the F-104's impressive performance, while overlooking its small payload, short range, high landing speed and unforgiving flight characteristics. In what was termed the 'sale of the century' the Starfighter was sold to the air forces of Canada, Belgium, Denmark, Greece, Italy, the Netherlands, Norway, Spain and Turkey as well as West Germany. A huge production program was set up with F-

In the United States it is not unusual to find high-performance ex-military aircraft such as the Lockheed F-104 in private ownership. This example is flown by the 'Starfighters' demonstration team and has appeared at a number of air shows (Photo: John Batchelor).

162

This gleaming U.S. Air Force Starfighter is an example of the initial single-seat production version of the type, the Lockheed F-104A. The Starfighter is, in reality, better known for its service with European NATO countries than with the American military.

104Gs built in Belgium, Canada (where it was built as the CF-104 and two-seat CF-104D), West Germany, Italy and the Netherlands. West Germany additionally acquired a batch of two-seat F-104Fs, while F-104Gs were also supplied to Taiwan, which converted some locally as Stargazer reconnais-

sance aircraft. After Lockheed delivered three F-104Js to Mitsubishi, the Japanese company built a further 207 for the Japanese Air Self Defence Force, and also assembled 20 F-104DJ two-seaters from Lockheed kits. It was Aeritalia of Italy that built the last of the 2,422 Starfighters. These were 246 F-104Ss, the S standing for the Sparrow air-to-air missile carried by the aircraft. The Italian air force was also the last military Starfighter operator, retiring them in 2004.

Specifications – Lockheed F-104C Starfighter

Wingspan	21 ft 9 in without wing-tip missile rails
Length	54 ft 8 in
Maximum speed	1,150 mph at 50,000 ft
Maximum take-off weight	27,853 lb
Range	1,500 miles with external fuel tanks
Service ceiling	55,000 ft
Armament	One 0.787 in (20 mm) cannon, provision for two or four AIM-9 Sidewinder air-to-air missiles, or up to 2,000 lb of unguided air-to-ground weapons
Engine	One General Electric J79-GE-7 turbojet engine, of 15,800 lb st with afterburning
Crew	One

Tupolev Tu-114

The Tupolev Tu-95 'Bear' series has been, since the 1950s, a highly-successful long-range bomber for firstly the Soviet armed forces and nowadays for those of Russia. The history of this very long-serving aircraft is covered on pages 146 to 147, but there is another important part to the Tu-95 story. The Tu-95 bomber formed the basis of an equally impressive, long-range civil airliner. It was not unusual for a military aircraft to be adapted for civil passenger use in the Soviet Union, the Tupolev Tu-104 jet airliner (see pages 118 to 119) being another example, having been devised using significant components and design aspects of the Tu-16 'Badger' bomber. The Tu-114 was developed to give the Soviet Union's state airline, Aeroflot, a long-haul airliner with intercontinental range. The Tu-95 was

a natural choice to form the basis of the Tu-114 due to its long-range capabilities. In fact, development of the Tu-95 as the basis of an airliner adaptation began with the Tu-116 (sometimes called the Tu-114D). At least two Tu-116 are known to have been built, the airframes concerned having been taken from the Tu-95 production line and suitably converted. They retained virtually all the Tu-95's main components, with the fuselage being converted to create a pressurised rear compartment with up to 30 seats. The first aircraft is thought to have flown in April 1957, and they were used for VIP transport and, apparently, for route-proving prior to the introduction of the Tu-114 itself into service. The Tu-114 airliner was a more complete adaptation of the Tu-95 bomber, with a new circular-section fuselage,

This example of the Tupolev Tu-114 airliner is preserved at the major Russian aviation museum at Monino outside Moscow (Photo: Malcolm V. Lowe).

The Tupolev Tu-114 was a giant propeller-driven airliner that served with the Soviet Union's State airline Aeroflot. It was known to NATO as 'Cleat.'

and seating in a high-density layout for up to 220 passengers. The first example is believed to have flown in November 1957, and the type was the largest and fastest propeller-driven airliner in the world – one example breaking several world records in its class prior to the type's service entry in 1961. Scheduled services began on the Moscow to Khabarovsk route in April 1961, and the type flew on Aeroflot's long-haul services from the Soviet Union to such countries as Japan, Cuba, and Canada. Eventually 36 were built, all at Samara under the Soviet Union's unwieldy aviation industry structure. They were eventually withdrawn and replaced by jets from the early 1970s, but the Tu-114 layout formed the basis for a military derivative. This was the Tu-126 (known to NATO as 'Moss'), which was an Airborne Warning and Control System (AWACS) aircraft for the Soviet air force, fitted with a large saucer rotodome-mounted radar above the fuselage. Nine were built, and they played an important role as AWACS aircraft until replaced by the Beriev A-50 'Mainstay' adaptation of the Ilyushin Il-76 (see pages 260 to 261).

Specifications – Tupolev Tu-114

Wingspan	167 ft 7.75 in
Length	177 ft 6 in
Maximum cruising speed	478 mph at 19,685 ft
Maximum take-off weight	376,987 lb
Range	3,852.5 miles
Service ceiling	39,370 ft
Engine	Four Kuznetsov NK-12MV turboprop engines, of 14,795 eshp each
Accommodation	Five crew plus stewards/stewardesses, normal seating for 120 to 170 passengers

Douglas (McDonnell Douglas) A-4 Skyhawk

The well-known American aircraft designer Ed Heinemann and his colleagues created the A4D (later A-4) Skyhawk to an exacting requirement for a light strike aircraft capable of carrying nuclear bombs from the decks of aircraft carriers. Compact, but with good performance and a useful warload, the Skyhawk evolved over the years to undertake the conventional attack role, became an advanced trainer, and was also produced in several export models. First flying on 22 June 1954 powered by a Wright J65 jet engine, the prototype was followed by 165 A4D-1s, 542 A4D-2s and 643 A4D-3s, later being re-designated as A-4As, Bs and Cs, for the U.S. Navy and Marine Corps. Rebuilt aircraft were export-

ed to Argentina as A-4P and Qs, and these saw action in the 1982 Falkland Islands conflict. Some also went to Singapore, where they were rebuilt to various A-4S standards, and to Malaysia as A-4PTMs. The second generation Skyhawks were the A-4E and F, and the two-seat TA-4F and J, all powered by versions of the Pratt & Whitney J52. They had two more pylons under the wings, and higher operating weights than the earlier versions. The prototype A-4E flew on 12 July 1961 and the A-4F on 31 August 1966, differing from the E by having a hump on its fuselage containing additional avionics. Alongside the earlier versions the A-4E and F flew combat missions over Vietnam from both

The Douglas (McDonnell Douglas) A-4 Skyhawk was a neat, compact warplane that fought a long war in Southeast Asia for U.S. forces.

166

The A-4 Skyhawk was an agile but powerful aircraft. This made it a useful type for aerobatics, and the type was flown by the U.S. Navy's aerobatic display team the 'Blue Angels'
(Photo: U.S. Navy).

airfields and aircraft carriers. The production two-seat versions were proceeded by the TA-4E prototype, first flying in June 1965. Production TA-4Fs were followed by the TA-4J, a simplified version with its navigation and attack systems deleted. The TA-4J was the last Skyhawk variant in U.S. Navy service, being replaced by the Boeing T-45 Goshawk (see pages 268 to 269) in the advanced training role. Export second-generation Skyhawks included versions for Australia, Israel and New Zealand. The final Skyhawk was designed for the U.S. Marine Corps as the A-4M Skyhawk II, featuring a J52-P-408 turbojet, more ammunition and upgraded electrical systems. It first flew on

10 April 1970 and the final example (also the last of 2,690 Skyhawks built) was delivered in February 1979. Export A-4M variants were supplied to Israel and Kuwait, while surplus U.S. examples were sold on to Argentina as the A-4AR Fighting Hawk. Kuwait used its Skyhawks in combat alongside U.S. Marine Corps OA-4M forward air control fire-spotting conversions during the 1991 Operation 'Desert Storm' campaign, before selling them to the Brazilian Navy.

Specifications – McDonnell Douglas A-4E Skyhawk

Wingspan	27 ft 6 in
Length	40 ft 1.5 in excluding refuelling probe
Maximum speed	673 mph at sea level
Maximum take-off weight	24,500 lb
Range	1,160 miles
Service ceiling	42,650 ft
Armament	One 0.787 in (20 mm) cannon in each wing root, up to 8,200 lb on four underwing and one lower fuselage pylons
Engine	One Pratt & Whitney J52-P-6A turbojet engine, of 8,500 lb st
Crew	One

Blackburn (Hawker Siddeley) Buccaneer

On 30 April 1958 the first of 20 planned prototype and pre-production Buccaneer S.Mk.1 (NA.39) took to the air. The initial aircraft were followed by a further 40 production examples, all powered by two 7,100 lb st de Havilland (Bristol Siddeley) Gyron Junior turbojets. The Buccaneer had been designed by Blackburn as its B-103 to a demanding requirement for a carrier-based strike aircraft outlined by Naval Staff Requirement 39. A robust aircraft with a crew of two and a rotary bomb-bay, the first production S.Mk.1 flew in January 1962 and entered operational Fleet Air Arm service in July with No.801 Squadron. It soon became clear that the aircraft was under-powered and so integration of Rolls-Royce Spey Mk.101 turbofans was studied, resulting in the Buccaneer S.Mk.2. The new powerplants allowed the aircraft to take-off from aircraft carriers at their intended full weight. First flying on 17 May 1963, several Fleet Air Arm squadrons received Buccaneer S.Mk.2s and the last unit, No.809

Squadron, continued to fly them until December 1978 from the Royal Navy aircraft carrier H.M.S. Ark Royal. Navy Buccaneers capable of using the Martel anti-ship guided missile became S.Mk.2Ds, while others receiving a less-capable avionics upgrade became S.Mk.2Cs. As the Royal Navy's aircraft carrier fleet was being run down, the surplus Buccaneer S.Mk.2s were transferred to the R.A.F. The R.A.F. had additionally ordered its own version of the type as the Buccaneer S.Mk.2B, also capable of firing Martels. This was to partly replace the cancelled F-111 and TSR.2 programs. The aircraft transferred from the Royal Navy without this capability became S.Mk.2As. No.12 was the first R.A.F. squadron to fly the type, and several others used the 'Brick' (as it was appropriately nicknamed) both in the overland attack role with R.A.F. Germany and for maritime strike. Indeed, the R.A.F. put Martel-capable Buccaneers into service before the Navy, prior to replacing the missile with the Sea Eagle. R.A.F.

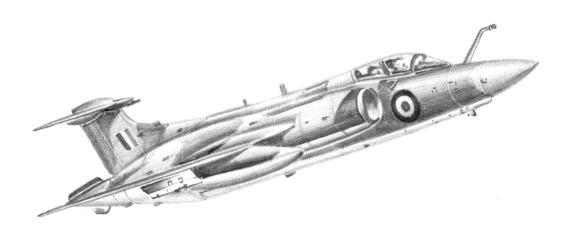

The Hawker Siddeley Buccaneer was a big, powerful carrier-based strike aircraft for naval use, although the type was also flown by the Royal Air Force as illustrated here.

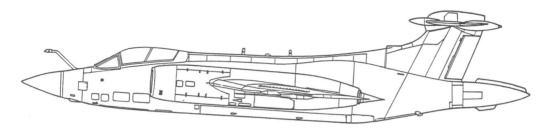

The large extension protruding from the nose ahead of the windscreen of this Buccaneer is an in-flight refuelling probe, the Buccaneer like most jet-powered aircraft from the 1960s onwards being capable of being refuelled in flight.

Buccaneers flew sorties during Operation 'Desert Storm' over Iraq in 1991, identifying targets for attack with the advanced 'Pave Spike' laser system. In this role the aircraft was highly effective, at last proving the operational capabilities of the big Buccaneer in British service. R.A.F. operations were concluded when No.208 Squadron stood-down in March 1994. However, the Royal Aircraft Establishment continued to operate the type for a short time after this on further trials work, retiring the last of its Buccaneer test-beds in early 1995. The only export customer

for the Buccaneer was South Africa, which received 16 S.Mk.50s in the mid-1960s. They differed from the Royal Navy's aircraft principally in that they could mount an 8,000 lb st Bristol Siddeley BS.605 rocket booster in the rear fuselage for additional power. South Africa's Buccaneers were used in action during operations over Angola, during the protracted fighting in that part of the world. The South African Air Force officially retired its Buccaneers in mid-1991, five aircraft still remaining operational at that time.

Specifications – Hawker Siddeley Buccaneer S.Mk.2

Wingspan	44 ft
Length	63 ft 5 in
Maximum speed	645 mph at sea level
Maximum take-off weight	62,000 lb
Radius of action	599 miles strike mission
Service ceiling	42,000 ft
Armament	Up to 4,000 lb of weapons in the fuselage rotary weapons bay, up to some 8,000 lb of weapons on four underwing pylons, including Sea Eagle anti-ship missiles, conventional and laser-guided bombs
Engine	Two Rolls-Royce Spey Mk.101 turbofan engines, of some 11,000 lb st each
Crew	Two

Lockheed C-130 Hercules

The Lockheed C-130 Hercules is the Western World's classic post-war transport aircraft. Still in production 50 years after its first flight, many air arms have come to the conclusion that the best replacement for their Hercules is a newer Hercules. Designed as a rugged tactical transport, the C-130's rear-loading ramp with its drive-on/off capabilities, useful load, turboprop performance and ability to operate from short runways or part-prepared surfaces made the aircraft a quantum leap over the U.S. Air Force's older piston-engined transports. The YC-130 prototype made its maiden flight on 23 August 1954, and production C-130As where delivered from April 1955. The C-130B followed with Allison T56-A-1A engines driving four-blade propellers and with increased fuel. It was followed by the C-130E and the C-130H. specialized transport versions were built for the U.S. Navy (C-130F and G, for land-based operations) and as the L-100 for civilian uses. Britain's Royal Air Force received 66 C-130Ks

as Hercules C.Mk.1s, later having 30 lengthened as Hercules C.Mk.3s. Several export customers also elected to have their existing Hercules lengthened, or buy new Hercules as C-130H-30s. Many specialist versions of the Hercules have been produced over the years for a variety of roles. Experience in the Vietnam War resulted in the development of gunship versions, initially AC-130As but followed by AC-130Es which were later upgraded as AC-130Hs. Early versions were replaced in the 1990s by the more capable AC-130U. U.S.-operated Hercules gunships have flown combat operations over Vietnam, Grenada, Panama, Iraq, and Afghanistan. specialized rescue versions with the capability to refuel helicopters were also built, with the U.S.A.F. also receiving 43 HC-130H rescue support aircraft. The HC-130H was additionally built for the U.S. Coast Guard to augment its earlier HC-130Bs. There have been a number of 'special forces' versions, and several in-flight refuelling models have been

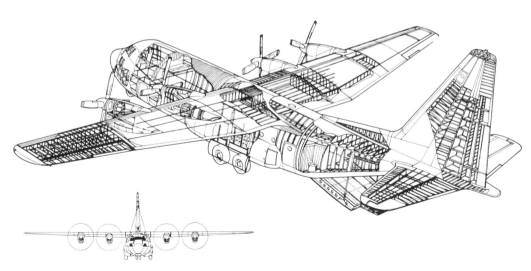

Visible in this cutaway drawing is the rear-loading ramp which helps to make the C-130 Hercules such a useful cargo transport. Small vehicles can be easily loaded, or large amounts of cargo.

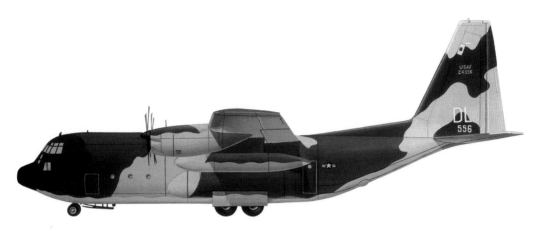

A U.S. Air Force Lockheed C-130 Hercules is illustrated here. The Hercules has been of great importance to the U.S.A.F. over the years, and will continue to serve for many years yet. It has gained several affectionate nicknames, including 'Fat Albert.'

built for U.S. military service. Other countries have modified their transports as tankers, including Canada and Britain, the R.A.F. requiring six Hercules C.Mk.1Ks because the Falklands conflict of 1982 showed a need for these aircraft. Electronic warfare versions include several variants of the EC-130E as airborne command posts and intelligence gatherers, and the EC-130H 'Compass Call' communications jammer. The U.S. Navy used two specially-equipped communications versions as relay aircraft to keep in touch with its nuclear submarine fleet. The latest family of Hercules variants is based on the C-130J with a two-man cockpit and Allison AE2100 turboprops driving six-blade propellers. The first customer was the R.A.F., but transport, weather reconnaissance and electronic warfare versions have been delivered to the U.S.A.F. and some other air arms. Over 2,100 Hercules have been built by 2005 and they are in service with over 50 air arms.

Specifications – Lockheed C-130E Hercules

Wingspan	132 ft 7 in
Length	97 ft 8 in
Maximum speed	384 mph at 10,000 ft
Maximum take-off weight	155,000 lb
Range	4,700 miles with external fuel tanks
Service ceiling	23,000 ft at 100,000 lb
Engine	Four Allison T56-A-7 turboprop engines, of 4,050 shp each
Crew	Four crew, various combinations of troop and paratroop seating available

English Electric/BAC Lightning

The BAC Lightning was one of the most powerful and impressive fighters of its day, and represented a huge leap forward in Britain's air defence capabilities when it entered service. It originated in the English Electric P.1/P.1A, which was designed by W.E.W. Petter (who also designed the English Electric Canberra bomber) in response to Specification ER.103, the first of two examples flying on 4 August 1954. The P.1/P.1A aircraft were supersonic test-beds, but they were designed so that they could also form the basis of a fighter. This was developed as the Lightning, which was destined to become the Royal Air Force's only wholly British-built Mach 2 fighter. The infamous 1957 Defence White Paper, that cancelled many of Britain's promising military aircraft programs, incorrectly stated that the Lightning would be the last manned fighter before missiles took over most combat roles. The three P.1B Lightning prototypes were basically militarised P.1As, with a raised cockpit, AI.23 nose radar and a cannon armament. The first example flew on 4 April 1957, going supersonic on its first flight. The P.1Bs were followed by a development batch of 20 Lightning F.Mk.1s used to test various aspects of the planned Lightning airframe and systems. Several Lightning F.Mk.1s were also delivered to equip the first R.A.F. squadron – No.74 – in the summer of 1960. The addition of an in-flight refuelling probe and other changes saw production switch to the F.Mk.1A, but this version was regarded as a stop-gap before the proposed F.Mk.2 could enter service in late 1962. The need for a two-seat conversion trainer resulted in the Lightning T.Mk.4, which first flew in May 1959 – some 20 production examples were built. The Red Top air-to-air missile (in place of the earlier Firestreak), a fin of increased area and a new cockpit layout were introduced on the subsequent Lightning F.Mk.3. This version dispensed with internal cannons, but could carry two in an optional ventral pack that also contained fuel. Further development led to the definitive F.Mk.6, which featured a revised wing design and could carry overwing fuel tanks in addition to a larger ventral fuel pack. The final versions for the R.A.F. were the T.Mk.5, a two-seat trainer version of the Mk.3, and an upgrade of the Mk.2 known as the F.Mk.2A for

The English Electric/BAC Lightning was built in a number of versions, including the two-seat T.Mk.4 illustrated here. This mark was a side-by-side seating, operational and conversion trainer.

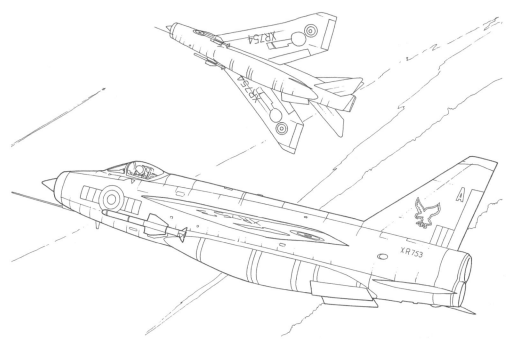

The English Electric/BAC Lightning was the first genuinely supersonic fighter used by the Royal Air Force. These two single-seaters are from a production batch of F.Mk.3A fighters, some of which were brought up to F.Mk.6 standard.

use by R.A.F. West Germany-based units. Export Lightning F.Mk.52/53s and T.Mk.54/55s were supplied or built for Kuwait and Saudi Arabia, the latter probably using them in combat operations during a confrontation with Yemen. The last R.A.F. operator was No.11 Squadron, which officially retired the Lightning in 1988. Nevertheless, a handful continued to fly on test duties with British Aerospace (the successor to BAC) into the early 1990s.

Specifications – BAC Lightning F.Mk.6

Wingspan	34 ft 10 in
Length	55 ft 3 in (including nose probe)
Maximum speed	1,390 mph at 40,000 ft
Maximum take-off weight	41,700 lb
Range	800 miles with ventral tank
Service ceiling	75,000 ft absolute
Armament	Two Red Top guided air-to-air missiles and, later in its service, two 1.18 in (30 mm) cannons in the forward section of the ventral fuel pack.
Engine	Two Rolls-Royce Avon Mk.301R turbojet engines, of some 11,100 lb st each (16,360 lb st each with afterburning)
Crew	One

Antonov An-24 and An-26 Series

In the post-World War Two period a number of transport aircraft have become famous for their highly successful and long-lived service. Amongst these are the ubiquitous Lockheed C-130 Hercules transport (see pages 170 to 171), used by many Western air forces and a participant in numerous conflicts and international aid efforts. From the former Eastern Bloc, there is a family of aircraft that can also claim many years of successful – and similarly continuing – service. This is the Antonov An-24 and An-26 family, which was created within the old Soviet Union in what is now independent Ukraine. The start of this successful line was the turboprop-powered Antonov An-24, which was developed to replace piston-engined transports then in service on internal civil routes within the vast Soviet Union, with military versions also planned. The prototype is believed to have first flown in late 1959, and over one thousand three hundred are thought to have been built of civil and military versions. The passenger-carrying An-24 examples generally had seating for 48/52 passengers. Production was also commenced in China as the Yunshuji Y-7. Continuing development led to the famous An-26 and its derivatives the An-30 and An-32. Whereas the An-24 was built either for civil passenger transport or military transport or cargo use, the An-26 was developed by Antonov specifically as a military cargo derivative. This involved detail refinement of the An-24 layout, and a re-design of the rear fuselage with a rear-loading ramp to make the An-26 into a dedicated cargo carrier. The first example is believed to have flown in 1968, and subsequently the type has seen literally world-wide service with operators in a variety of countries. These included Warsaw Pact nations and those elsewhere that were friendly towards the Soviet Union, but the type continues in service today in significant numbers. The An-26 was known to NATO by the reporting name 'Curl.' Several specialized versions were built including the capability to carry palletised cargo within the fuselage, and an electronic-warfare model also exists. Approximately 1,410 (probably more) An-26s were built, and production has also taken place in China as the Y-7H. An important An-24/An-26 derivative was the An-30 (NATO reporting name 'Clank'), developed specially for aerial survey/mapping and reconnaissance (but with secondary transport capability), and

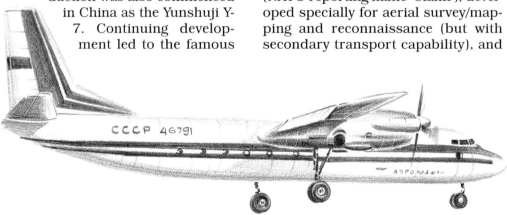

An Antonov An-24B of the Soviet Union's State airline Aeroflot.

There have been many different versions in the Antonov An-24 and An-26 family. This aircraft is a reconnaissance Antonov An-30FG of the Czech Air Force, used for post-Cold War 'Open Skies' arms reduction verification flights, an important role carried out by the Czech Republic and several other countries (Photo: Malcolm V. Lowe).

much-used in the 1990s by several air forces for post-Cold War 'Open Skies' arms reduction verification missions. The type is thought to have first flown in 1973 or 1974, with approximately 160 being built. A final important derivative is the An-32 ('Cline'), with high-mounted, more powerful engines and other refinements for operations in difficult (for example, 'hot and high') conditions. This model probably first flew in 1976 or 1977, and approximately 346 are thought to have been built.

Specifications – Antonov An-26B

Wingspan	95 ft 9.5 in
Length	78 ft 1 in
Maximum speed	270.3 mph plus at 19,685 ft
Maximum take-off weight	52, 910 lb
Range	1,653 miles
Service ceiling	24,606 ft
Engine	Two ZMKB Progress/Ivchenko AI-24 VT turboprop engines, of 2,780 ehp each, and one auxiliary RU 19A-300 turbojet, of 1,765 lb st (for additional power or main engine starting)
Crew	Five

Boeing B-52 Stratofortress

The Boeing B-52 Stratofortress strategic bomber has had a very long and active service life with the U.S. Air Force, having become as important in the conventional attack role as it once was as a nuclear deterrent during the Cold War. Present plans call for the remaining B-52Hs to remain operational until around 2040, meaning that most will be nearly 80 years old by the time they are retired! The B-52 was designed to carry nuclear bombs to targets deep inside the Soviet Union at high altitude, as a replacement for the Consolidated B-36 Peacemaker (see pages 82 to 83). The initial YB-52 first flew on 15 April 1952, with three B-52As being subsequently used as development aircraft. The initial production B-52B entered the U.S.A.F.'s Strategic Air Command

(SAC) bomber force in mid-1955. The fifty B-52B-standard aircraft were followed by 35 B-52Cs, the first with white undersides to protect the aircraft from thermal blast damage from nuclear explosions. 101 B-52Ds were built at by Boeing at Seattle and a further 69 at Wichita, while 42 and 58 B-52Es with improved navigation and electronics were built at the two sites. The last of the pure bomber versions was the B-52F, because the B-52G and B-52H models were designed as stand-off missile carriers. The first B-52G flew in October 1958 and 193 were built, introducing a shorter vertical tail, and underwing pylons to carry AGM-28 Hound Dog missiles. The B-52H was designed to carry the GAM-87A Skybolt, but this missile was cancelled and the Hound Dog

Affectionately known as the BUFF (big ugly fat 'feller), the Boeing B-52 Stratofortress is one of aviation's classic bombers, and has served with great effect in a number of wars.

substituted. It was powered by the TF33-P-3 turbofan in place of the previous J57 jet engines. The Hound Dog was phased out in the early 1970s and replaced by the AGM-69 Short Range Attack Missile (SRAM), itself supplemented by the AGM-86B Air Launched Cruise Missile (ALCM) from 1982. The B-52B, C, E and F fleets were ultimately retired, and the remaining bomber fleet was switched to low-level operations. The final B-52G was retired in 1994, leaving the B-52H version (102 built) to fly alongside Air Combat Command's Rockwell/Boeing B-1B Lancers and Northrop B-2A Spirit stealth bombers. Between 1965 and August 1973 B-52Fs and later B-52Ds flew over one hundred thousand combat mission over Southeast Asia, sorties from Guam taking over 13.5 hours. B-52G and B-52Hs have since been used over Iraq in 1991, and by the B-52H in 2003, the Balkans and Afghanistan, usually launching conventionally armed cruise missiles or free-fall bombs, although recent operations have involved precision munitions. Around 93 of the 744 B-52s built remain in service in 2005.

This Boeing cutaway illustration shows the configuration of some earlier B-52 Stratofortress versions with a tail armament and a bomb load of AGM-69 SRAM missiles (courtesy of the Boeing Military Airplane Company).

Specifications – Boeing B-52H Stratofortress

Wingspan	185 ft
Length	160 ft 10.9 in
Maximum speed	approximately 595 mph at 35,000 ft
Maximum take-off weight	505,000 lb
Range	10,130 miles un-refuelled
Service ceiling	55,000 ft
Armament	One 0.787 in (20 mm) tail turret-mounted cannon (sometimes removed); various air-launched guided missiles, or up to 50,000 lb of conventional unguided bombs, or nuclear weapons
Engine	Eight Pratt & Whitney TF33-P-3 turbofan engines, of 17,000 lb st each
Crew	Six, or five when rear gun and gunner deleted

BAC TSR.2

Another of Britain's famous post-World War Two cancelled aircraft projects, the TSR.2 only completed test flying totalling just over 13 hours before the whole program was cancelled in April 1965 – possibly due to pressure from the United States. Seeking a replacement for the highly-capable BAC Canberra bomber (see pages 112 to 113) suited for low-level tactical strike and reconnaissance (TSR) duties, General Operational Requirement (GOR) 339 was issued in Britain in September 1957. Unfortunately this requirement was subsequently amended several times, one of the many problems in the whole TSR.2 program. The English Electric company had already been working on its related P.17/P.17A project, while rivals Vickers proposed its Type 571. Both companies were subsequently awarded a joint development contract for what was to become the TSR.2, with Vickers being made lead (main) contractor. Friction between these two companies did not help the TSR.2 project, and the two eventually came

to be a part of the amalgamated British Aircraft Corporation (BAC). The final design was a refined Type 571, with the delta wings of the P.17, powered by Bristol Siddeley Olympus engines – whose development was also proving to be a difficult process at the time. The TSR.2 in fact had to meet several demanding requirements, especially a need for a short take-off capability, and terrain-following flight on its way to its target. Meanwhile, GOR.339 had become Operational Requirement 343, and finally Specification RB.192D was issued for the development aircraft. Six Type 571 development aircraft were eventually ordered during 1960 to be built at Weybridge, while all further examples were due to be built at Preston in Lancashire as Type 579s. Preston was scheduled to produce three more development aircraft, 11 pre-production and 30 production TSR.2s at the time of cancellation. The first TSR.2 made a successful maiden flight at Boscombe Down, Wiltshire, on 27 September 1964, but three months

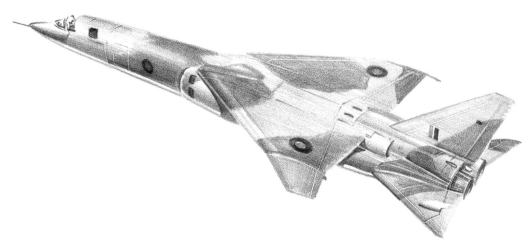

This is what the TSR.2 might have looked like if it had ever reached Royal Air Force service. One of the advances that the TSR.2 would have brought into operation was low-level terrain-following flight at high-speed, some very advanced avionics having been developed for the type.

Several views of a preserved TSR.2, showing in particular some details of the undercarriage (Photos: John Batchelor).

elapsed before the second test. The TSR.2 attained supersonic speed in February 1965, but made its last flight on 31 March 1965. At the time of cancellation two others were ready to fly, 17 more were in an advanced state of construction and components of 30 more were being produced. The only example to fly was ultimately used as a ballistics target. However, two pre-production/development examples have survived, and in 2005 were on display at the museums in Britain at Cosford, Shropshire, and Duxford, Cambridgeshire.

Specifications – BAC TSR.2 (some data estimated)

Wingspan	37 ft 1.5 in
Length	89 ft 0.46 in (including nose probe)
Maximum speed	Mach 2 plus at 36,000 ft
Maximum take-off weight	105,000 lb
Range	2,870 miles ferry range
Service ceiling	55,000 ft
Armament	None ever carried, but designed for two tactical nuclear weapons or six 1,000 lb conventional bombs in the bomb-bay. Two wing pylons (never fitted) intended for a tactical nuclear bomb each, or a 1,000 lb conventional bomb. Alternatively four air-to-surface missiles or four 37-missile rocket packs were planned.
Engine	Two Bristol Siddeley Olympus 22R Mk.320 turbojet engines, of 19,600 lb st each (30,610 lb st each with afterburning and water injection)
Crew	Two

Bell H-1 Huey and HueyCobra Family

One of the most famous helicopter families yet produced, the Bell UH-1 series commenced its long and celebrated career by becoming the U.S. Army's standard utility helicopter from the mid-1960s. It first flew on 22 October 1956 as the XH-40, after the Bell Model 204 was selected as the winner of an Army utility helicopter competition. The three XH-40s used an 825 shp XT53 turboshaft engine mounted above the cabin. They were followed by six YH-40s. Nine pre-production HU-1s (from which the 'Huey' nickname was derived) preceded 182 HU-1As and 1,014 HU-1Bs, redesignated as UH-1As and Bs from 1962. Between 1965 and 1967 767 UH-1Cs with improved main rotor systems and increased fuel capacity were delivered to the Army. The Bell Model 205, with an enlarged cabin to carry 12 troops was produced as the UH-1D, over 2,000 examples being delivered to the U.S. Army alone. While increasingly

more powerful T53 turboshaft variants had been used by the previous Huey versions, the UH-1H introduced the 1,400 shp T53-L-13. It became the most numerous version for the Army, with over 5,000 (including upgraded D-models) being acquired, becoming a workhorse in the Vietnam War. While largely replaced in the utility role by UH-60 Black Hawk variants from the early 1980s, upgraded examples continued to serve in the aero-medical role as UH-1Vs, the Army still using around 380 Hueys in 2005. The U.S.A.F., Navy and Marines also acquired numerous versions of the Model 204 and 205. Development of a twin-engined version, powered by the Pratt & Whitney Canada PT6T Turbo Twin-Pac produced the Model 212, ordered as the UH-1N by the three U.S. services. The Marines are currently upgrading their fleet of UH-1Ns as UH-1Ys, with a four-blade rotor and improved systems. The Iranian Army ordered a version of the 212 as the Model 214 Isfahan, 287 being delivered. An uprated power-

The Bell UH-1
series of helicopters
represents one of the most
famous and widespread
helicopter series in history.
The example illustrated is typical
of the many hundreds operated
by the U.S. Army

The Bell UH-1 series helicopters are justifiably famous for their long-running service in Southeast Asia during the Vietnam War. The example shown here is flying over typical terrain in South Vietnam (Photo: M.V. Lowe Collection).

plant and four-blade rotor formed the basis of the Model 412, Canada acquiring 100 as CH-146 Griffons. Production of the Huey family has been undertaken in West Germany, Indonesia, Italy, Japan and Taiwan as well as in the U.S.A. and Canada. The Bell Model 209 AH-1 HueyCobra attack helicopter is a Huey variant with a new, slim fuselage and stub-wings for weapons. A total of 1,119 AH-1Gs were followed by several other models for the U.S. Army. The U.S. Marine Corps also adopted twin-engined versions as AH-1J and AH-1T SeaCobras, replacing them with even more capable AH-1W SuperCobras. The AH-1W is currently being upgraded for further service as the AH-1Z with a four-bladed rotor and host of other improvements. Cobra versions have also served with Bahrain, Iran, Israel, Japan, Jordan, Pakistan, South Korea, Spain, Thailand and Turkey, while thousands of utility Hueys continue to fly with many military and civil operators world-wide.

Specifications – Bell UH-1H

Main Rotor Diameter	48 ft
Fuselage Length	41 ft 10.75 in
Maximum speed	128 mph at 5,700 ft
Maximum take-off weight	9,500 lb
Range	318 miles
Service ceiling	12,600 ft
Armament	Usually none, although door-mounted machine guns saw widespread use in Vietnam
Engine	One Lycoming T53-L-13 turboshaft engine, of 1,400 shp
Crew	Two or three crew, up to 14 troops

Dassault Mirage III Series

One of the most famous series of combat aircraft ever produced, the French Dassault Mirage family dates from the 1950s but is still very active in several forms today. Dassault gained post-World War Two success with its Mystère series of fighters (see pages 92 to 93), but much experimentation took place in France towards future combat aircraft design, and in early 1953 the French air force launched a competition for a lightweight supersonic-capable fighter. Dassault's proposal was for a radical delta-wing interceptor powered by two small turbojets augmented by a rocket motor. The initial MD.550 Mirage first flew on 25 June 1955, and eventually attained Mach 1.3. It was too small to be an effective fighter, however, and a complete re-design and re-think led to the larger, delta-wing single-engined Mirage III. Pursued as a company-funded project, the type flew in November 1956. It at once showed promise, and was soon regularly reaching Mach 1.5. A developed, pre-production batch of ten Mirage IIIA was duly built, the first of these flying in May 1958, and this type was found to be Mach 2-capable. The first production model for the French air force was the Mirage IIIC single-seat radar and guided missile-equipped interceptor, and the two-seat Mirage IIIB trainer. It was the start of a very successful line of Mirages IIIs and derivatives that eventually ran to over 1,400 production examples and a very large number of derivatives, sub-types, foreign sales, foreign-developed derivatives, as well as combat in several wars and smaller conflicts. The initial French air force Mirage IIIC flew in October 1960, and the type proved successful from the start. Initial foreign orders came from Switzerland, South Africa, and Israel. The latter used their Mirage IIICJ in combat, very successfully against Arab-operated MiG-21s in the Six Day War of June 1967, but the first air-to-air successes came against Syrian-flown MiG-17s in August 1963. Further development by Dassault resulted in the Mirage IIIE, with a redesigned wing and other changes capable of all-weather ground attack as well as fighter operations. Deliveries to the French air force commenced in March

Israel has used many Mirage III or their Israeli-derivatives in her struggle for freedom against her Arab neighbors. The configuration shown here is the Mirage IIIE which was never flown by Israel as such, but was used by many export customers world-wide as well as by the French.

A Dassault Mirage IIIE of the French air force (Armée de l'Air). The Mirage IIIE is the ground attack version of the successful Mirage III family (Photo: Christian Durand).

1964, but the type was also licence-built in Australia (Mirage IIIO) and Switzerland (Mirage IIIS). A simplified export model was the Mirage 5 which gained many overseas sales, and the more powerful Mirage 50. There was also a line of reconnaissance Mirage IIIRs, and a two-seat Mirage 5 version. Continuing development led to the Mirage 2000 – see pages 274 to 275. Israel re-built some earlier Mirages, and then built unlicensed copies of the Mirage III line to beat arms embargoes. The brand-new models included the IAI Nesher, and the American General Electric J79-engined IAI Kfir. Chile and South Africa also much modified their Mirages, South Africa creating the Atlas/Denel Cheetah C fighter which is possibly the best Mirage III derivative and is still in service.

Specifications – Dassault Mirage IIIC

Wingspan	26 ft 11.75 in
Length	48 ft 4 in
Maximum speed	Mach 2.15 at 39,370 ft
Maximum take-off weight	26,455 lb
Radius of action	approximately 186.5 miles
Service ceiling	58,071 ft
Armament	Two 1.18 in (30 mm) cannons in lower forward fuselage, two short-range guided air-to-air missiles and one medium-range guided air-to-air missile
Engine	One SNECMA Atar 9B3 turbojet engine, of 13,228 lb st with afterburning
Crew	One

McDonnell Douglas F-4 Phantom II

The F-4 Phantom II was one of the Western World's most famous jet fighters. It was a large, twin-engined, missile-armed fighter with a crew of two, and was designed in response to a U.S. Navy requirement for a new carrier-based fighter-bomber. The prototype YF4H-1F Phantom II made its first flight on 27 May 1958. This entered production as the F4H-1F (after 1962, F-4A), followed by the first major production version the F4H-1, which later became the F-4B. These were procured for the U.S. Navy, as were the reconnaissance-configured RF-4B, and F-4J. Phantoms first entered service with U.S. Navy fighter squadron VF-121 in late 1960, and were first deployed on-board an aircraft carrier by VF-102. The F-4N and S were upgrades of the F-4B and F-4J. These served with the U.S. Navy and Marine Corps until being replaced by Grumman F-14 Tomcats, and F/A-18 Hornets in the later 1980s. The Phantom was unique in that it was adopted by the U.S.A.F. – the first time a Navy fighter had been selected for the Air Force. Initially U.S. Navy F-4Bs were loaned, before the genuine land-based F-4C version was delivered. It was followed by the F-4D, with extensive avionics

modifications. The F-4E was developed after experience gained in air-to-air combat over Southeast Asia, becoming the first Phantom variant with an internal gun when the previous all-missile armament was found to be operationally inadequate. It first flew in the summer of 1967 and over 1,300 were built, of which around two-thirds went to the U.S.A.F. A photo-reconnaissance version, the RF-4C was the only other new-build Phantom for that service. However, over one hundred F-4Es were converted as F-4G 'Wild Weasels' for the suppression of enemy ground-based air defences. U.S. Phantoms were heavily tasked in the Vietnam War, and U.S.A.F. RF-4Cs and F-4Gs also served over Iraq in 1991. Phantoms were replaced in U.S.A.F. service by General Dynamics F-16 Fighting Falcons, although surplus examples were converted as un-manned target drones. The Phantom was widely exported. Britain's Royal Air Force flew the Rolls-Royce Spey-powered F-4M Phantom FGR.Mk.2, and also the F-4K Phantom FG.Mk.1 after this mark had been retired by the Fleet Air Arm. The R.A.F. also flew the General Electric J79-powered F-4J(UK). Other Phantom operators were Australia,

A McDonnell Douglas RF-4C Phantom II, wearing the markings of the U.S. Air Force's 432nd Tactical Reconnaissance Wing. This unit was based at the air base in Udorn, Thailand, for operations during the Vietnam War.

Both the Americans and Israelis have flown their F-4s Phantoms successfully in combat, the U.S. Navy example here operating during the Vietnam War.

Egypt, West Germany, Greece, Iran, Israel, Japan, South Korea, Spain and Turkey, some flying the RF-4E export reconnaissance version. Both Iran and Israel used their examples operationally. Major upgrades have been planned for the German and Israeli Phantoms. Historians disagree as to how many Phantoms were actually completed and flown, but McDonnell Douglas built at least 5,068 F-4s, while over one hundred F-4EJs were constructed by Mitsubishi in Japan.

Specifications – McDonnell Douglas F-4E Phantom II

Wingspan	38 ft 4.875 in
Length	63 ft
Maximum speed	Mach 2.2 at 36,000 ft
Maximum take-off weight	61,795 lb
Radius of action	786 miles
Service ceiling	62,250 ft
Armament	One 0.787 in (20 mm) multi-barrel rotary cannon under the nose, four semi-recessed air-to-air missiles under the fuselage and up to 16,000 lb of ordnance on four wing and one under fuselage pylons, including air-to-air and air-to-surface missiles, free-fall bombs or rocket pods
Engine	Two General Electric J79-GE-17 or -17A turbojet engines, of 11,810 lb st each (17,900 lb st each with afterburning)
Crew	Two

Westland Sea King/Commando

One of the West's classic military helicopters is the Sikorsky S-61/H-3 and Westland Sea King series. This large family of helicopters can trace its ancestry back to the later 1950s, yet in various forms, the type remains in widespread and important service with various air arms and some civil operators today. The American company Sikorsky was already famous for such types as the S-55/H-19 series (see pages 76 to 77) when it began design work to meet a 1957 U.S. Navy requirement for an anti-submarine helicopter able to carry out hunter and killer roles in the same airframe. The result was the basic HSS-2 Sea King design. As a testimony to the soundness of this layout, all subsequent Sea King versions have generally kept to the same original design. The prototype first flew on 11 March 1959, and the type was an immediate success. Series production followed with hardly a hitch, the type being redesignated from HSS-2 to H-3 in 1962. Sikorsky Sea Kings have subsequently served very widely with U.S. forces, Sea Kings serving in the

Vietnam War alongside combat search and rescue models and related derivatives such as the HH-3E 'Jolly Green Giant.' A civil passenger derivative is well-known for supporting oil and gas rigs in various parts of the world. Perhaps the best known of all American Sea Kings are the small fleet of special VIP-configured U.S. Marine Corps-controlled VH-3D which transport the American President. Three countries obtained licence-manufacturing rights for the Sea King, these being Britain, Italy, and Japan. In Britain, the famous helicopter company Westland obtained a manufacturing licence as early as 1959. Westland had already constructed and developed licence-built versions of the Sikorsky S-55 series as the Whirlwind, and the Sea King proved to be just as successful. The first production model was the Sea King HAS.MK.1 for Royal Navy anti-submarine work. The first example flew in May 1969, and the type entered front-line service in 1970. A number of further specific versions followed for the Fleet Air Arm or the Royal Air Force, some of these seeing action during the Falkland Islands

The Westland Sea King has served with Britain's Royal Navy from 1969/1970, when the Sea King HAS.Mk.1 anti-submarine version illustrated first entered service.

An important derivative of the basic Westland Sea King layout is the Westland Commando. The Commando Mk.2A shown here was built for service in Qatar (Photo: Westland Helicopters).

campaign against Argentina in 1982. There have also been a number of export successes for the Westland Sea King line. A highly-important but improvised model was the airborne early warning AEW.Mk.2, a makeshift radar-equipped model which hastily came about when Argentine success against British shipping in the Falkland Islands war showed the total lack of this type of aerial cover for the British fleet. This model in particular has been the subject of subsequent upgrades. A significant spin-off from the Westland Sea King line is the troop-carrying Commando series, which can be specially-configured to customer choice, British-operated examples (called Sea King HC.Mk.4) being assault transports. The type has seen limited export successes, with several being configured for VIP transport. Some 328 Westland Sea King/Commando of all marks have been built. The long-term replacement for the British-operated Sea Kings is the EH Industries EH 101 (see pages 298 to 299).

Specifications – Westland Commando Mk.2

Main Rotor Diameter	62 ft
Fuselage Length	55 ft 10 in
Maximum speed	169 mph at sea level
Maximum take-off weight	21,500 lb
Range	246 miles
Service ceiling	10,000 ft
Armament	Various machine guns, cannons and rockets/missiles could be fitted to customer choice
Engine	Two Rolls-Royce Gnome H.1400-1T turboshaft engines, of 1,660 shp each
Crew	Two crew, up to 28 troops

Lockheed P2V/P-2 Neptune

Originally designed during World War Two as a long-range land-based maritime patrol aircraft for the U.S. Navy, the first of two prototype P2V Neptunes made its first flight on 17 May 1945. Fifteen initial production P2V-1s were built, and these started to enter service in the first half of 1947. Early production models retained the 'solid' unglazed nose of the P2V-1, but the P2V-5 introduced forward defensive armament in a nose ball turret. Later, a pair of J34 turbojet engines were added under the wings for additional power, along with a submarine-hunting magnetic anomaly detector (MAD) tail boom to create the P2V-5F (P-2E post-1962) anti-submarine warfare aircraft. Some 372 P2V-5 series were built to become the most numerous Neptune variant. The P2V-6 was primarily a mine-laying aircraft but (in its P2V–6B version) could carry Petrel anti-ship missiles. In April 1954 the final version of the Neptune built by Lockheed, the P2V-7 (P-2H post 1962) made its maiden flight. Some 318 were constructed, approximately 205 entering service with the U.S. Navy. Most were later equipped with Julie/Jezebel submarine detection gear as SP-2Hs. At its peak over thirty U.S. Navy patrol squadrons flew Neptunes, the type eventually being retired from the Navy Reserve in 1978. Alongside the patrol versions, the U.S. Navy used Neptune variants as drone carriers, combat transports, for Antarctic supply, trainers, and as heavy attack aircraft and sensor droppers in the Vietnam War (AP-2H and OP-2E versions). There was even a carrier-borne nuclear bomber model, the P2V-3C, although these aircraft were intended to ditch after attacking their targets and not to land back onboard their aircraft carrier. The U.S. Army also used AP-2E Neptunes over Vietnam for electronic warfare, while the C.I.A. used several RB-69As in U.S. Air Force colors to gather intelligence on Soviet radars. U.S. Navy Neptunes were similarly used for clandestine intelligence purposes, but at least three were shot down in the early 1950s. Export Neptunes were operated by several countries including France, Japan, the Netherlands, and Britain's Royal Air Force. Kawasaki in Japan produced 48 P2V-7, a further 83 (including a prototype conversion) P2V-7 KAIs (later P-2J) being built. The P-2J featured many improvements, including General

Amongst the many operators of the Lockheed P2V/P-2 Neptune was France's naval air arm the Aéronavale. This French example shows the large pod on the right-hand wingtip which mounted a powerful searchlight.

There were many special versions and sub-types of the Lockheed Neptune family. The aircraft illustrated here has been fitted with skis for Antarctic exploration and wears a special high-visibility paint scheme (Photo: U.S. Navy).

Electric T64-series turboprops and Japanese-built J3-IHI turbojets in place of the original Wright piston engines and J34 turbojets respectively. Japan was the last military user of the Neptune, retiring the type well into the 1990s. Some surplus ex-military Neptunes had a useful second life as civil-operated fire-bombers. A worthy successor to the Neptune, the four-engined Lockheed P-3 Orion, is in widespread service today.

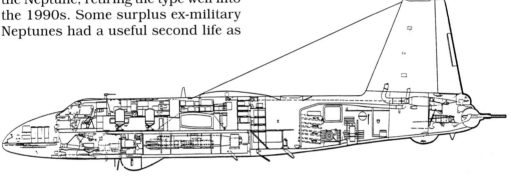

A cutaway drawing showing the internal features of an early unglazed-nose Lockheed Neptune of the P2V-2 or similar series. Note the mid-fuselage bomb-bay and the tail-mounted gun armament of these early production aircraft.

Specifications – Lockheed SP-2H Neptune

Wingspan	103 ft 10 in
Length	91 ft 8 in
Maximum speed	364 mph at 10,000 ft
Maximum take-off weight	79,895 lb
Range	2,200 miles
Service ceiling	38,550 ft
Armament	Up to 8,000 lb of ordnance in internal bomb-bay, including torpedoes, mines, depth charges or bombs, up to eight 5 in rockets beneath the wings
Engine	Two Wright R-3350-32W Turbo-Compound Duplex Cyclone radial piston engines, of 3,500 hp each, and two Westinghouse J34-WE-34 or -36 turbojet engines, of 3,400 lb st each
Crew	Seven to nine

Boeing 727

Design work on what became the Boeing Model 727 commenced in February 1956, when Boeing started investigating a short- to medium-range and medium-capacity jet-powered airliner layout with good take-off performance and able to cruise at high speed. The secret that Boeing found was an efficient wing design, with lift-augmentation flaps and slats as well as spoilers to decrease the aircraft's landing run. This was at a time when jet airliners were still in their relative infancy, and Boeing's initiatives during that period were eventually to put the company at the forefront of airliner design and manufacture. The Model 727 had a significant advantage in the market because of the good fuel economy of its Pratt & Whitney JT8D turbofans, six-abreast passenger seating, and integral equipment allowing operations from austere airfields (including an auxiliary power unit to start the aircraft's engines, and foldable airstairs). Eastern Air Lines and United Air Lines ordered the Boeing 727 as launch customers in December 1960. The prototype made its maiden flight on 9 February 1963, the second flying on 12 March 1963. Ansett-ANA, American Airlines, Lufthansa, TAA and TWA followed these two launch customers in making early orders for the type. The 727-100 received its FAA Certification in December 1963, Eastern putting the type into service in February 1964. To capitalise on the air cargo market the Model 727-100C convertible cargo/passenger version was introduced in mid-1964, Northwest Orient becoming the first customer. The 727-100QC with palletised interiors and the –100 Business Jet were also built. By April 1967 the 727 was the most widely used commercial jet airliner in service, peak production at Boeing's Renton factory reaching some 315 examples between 1967 and 1968. Two fuselage extensions fore and aft of the wing produced the longer 727-200, destined to become the standard model with over 1,000 built – later examples as the Advanced 727-200 with increased fuel capacity, higher operating weights and extended range. Freighter versions were built as the 727-200F, with over 160 delivered to Federal Express including the last production 727, which flew in August 1984. A total of 1,832 727s were produced, making it the world's best selling airliner until it

Eastern Air Lines was a major supporter of the Boeing Model 727, being one of the launch customers for the type.

A rear view of a Boeing 727, showing the three-engine layout of the type, and the rear fuselage airstairs (Photo: Boeing).

was eventually overtaken by the Boeing 737 described on pages 218 to 219. In major airline service the 727 was replaced by the latest generation of efficient turbofan-powered airliners, and it quickly disappeared from operators in Europe and Asia. However, it continues to thrive with smaller airlines in the United States serving the domestic routes it was originally designed for. Only a small number served with military forces, although six flew as C-22s with the U.S. Air Force, while Belgium, New Zealand and Taiwan also used the type.

Specifications – Boeing 727-200

Wingspan	108 ft
Length	153 ft 2 in
Maximum speed	622 mph at 20,500 ft
Maximum take-off weight	190,500 lb
Range	2,510 miles with reserves
Service ceiling	33,000 ft
Engine	Three Pratt & Whitney JT8D-15 turbofan engines, of 15,500 lb st each
Accommodation	Three crew plus stewards/stewardesses, maximum of 189 passengers (155 often standard)

BAC One-Eleven

The BAC One-Eleven was one of Britain's major post-war jet airliners. The first example flew from Hurn airport in southern England on its maiden flight on 20 August 1963. By then the Type 111 already had orders for approximately 60 examples, half of them very importantly from airlines in the United States. Production amounted to 236 examples at Weybridge and Hurn and a further nine (plus several uncompleted examples) in Romania, where the aircraft was built under licence in a rather unsuccessful deal by ROMBAC. The One-Eleven design started as a project of the Hunting company, before that organisation was incorporated into the British Aircraft Corporation (BAC). Unfortunately the prototype crashed on 22 October 1963 after a deep stall, but customer confidence was not lost and testing resumed when the second aircraft took to the air on 19 December 1963. The Series 200 entered revenue earning service with British United Airways on 9 April 1965, the first time a British aircraft started its career with an independent airline instead of one of the major national airlines. The Series 200 was powered by the 10,300 lb st

Spey 506 turbofan, but this was replaced by the 11,400 lb st Spey 511 in the Series 300, which could also carry more fuel. Nine were built to add to the 56 Series 200s. A total of 69 Series 400s followed, capable of two-crew operations due to their advanced avionics. A lengthened fuselage, 12,550 lb st Spey 512s and a slightly increased wingspan were the features of the Series 500 that made its maiden flight on 17 February 1968. Aimed as a replacement for the turboprop-powered Vickers Viscount (see pages 80 to 81), 89 were built including 18 for British European Airways. The wings and powerplant of the Series 500 were combined with the short fuselage of the Series 400 to produce the 'hot-and-high' Series 475, but only nine of

The BAC One-Eleven was a classic British airliner that continues to fly today in some parts of the world. A set of airstairs in the rear fuselage below the tail allowed entrance and exit in addition to the conventional passenger side doors.

A BAC One-Eleven 500 Series of British Airways. Registered G-BGKE, it was delivered in February 1980, and was one of several examples fitted with 'hush-kits' to reduce the type's engine noise. British Airways-operated One-Elevens served faithfully on the short-range air routes within Western Europe for which the type was particularly well suited (Photo: British Airways).

these were sold. The prototype Series 475 was converted as the one-off Series 670 for the Japanese market, but failed to find a buyer. British Aerospace (the successor to BAC) investigated several other potential versions of the One-Eleven, but none ever made it into the air. With the end in sight for the British production line the Romanian aerospace industry took an interest in producing the type behind the Iron Curtain. The last three built in Britain were delivered to the Romanian airline TAROM and nine where constructed in Romania

before interest ended. Eventually the One-Eleven fell victim to the environmental lobby due to its alleged high noise levels. A re-engining program to replace Speys with the quieter Tay turbofan engine was started by Dee Howard – the first flying as the One-Eleven Series 2400 on 2 July 1990 – but only one more conversion was undertaken. The last commercial flight of a One-Eleven in Europe took place in March 2002 but operations in Africa – notably Nigeria – continued beyond this date.

Specifications – BAC One-Eleven Series 500

Wingspan	93 ft 6 in
Length	107 ft
Maximum speed	541 mph at 21,000 ft
Maximum take-off weight	104,500 lb
Range	2,165 miles maximum, with reserves
Service ceiling	35,000 ft
Engine	Two Rolls-Royce Spey Mk.512-14DW turbofan engines, of 12,550 lb st each
Accommodation	Two crew plus stewards/stewardesses, up to 119 passengers, 99 standard

North American XB-70 Valkyrie

The Boeing B-52 Stratofortress jet-powered bomber (see pages 176 to 177) was expected to have a service life of around ten years while operational with the U.S. Air Force's bomber force the Strategic Air Command (SAC). The Command's forceful leader, Curtis LeMay, wanted a replacement aircraft with the range of the B-52 and the speed of the Convair B-58 Hustler (pages 144 to 145) – the larger-than-life B-70A Valkyrie program was the product of this vision. The requirement Weapon System (WS) 110A was born which called for a chemical-powered bomber with intercontinental range and supersonic speed. The basic SAC demand was for an unrefuelled range of 6,325 miles (10,179 km), with a 1,000 mile (1,609 km) supersonic dash over the target. In response, North American Aviation started investigating boron-based fuel to provide an aircraft with the performance demanded, coupled to the phenomenon known as compression lift allowing an aircraft to ride on its own shockwave to reduce fuel consumption. Compression lift would allow the aircraft, unbelievably, to fly its entire mission at Mach 3. Two pro-

totypes were ordered as XB-70 (later XB-70A) Valkyrie in October 1961, a further prototype later being cancelled. However, a debate had by then started between the merits of bombers and intercontinental missiles. Development of surface-to-air anti-aircraft missiles was also proceeding to the point where they would be able to destroy even an aircraft with the speed and height capabilities of the Valkyrie. One of the Valkyrie's leading critics was Secretary of Defence Robert S. McNamara. During 1962 the U.S. Air Force switched its requirement from 200 B-70A bombers to 150 revised RS-70 reconnaissance/strike aircraft. But when U.S. President Johnson revealed the hitherto-secret Lockheed SR-71A reconnaissance aircraft, the American Congress had enough justification to virtually kill off the program. This was the situation when the first XB-70A was rolled out during 1964, becoming the longest, heaviest, most powerful and most expensive aircraft then in existence. The first flight was made by this aircraft on 21 September 1964. The Valkyrie was revolutionary in many respects, and the amazing speed of

Two photographs showing details of the preserved North American XB-70A Valkyrie at the U.S. Air Force Museum (Photos: John Batchelor).

The North American XB-70A Valkyrie was an amazing feat of engineering, and required special heat-resisting metals in its structure. The installation of the type's six engines is particularly evident in this drawing.

Mach 3 was achieved on its seventeenth flight. The second prototype flew in July 1965, but by that time much of the Valkyrie's flight development work had been redirected to supporting the (ultimately unsuccessful) U.S. civil supersonic transport program. Sadly, disaster struck on 8 June 1966 when the second prototype was lost in a fatal collision with a Lockheed F-104 Starfighter during (of all things) an air-to-air photo shoot. The pilot successfully ejected, but the aircraft's co-pilot died in the crash. The first XB-70A continued to be used on various NASA test programs until it was delivered to the U.S. Air Force Museum at Wright-Patterson Air Force Base, Ohio, in February 1969.

Specifications – North American XB-70A Valkyrie (some data provisional)

Wingspan	105 ft
Length	196 ft 6 in (including nose probe)
Maximum speed	Mach 3.08 at 50,000 ft
Maximum take-off weight	550,000 lb
Range	approximately 5,000 miles un-refuelled
Service ceiling	75,000 ft
Armament	None ever carried, but intention for 14 nuclear or thermonuclear weapons, or various conventional weapons
Engine	Six General Electric J93-GE-3 turbojet engines, of some 30,000 lb st each with afterburning
Crew	Two, possibly four in planned operational aircraft

Mikoyan-Gurevich MiG-21

The Mikoyan-Gurevich MiG-21is one of the world's most famous and widely-used jet fighters, and one that has seen very long-lasting front-line service. The MiG-21's design arose partly as a result of combat experience with the MiG-15 (see pages 58 to 59) during the Korean War in the early 1950s, but it also came about from continuing design work by the MiG design bureau into high-performance jet fighter technology. An official requirement was developed in the Soviet Union during 1953/1954 for the creation of an interceptor fighter with various capabilities including the ability to fly at over Mach 1. This was a demanding specification at that time, and MiG responded with two different prototype designs. One had sharply swept wings, the other a delta wing layout with a conventional tailplane. The latter, 'tailed-delta' aircraft was initially called the Ye-4, and it first flew in June 1955. During that era many developments were being made with materials suitable for the construction of aircraft able to fly at supersonic speeds, and with jet engines that were light enough and powerful enough to provide sufficient thrust for super-sonic flight. This led to further development aircraft that included the Ye-5, which first flew in 1956 and was a precursor of the MiG-21 family. Continuing development led to the Ye-6, which was effectively a pre-production layout for the MiG-21 and initially flew in the first half of 1958. The first true production MiG-21 was the MiG-21F, the type receiving the strange NATO reporting name 'Fishbed.' Initial deliveries were made in late 1958/early 1959 for evaluation and service introduction by the Soviet air force, with the type entering Soviet service in its MiG-21F-13 ('Fishbed-C') version in the early 1960s. It was the start of a vast number of MiG-21 single-seat fighter models, for Soviet and very widespread export service, in addition to related reconnaissance-configured variations as well as the two-seat MiG-21U (initially Ye-6U and MiG-21UTI) series of operational trainers (named 'Mongol' by NATO). Continuing development led to successful fighter marks such as the MiG-21MF ('Fishbed-J') fighter, then to the improved multi-role MiG-21bis ('Fishbed-L') which entered Soviet service in the early 1970s. Licence-production of early

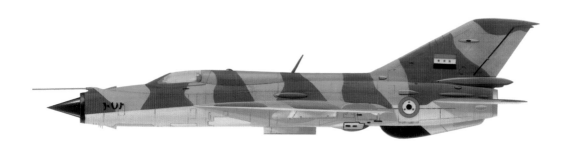

Sleek and purposeful, the MiG-21 was built in large numbers and served very widely around the world with countries that were friendly towards the Soviet Union. This drawing approximates to the MiG-21PF or PFM layout.

MiG-21 versions began in Czecho-slovakia and India in the early 1960s, and was later pursued by Communist China which has subsequently developed the type into a variety of additional versions. North Vietnamese-operated MiG-21s proved to be worthy opponents of U.S. fighters during the Vietnam War, although those flown by Arab air forces were less successful against Israeli-operated fighters during conflicts in the Middle East.

Although the Russians have now withdrawn the MiG-21 from front-line service, in early 2005 a number of other air forces were continuing to use the type, including the Czech Republic and India. Some of these MiG-21s have received major upgrades, such as the Romanian-operated examples which are now called MiG-21 Lancer. Altogether, approximately eight thousand MiG-21s of all types were built.

Unfortunately neither of the two drawings on these pages show the beautiful delta wing of the MiG-21 series. The example illustrated here was flown by one of the Arab air forces that operated the type. Early MiG-21s were Tumansky R-11F powered, later MiG-21s had the Tumansky R-13 powerplant.

Specifications – Mikoyan-Gurevich MiG-21MF

Wingspan	23 ft 5.65 in
Length	51 ft 8.5 in (including nose probe)
Maximum speed	approximately Mach 2.15 at 36,090 ft
Maximum take-off weight	20,723 lb
Range	746 miles on internal fuel
Service ceiling	59,711 ft
Armament	One 0.9 in (23 mm) cannon in lower fuselage, four K-13 short-range guided air-to-air missiles
Engine	One Tumansky R-13-300 turbojet engine, of 14,307 lb st with afterburning
Crew	One

Lockheed U-2

Lockheed has been responsible for several pioneering and top secret aircraft programs. One of these is the famous U-2 'spyplane.' America's Central Intelligence Agency (CIA) was responsible for the early U-2 program, as it saw the aircraft as a way of obtaining firm information on military developments within the Soviet Union. A high-altitude, long-range reconnaissance aircraft, the prototype first flew on 4 August 1955 from Groom Dry Lake, Nevada. A team of pilots was trained on the U-2 – which proved to be demanding to fly – for the CIA's 'Overflight' program. 'Overflight' involved flying over the Soviet Union's most sensitive military facilities taking photographs. One of its early successes was confirmation that the so-called 'bomber gap' (a feared disparity between the West and the Soviet Bloc in combat aircraft) was a myth. However, on 1 May 1960 a U-2C flown by Francis Gary Powers was shot down over Sverdlovsk in the

Soviet Union and the pilot captured, thrusting the aircraft into the limelight. U-2As were powered by the Pratt & Whitney J57 jet engine, while the U-2B used the Pratt & Whitney J75 and also had an increased fuel capacity and strengthened airframe. The U-2C could carry a larger load of sensors, a two-seat version (U-2CT) having a second cockpit in the position behind the pilot for conversion training. Although the U-2D also had two cockpits, it was used for high-altitude research. The U.S. Air Force acquired its own U-2s in time to use them to discover ballistic missiles on Cuba in 1962, triggering the Cuban Missile Crisis which threatened to lead to major war between the Soviet Union and the West. In order to increase the sensor carrying capability of the aircraft the redesigned U-2R was produced, six examples going to the CIA for operations from Taiwan over Communist China and six to the U.S. Air Force for operations over

Lockheed's famous 'Skunk Works' has been responsible for the design of some fascinating and remarkable aircraft, of which the U-2 series is but one.

Southeast Asia. It first flew in August 1967. The U-2R was a larger version of the earlier U-2s with a longer wingspan and a lengthened fuselage, but retained the J75 powerplant. Surviving CIA U-2Rs were transferred to the Air Force in 1974. The U-2 production line was re-opened again in November 1979 to build 37 aircraft, a mixture of U-2Rs, TR-1As, TR-1Bs, ER-2s and a single U-2RT. The TR-1A was intended for tactical (shorter-range) reconnaissance missions, although the missions and sensors of the aircraft were interchangeable with the U-2R. TR-1As were based at R.A.F. Alconbury in England to monitor Eastern Europe. The TR-1B was a two-seat trainer version, while the ER-2s were Earth resource monitoring and test aircraft for NASA. In December 1991 the TR-1 designation was dropped, with surviving aircraft becoming U-2Rs and U-2RT trainers. From October 1994 the surviving U-2R fleet was re-engined with General Electric F118 jet engines as U-2Ss, the U-2RTs becoming U-2STs. Total U-2 production appears to have amounted to 55 smaller first generation aircraft and 49 larger later versions.

A pair of Lockheed U-2s of the U.S. Air Force. The type has become well-known as a so-called 'spyplane,' and was very active during the Cold War (Photo: U.S. Air Force).

Specifications – Lockheed U-2R

Wingspan	103 ft
Length	62 ft 9 in
Maximum speed	430 mph at 70,000 ft
Maximum take-off weight	41,000 lb
Range	6,250 miles
Service ceiling	80,000 ft
Engine	One Pratt & Whitney J75-P-13B turbojet engine, of 17,000 lb st
Crew	One

Northrop F-5 Series

The F-5 family was developed from the Northrop N-156 proposal for a lightweight fighter to be supplied under the various American military aid programs to allied countries. Development split between the N-156T, that emerged as the two-seat T-38 Talon supersonic advanced trainer, and the N-156F that became the single-seat F-5 Freedom Fighter. The T-38A Talon first flew on 10 April 1959 and 1,139 production examples were built for the U.S. Air Force and West Germany, entering service in March 1961. Subsequently 132 were modified as more advanced T-38B lead-in fighter trainers, while others were supplied to Portugal, South Korea, Taiwan and Turkey. NASA flew a number of T-38As to allow its astronauts to keep up their normal flying hours, while a small number also served with the U.S. Navy. Currently the U.S. Air Force's long-surviving fleet is being upgraded as T-38Cs with more up-to-date avionics. The prototype single-seat N-156F flew on 30 July 1959. The subsequent F-5A Freedom Fighter initial production model flew in May 1963. A two-seat conversion trainer related model was designated the F-5B, and a recon-naissance version the RF-5A. Several F-5As were deployed to Vietnam for an extended combat test period between 1965 and 1967 as F-5Cs. Licence production was set up in Canada (CF-5A/D) and Spain (SF-5A/B and SRF-5A) while other export operators include Botswana, Brazil, Ethiopia, Greece, Iran, Jordan, Morocco, the Netherlands, Norway, Philippines, Saudi Arabia, South Korea, South Vietnam, Thailand, Turkey, and Venezuela. The type's General Electric J85-GE-13 turbojet engines were replaced by more powerful –21s in the subsequent, improved F-5E Tiger II. The F-5E was designed in response to a U.S. Air Force international fighter requirement, the first production example flying on 11 August 1972, and was followed by the combat-capable F-5F two-seat conversion trainer and RF-5E TigerEye reconnaissance aircraft. The Tiger II was supplied to Bahrain, Brazil, Chile, Ethiopia, Honduras, Indonesia, Iran, Jordan, Kenya, South Korea, Malaysia, Mexico, Morocco, Saudi Arabia, Singapore, Sudan, Switzerland, Taiwan, Thailand, Tunisia, South Vietnam and Yemen, as well as the U.S. Air Force, Navy and Marines for air combat training. Several countries have put their F-5s through upgrade programs. The final ver-

The Northrop F-5 family of no-frills fighters is one of the most widely-exported combat aircraft in history. This example is in South Vietnamese markings.

Four two-seat Northrop T-38 Talon jet trainers fly in formation. In addition to training U.S. Air Force pilots, T-38s based in the United States were also used to train pilots from West Germany (Photo: Northrop).

sion of the F-5 family offered by Northrop was the F-5G, powered by a single General Electric F404 engine. Later redesignated the F-20A Tigershark, only three prototypes were built as the program was cancelled. In total, over 2,200 F-5s were built. They have fought in several wars, including the 1980 to 1988 Iran-Iraq conflict, in Ethiopian service against Somalia, and in the Vietnamese invasion of Cambodia.

Specifications – Northrop F-5E Tiger II

Wingspan	28 ft (including wing-tip missiles)
Length	47 ft 4.75 in
Maximum speed	1,056 mph at 36,000 ft
Maximum take-off weight	24,664 lb
Radius of action	873 miles
Service ceiling	51,800 ft
Armament	Two 0.787 in (20 mm) nose-mounted cannons, up to 7,000 lb of weapons on one lower fuselage and four underwing pylons, including air-to-air missiles, air-to-surface missiles or bombs, plus two AIM-9 Sidewinders on wing-tip rails
Engine	Two General Electric J85-GE-21B turbojet engines, of 3,500 lb st each (5,000 lb st each with afterburning)
Crew	One

de Havilland Canada DHC-6 Twin Otter

Using the experience gained from its earlier DHC-3 Otter short take-off and landing design, de Havilland Canada started work on a new 20 passenger aircraft in 1964 for operations in the outback and remote regions, aiming to produce an aircraft with good short take-off and landing performance. Construction of an initial batch of five of the resulting DHC-6 Twin Otter started in late 1964. The type made its maiden flight on 20 May 1965 powered by a pair of 579 shp Pratt & Whitney PT6A-6 turboprops, certification being achieved in the early summer of 1966. From the fourth aircraft PT6A-20s were substituted for –6s, still rated at 579 shp but with increased reliability. Early production

consisted of the DHC-6-100, the first example being delivered to launch customer Trans Australia Airlines in the summer of 1966. After approximately 115 DHC-6-100s had been built the –200 (with an increased luggage capacity in an extended nose cone) entered production. A total of 115 were completed. The most numerous version was the DHC-6-300 introduced from 1969, with several sub-variants such as the military –300M troop transport and –300MR maritime reconnaissance versions, built alongside the civil aircraft. The DHC-6-300 had a larger two-part passenger/cargo door, increased fuel capacity and separate crews doors. Later versions of the DHC-6 300 Series were powered by the 620 shp PT6A-27, allowing an increase in maximum take-off weight. The last of

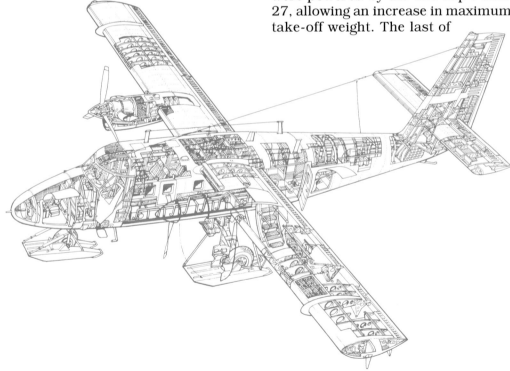

The de Havilland Canada Twin Otter is a very versatile aircraft, able to operate from a variety of prepared or semi-prepared surfaces. Shown here is a ski arrangement for the aircraft's undercarriage.

844 Twin Otters was delivered on 30 December 1988. They have operated in all major Continents, including service with the British Antarctic Survey flying from the polar ice cap in support of scientific expeditions during that Continent's brief summer period. Others are flown with floats as seaplanes, with the original short-nose configuration adopted for such aircraft to facilitate the pilot's downward view when landing. Military versions have been operated by the U.S. Alaskan Army Reserve as UV-18As, U.S. Air Force as UV-18B parachute jump trainers, the Canadian Armed Forces as CC-138s and in small numbers by around 14 other military operators. Although designed as a bush aircraft the Twin Otter attracted the interest of feeder and commuter airlines and served with airlines such as Air Mali, the Civil Aviation Administration of China, and Loganair. However, Twin Otters were soon replaced in this role by larger designs, but ex-airline examples found a ready market with smaller air taxi and other specialist firms. Around 600 remained active in 2005.

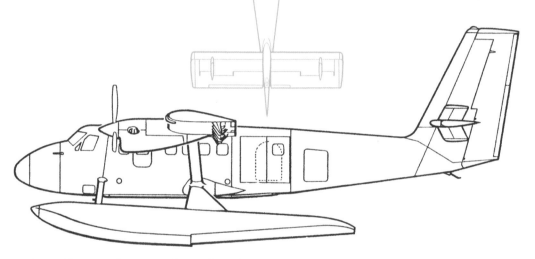

A twin-float attachment can be made to the Twin Otter, to allow it to operate from water as a floatplane. This is particularly useful for operations in the outback of such countries as Canada, where there are few airfields but many lakes and coastal inlets.

Specifications – de Havilland Canada DHC-6 Twin Otter 300 Series

Wingspan	65 ft
Length	51 ft 9 in
Maximum cruising speed	210 mph at 10,000 ft
Maximum take-off weight	12,500 lb
Range	806 miles with reserves
Service ceiling	26,700 ft
Engine	Two Pratt & Whitney Canada PT6A-27 turboprop engines, of 620-652 eshp each
Crew	Two crew, maximum of 20 passengers (often less)

Grumman E-2 Hawkeye

The E-2 Hawkeye entered service with the U.S. Navy as its carrier-borne airborne early warning (AEW) aircraft in 1964, augmenting before replacing the previous Grumman E-1B Tracer. It has remained in service and production ever since in progressively upgraded versions. The W2F-1 (E-2A from 1962) made its maiden flight on 21 October 1960, with an APS-96 surveillance radar mounted in a saucer-shaped radome above the fuselage. A total of 59 production E-2As were built, the majority being upgraded as E-2Bs from 1969 with an improved mission computer and provision for in-flight refuelling. Continuing development led to the E-2C, identified by the addition of a cooling intake behind the cockpit and equipped with the new APS-125 radar and other improvements. The E-2C extended radar coverage around an aircraft carrier battle group to around 300 miles (483 km), but also allowed control of the carrier's fighters to be undertaken from the aircraft. Progressive upgrades of the mission electronics and main radar (the APS-125 being replaced by the APS-138, -139, and -145) have greatly increased the capabilities of the aircraft, successive versions being known as E-2C Group O, I and II aircraft. Recent additions have included the Co-operative Engagement Capability system to increase information-sharing between the E-2C and U.S. Navy warships. While these improvement have had little impact externally on the Hawkeye, the introduction of the E-2C Hawkeye 2000 saw the traditional metal four-blade propellers replaced with eight-blade composite units. Low rate production of the E-2C Hawkeye 2000 for the U.S. Navy continues, to re-equip each squadron of the existing

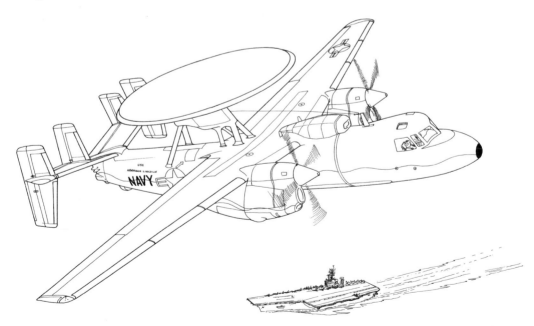

The Grumman E-2C Hawkeye is typical of the various types of military aircraft that are perhaps not as glamorous as front-line fighters or bombers, but nevertheless perform equally important functions within a modern military organisation.

Functional rather than beautiful, the Grumman E-2 Hawkeye has been in service since the 1960s but is still a very important warplane today.

U.S. Navy aircraft carrier-based battle groups. Several TE-2C conversion trainers have also been delivered. The E-2C Hawkeye has been exported to Egypt, Israel, Japan, Singapore and Taiwan, while the French Navy's four are sometimes known as E-2Fs. Hawkeyes have supported all of the conflicts that the U.S. carrier groups have fought in, from the Vietnam War onwards. In addition, Israeli aircraft were used to provide warnings of Syrian fighters during the fighting over Lebanon in the early 1980s. Israeli Hawkeyes were later sold to Mexico. In total, over 185 Hawkeyes have been built, with production continuing. A transport version of the Hawkeye for making deliveries to aircraft carriers called the carrier on-board delivery (COD) aircraft, with a new fuselage arrangement, no radar saucer and simplified tail surfaces, first flew in November 1964 as the YC-2A. It was followed by a second prototype and 17 production C-2A Greyhounds. An additional 39 C-2As from a re-opened production line were delivered between 1985 and 1989, and the type remains the U.S. Navy's standard COD aircraft.

Specifications – Grumman E-2C Hawkeye

Wingspan	80 ft 7 in
Length	57 ft 7 in
Maximum speed	372 mph at 10,000 ft
Maximum take-off weight	51,900 lb
Endurance	6 Hours 15 minutes
Service ceiling	30,800 ft
Engine	Two Allison T56-A-425 turboprop engines, of 4,910 shp each
Crew	Five

McDonnell Douglas DC-9 and MD-80 Series

The development of the DC-9 by McDonnell Douglas was spurred by the company's need to compete in the short-range airliner market against the turboprop-powered Lockheed Electra and Vickers Viscount, and the jet-powered Sud-Aviation Caravelle, BAC One-Eleven and Boeing 727 – many of which are covered elsewhere in this book. The type proved to be remarkably adaptable, its basic configuration spawning not only the DC-9 and MD-80 families, but the MD-90 and MD-95/Boeing 717 as well. Indeed, the DC-9 became the backbone of many airlines' short-haul fleets. The DC-9-10 was the initial model, with seating for up to 90 passengers and powered by a pair of Pratt & Whitney JT8D-5 turbofan engines. Delta Air Lines placed the launch order in 1963. The first example flew on 25 February 1965, a record 30 months after the program had been launched. An order from Eastern Air Lines launched the DC-9-30 with a length-

ened fuselage and slightly greater wingspan. It first entered service with the airline in early 1967, having made its maiden flight on 1 August 1966. The DC-9-30 proved to be the most popular version, accounting for well over 600 of the 976 DC-9s that were built. A comparatively small number of these were military DC-9s, produced for the U.S. Air Force as C-9A Nightingale aero-medical aircraft and VC-9C VIP transports, and for the U.S. Navy as C-9B Skytrain IIs. Further development of a 'super-stretched' version of the DC-9 resulted in the MD-80 series, initially produced as the Super 80. The first example that was built, an MD-81, flew on 18 October 1979 as a 135 passenger aircraft powered by JT8D-209 turbofans. It was followed by the MD-82, –83 and –88, and short fuselage MD-87. The MD-80 family was even more successful than the DC-9, a total of some 1,191 being built, including 35 assembled under licence

An in-flight study of a Douglas DC-9. The particular aircraft shown is a DC-9-51, registered N991EA of Eastern Air Lines, which was delivered to the airline in July 1977 (Photo: McDonnell Douglas).

in China. American Airlines became the largest operator of the MD-80 family with at least 279 examples flown by the airline, while Delta Air Lines employed 120 MD-88s with a 'glass' cockpit featuring advanced instrumentation and incorporating a large percentage of composite materials in their structure. Production of the MD-80 family was terminated in the late 1990s when McDonnell Douglas was acquired by Boeing. The MD-90 family was designed as an advanced technology follow-on to the MD-80 series. MD-90s used IAE V2525-D5 turbofans and had a lengthened fuselage compared to the MD-81 to accommodate up to 172 passengers. A 1989 order from Delta launched the program, the first example flying in February 1993. Plans to build the aircraft in China as the MD90-30T Trunkliner floundered after two were produced, adding to the 114 built at Long Beach in California before Boeing cancelled the program. The last aircraft that could trace its roots back to the DC-9 was the MD-95, a smaller version of the MD-80 powered by Rolls-Royce BR715 turbofans. It was built as the Boeing 717-200, first flying in September 1998. Boeing cancelled production in early 2005 because of comparatively slow sales, bringing airliner production at the historic Long Beach facility to an end.

The Scandinavian airline SAS was a loyal supporter of the DC-9 line of airliners. This example in SAS service registered as OY-KGA was a DC-9-41 delivered in February 1968.

Specifications – McDonnell Douglas DC-9-30

Wingspan	93 ft 5 in
Length	119 ft 3.5 in
Maximum cruising speed	565 mph at 25,000 ft
Maximum take-off weight	108,000 lb
Range	1,725 miles with 80 passengers
Service ceiling	35,000 ft
Engine	Two Pratt & Whitney JT8D-15 turbofan engines, of 15,500 lb st each
Accommodation	Two crew plus stewards/stewardesses, a maximum of 115 passengers, but 105 standard

Mil Mi-6 and Mi-8

One of the most widely-used helicopter types yet produced, the ubiquitous Mil Mi-8 family is one of the world's most important helicopter series. It was designed by the Mil design bureau in the Soviet Union, an organisation that is responsible for many helicopter types from the Cold War era. Mil began creating military helicopters in the late 1940s, firstly with the successful and widely-produced Mi-1 and Mi-2 light utility helicopters before progressing to larger transport types including the Mi-4. More recent combat helicopter studies led to the Mil Mi-24 'Hind' series of attack helicopters (see pages 256 to 257). A very powerful early Mil heavy-lift military helicopter design was the Mi-6, which received the appropriate NATO reporting name 'Hook.' The original prototype flew in June 1957, and 874 are believed to have been built. As usual for Soviet military types, the Mi-6 was made in a wide variety of versions and sub-types. The basic heavy-lift Mi-6 and Mi-6A could carry a massive 26,455 lb (12,000 kg) internal payload and an underslung load externally of up to 19,841 lb (9,000 kg), but there were also specialized versions such as airborne command post and troop transports. These venerable but still useful helicopters have been gradually withdrawn from service as their irreplaceable wooden tail rotors reach the end of their fatigue lives. In 1960 Mil began the development of a helicopter to replace the Mi-4 'Hound,' and this matured into the world-famous Mi-8. Known to NATO as 'Hip,' this workhorse has also been built in a vast number of different versions. The prototype (called V-8) first flew on 24 June 1961, two prototypes being followed by various development

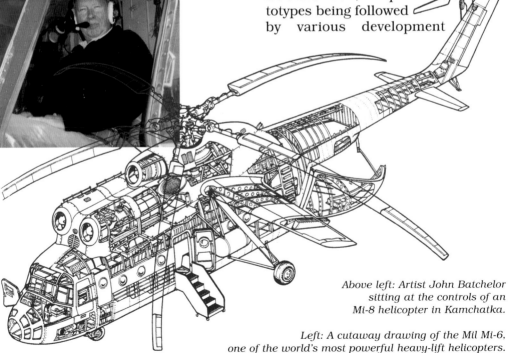

Above left: Artist John Batchelor sitting at the controls of an Mi-8 helicopter in Kamchatka.

Left: A cutaway drawing of the Mil Mi-6, one of the world's most powerful heavy-lift helicopters.

machines which pioneered the Mi-8 production standard and special versions, including the use of a five-blade main rotor. Since the early 1960s there have been many versions, including civil as well as military derivatives. The basic troop transport for the Soviet Union's army aviation was the Mi-8T ('Hip-C'), and this has formed the basis of many upgraded versions. Some Mi-8 models are armed as dual-purpose attack/transport helicopters. Civil versions used by Aeroflot include the civil derivative of the Mi-8T with seating for up to 26 passengers. Further development led to the Mi-17 ('Hip-H'), which is a modified version with elements of the Mi-14 ('Haze') incorporated. The Mi-14 is a completely different Mi-8 derivative used by Russia's naval air arm as an amphibious helicopter with a redesigned fuselage and other changes. Continuing development work has led to the Mi-171, an export derivative of one of the Mi-8 development lines. Over 17,000 Mi-8/Mi-17/Mi-171 are thought to have been built, including some 3,500 for export to well over fifty countries.

Specifications – Mil Mi-8T

Main Rotor Diameter	69 ft 10.25 in
Fuselage Length	60 ft 1 in
Maximum speed	155 mph at sea level
Maximum take-off weight	26,455 lb
Range	612 miles with auxiliary fuel
Service ceiling	14,764 ft
Armament	Usually unarmed, but can carry anti-personnel mine dispenser; armed Mi-8 versions carry unguided rocket pods, machine guns, and various guided anti-tank missiles
Engine	Two Klimov (Isotov) TV2-117A or -AG turboshaft engines, of 1,677 shp each
Crew	Two or three crew, 24 troops

Hawker Siddeley (BAe) Harrier and Harrier II Series

The Harrier is the world's only operational vertical take-off and landing aircraft, powered by the vectored thrust Pegasus jet engine. It started life as the Hawker P.1127, of which two prototypes (with the 12,000 lb st Pegasus 2 engine) and four pre-production aircraft (using the 13,500 lb st Pegasus 3) were built. The first tethered hovering flight was made on 19 November 1960, a conventional flight following on 13 March 1961. Nine Kestrel F(GA).Mk.1s powered by the 15,500 lb st Pegasus 5 followed for operational evaluation by British, West German and American pilots. Following the cancellation of the supersonic P.1154 design (yet another of Britain's cancelled post-World War Two designs), a developed version of the Kestrel was ordered as the Hawker Siddeley Harrier. The first Harrier flew on 31 August 1966 with a Pegasus 101 powerplant. 124 single-seaters were duly built for the R.A.F. as Harrier GR.Mk.1s, 1As (Pegasus 102) and 3s (Pegasus 103), earlier variants being upgraded to the later standard with the improved powerplant. Two-seaters were built as T.Mk.2s, 4s and 4As for the R.A.F. and as T.Mk.4Ns for the Royal Navy, which later upgraded its fleet as T.Mk.8s. In a very significant export order, the U.S. Marine Corps acquired 110 first-generation Harrier Mk.50s as AV-8As, 47 later being upgraded as AV-8Cs. Spain acquired 11 AV-8S and two TAV-8A(S) Matadors, but it later sold the survivors to the Thai Navy. The Sea Harrier was a first generation Harrier fighter for the Royal Navy with a Blue Fox radar. First flying on 20 August 1978, a total of 57 Sea Harrier FRS.Mk.1s were built. Their finest hour was in the 1982 Falklands conflict, when they helped to win the war for Britain with several aerial victories against Argentine aircraft. Upgraded with the Blue Vixen radar as the Sea Harrier FA.Mk.2, the survivors were joined by 18 new-build Mk.2s. The Indian Navy received 23 Sea Harrier FRS.Mk.51s, plus Harrier T.Mk.60 and 4(I) two-seaters. British Aerospace (successor to

The Hawker Siddeley/BAe Harrier has seen success both as an attack aircraft and as a fighter. The illustration here shows an early configuration for what became the Royal Navy's Sea Harrier carrier-based fighter.

The Harrier layout is unique amongst modern combat aircraft, with swivelling nozzles to direct the Pegasus engine's thrust so that the aircraft can take-off and land vertically, but fly horizontally like a normal aircraft.

Hawker Siddeley) and McDonnell Douglas of the U.S. later collaborated on the Harrier II, with a larger wing, raised cockpit and advanced lift-enhancing devices. The new wing first flew on a YAV-8B on 9 November 1978 and the first production AV-8Bs were delivered to the U.S. Marines in 1983. From the 167th example they had a night-attack capability. Continued development added an AN/APG-65 radar as the Harrier II Plus, earlier examples being upgraded. The Marines also acquired TAV-8B conversion trainers. The Harrier GR.Mk.5 (first flying in April 1985) and interim GR.Mk.5A were the R.A.F.'s initial Harrier II variants, most being upgraded as GR.Mk.7s. Thirteen two-seaters were acquired as Harrier T.Mk.10s. An avionics and powerplant upgrade was underway in 2005 to bring the R.A.F.'s fleet up to GR.Mk.7A, 9, 9A and T.Mk.12 standards. Export customers for the Harrier II were the Italian and Spanish navies.

Specifications – British Aerospace (Hawker Siddeley) Harrier GR.Mk.3

Wingspan	25 ft 3 in with combat wingtips
Length	46 ft 10 in
Maximum speed	730 mph at sea level
Maximum take-off weight	25,200 lb
Radius of action	approximately 500 miles strike mission
Service ceiling	51,200 ft
Armament	Two 1.18 in (30 mm) cannons in underbelly pods, up to 5,000 lb of weapons on one lower fuselage and four underwing pylons
Engine	One Rolls-Royce Pegasus Mk.103 turbofan engine, of 21,500 lb st
Crew	One

General Dynamics F-111

The 1960s Tactical Fighter Experimental (TFX) requirement in the U.S. outlined the need for a long-range strike aircraft for the U.S. Air Force and a carrier-based missile-armed fighter for the U.S. Navy. Won by General Dynamics with what became the F-111, these two contradictory needs – rather unwisely put together by U.S. Defence Secretary Robert S. McNamara – added millions to the cost of the project and produced an aircraft that was unacceptable to the Navy. In 1968, after seven F-111Bs had been built, the Navy pulled out of the program. The Air Force continued with a long development program that resulted in a capable tactical long-range strike aircraft for the U.S.A.F.'s Tactical Air Command and a medium-range strategic bomber for Strategic Air Command. The Air Force acquired 533,

consisting of 159 F-111As (including the sole RF-111A and FB-111A prototype), two YF-111As, 76 FB-111As, 96 F-111Ds, 94 F-111Es and 106 F-111Fs. The F-111A was the first, making the type's maiden flight on 21 December 1964, 27 aircraft being used in the development program. Initial Combat Lancer deployments to Southeast Asia were marked by unexplained losses, which were later explained by tailplane failure. However, the F-111 later proved to be a capable strike aircraft during the later stages of the Vietnamese conflict. The F-111E was the next version to enter TAC service, with modified air inlets and an improved navigation and attack system. A new avionics system and TF30-P-9 engines were introduced in the F-111D. The last version to enter service was the F-111F with more powerful TF30-P-100 powerplants and a simplified avionics system compared to

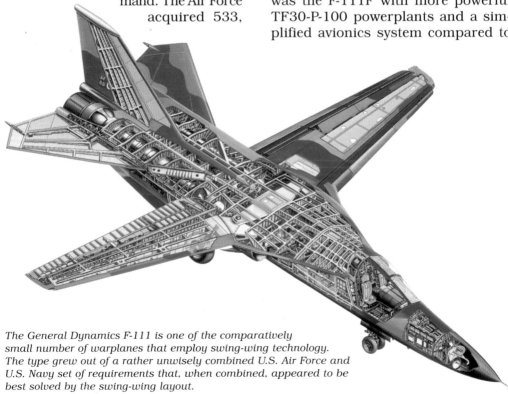

The General Dynamics F-111 is one of the comparatively small number of warplanes that employ swing-wing technology. The type grew out of a rather unwisely combined U.S. Air Force and U.S. Navy set of requirements that, when combined, appeared to be best solved by the swing-wing layout.

212

The EF-111A Raven was a Grumman-developed dedicated jammer electronic warfare aircraft, the need for which was not in the minds of the General Dynamics design team when the F-111 design was first drawn-up (Photo: Grumman History Center).

that of the F-111D. The F-111K and TF-111K were ordered for Britain's Royal Air Force instead of the cancelled TSR.2 (see pages 178 to 179) before themselves also being cancelled. The FB-111A was built for the Strategic Air Command, using the longer wings of the F-111B and provision for up to 50 750 lb (340 kg) bombs. Deliveries started in 1971, and they served until 1991, although 30 were converted as F-111Gs for further service. Another conversion program created 42 EF-111A Raven escort jammer electronic warfare aircraft from F-111As. They flew alongside F-111Fs from R.A.F. Lakenheath to attack Libyan targets on the evening of 14/15 April 1986. The F-111F's ability to use precision-guided munitions (PGM) also gave it a starring role in operations over Iraq in 1991, where it was joined by the non-PGM-configured F-111E. Australia was the only export customer to actually receive F-111s, by acquiring 24 F-111Cs. Some of these were later modified for the reconnaissance role. They were eventually supplemented by some ex-U.S.A.F. examples, the Royal Australian Air Force being the sole operator in the 21st Century.

Specifications – General Dynamics F-111A

Wingspan	63 ft (wings un-swept)
Length	73 ft 6 in
Maximum speed	1,650 mph at 40,000 ft
Maximum take-off weight	92,500 lb
Range	3,800 miles
Service ceiling	60,000 ft
Armament	One 0.787 in (20 mm) multi-barrel cannon, up to 30,000 lb of weapons in an internal weapons bay and on six underwing pylons
Engine	Two Pratt & Whitney TF30-P-3 turbofan engines, of 18,500 lb st each with afterburning
Crew	Two

Tupolev Tu-22M

The premier designer of high-performance bomber aircraft in the Soviet Union during the Cold War period was the Tupolev design bureau. This organisation crated a number of significant combat aircraft for Russia's armed forces, including the long-standing Tu-95 'Bear' series (see pages 146 to 147). Tupolev began work on a high-performance jet bomber layout in the 1950s, and after considerable development work the Soviet Union's first major jet-powered bomber emerged as the Tu-22. Known to NATO as 'Blinder,' the type entered service in the mid-1960s. It was distinctive by its two turbojet engines being mounted side-by-side beside the vertical tail. Continuing development by Tupolev led to a production bomber that was given the uncomplimentary NATO reporting name 'Backfire,' and was thought at first to be designated Tu-26. This new aircraft was in fact the Tu-22M, and typical of the secrecy surrounding Cold War-era Soviet aircraft little was known of the type in the West until the Cold War

ended in the later 1980s and early 1990s. Development of the Tu-22M commenced during the early 1960s. A significant alteration in the design of the Tu-22M was the adoption of a 'swing-wing' variable geometry layout, and the re-positioning of the type's two jet engines to the rear fuselage – these being turbofans related to those developed for the Soviet Union's supersonic civil transport, the Tu-144, instead of the tail-mounted turbojets of the Tu-22. A prototype of the Tu-22M was first observed by Western intelligence sources in July 1970, the first flight being in the previous year. The original prototype was followed by nine or ten Tu-22M-1 pre-production/development aircraft, after which 211 Tu-22M-2 ('Backfire-B') production machines are thought to have been built. The definitive series version was the Tu-22M-3 'Backfire-C,' production of which is believed to have reached 268 – construction ended in 1993. The more powerful Tu-22M-3 features revised engine air intakes of

This drawing is based on an artist's impression from 1979 of what was believed to be the Tupolev 'Backfire' layout. It is actually comparatively close to the Tu-22M-2 ('Backfire-B') configuration, the color scheme should be a much lighter blue-grey. Note the 'swing-wings' in the fully swept position.

The break-up of the Soviet Union at the end of the Cold War resulted in the creation of many newly-independent countries, which 'inherited' former Soviet-operated aircraft based on their soil. This Tu-22M-3 ('Backfire-C') was acquired in this way by the Ukraine, in whose colors (probably of the 185th Regiment) it is shown here. Note the type's upward-swept nose and wedge-shaped air intakes (Photo: via John Batchelor).

'wedge' shape rather than the upright intakes of the Tu-22M-2, and an upturned nose instead of the symmetrical nose cone of the Tu-22M-2. The type entered service with the Soviet air force's 185th Guards Heavy Bomber Regiment in the mid-1980s. Despite its all-round high performance (including low-level high dash speed), the Tu-22M is called a medium bomber (due to un-refuelled range limitations). In addition to conventional and nuclear strike missions, it can also be configured for maritime reconnaissance and electronic warfare. Several served as high-level bombers over Afghanistan during the Soviet intervention there in the 1980s. In 2004-2005 the Tu-22M-3 remains in service with the Russian air force and naval air arm, and Ukrainian forces, with upgrades a possibility including the installation of terrain-following radar.

Specifications – Tupolev Tu-22M-3 ('Backfire-C')

Wingspan	112 ft 5.75 in (wings spread)
Length	139 ft 3.75 in
Maximum speed	Mach 1.88 at 36,090 ft
Maximum take-off weight	273,370 lb
Radius of action	1,034.5 miles subsonic low-level attack
Service ceiling	43,635 ft
Armament	One rearward-firing tail-mounted 0.9 in (23 mm) twin-barrel cannon, three Kh-22 (AS-4 'Kitchen') air-to-surface guided missiles, or up to 52,910 lb of conventional bombs or mines
Engine	Two Kuznetsov/KKBM NK-25 turbofan engines, of 55,115 lb st each with afterburning
Crew	Four

Cessna Light Aircraft

The history of aviation is not just the story of high-performance military aircraft and large civil airliners. There are many other types of aircraft, and a significant proportion of these fall into a variety of categories of privately-owned and privately-operated aircraft. Private aircraft owned by individuals or companies include light aircraft of many shapes and sizes from light single-engined aircraft for one or two occupants upwards (often called 'general aviation' types), and also includes high-performance business jets used to transport executives of companies from one business meeting to another. As explained in the first Volume of this 'Compete encyclopedia of Flight,' aviation in the early pioneering days of manned powered flight prior to World War One was very much in the hands of private individuals before the creation of military air arms and major civil airlines. Over the years a number of compa-

nies have specialized in the manufacture of aircraft primarily for private ownership. Probably the most famous of these is the Cessna Aircraft Company of the United States. This company is well-known for its light 'general aviation' aircraft, but it has also created some military aircraft such as the A-37/T-37 (see pages 158 to 159). It was originally formed in 1927 by Clyde V. Cessna, one of America's aviation pioneers. A number of modestly successful light aircraft designs were produced by Cessna during the 1930s, some of these establishing the high-wing cabin monoplane configuration that persists so successfully to this day in Cessna's light aircraft line. Cessna subsequently produced the twin-engined light T-50 as the AT-17/UC-78 Bobcat, which became a comparatively widespread type for military use particularly as a trainer during World War Two. However, the company was already looking towards the prospects of a large demand for light aircraft in the post-war world. In June 1945 the prototype of the two-seat Cessna Model 120 was flown, this again being a high-

An historic moment for the artist and illustrator of this book, John Batchelor, as he performs his first solo loop. He is flying a Cessna FRA.150M, registered in Britain as G-BDEX.

The long-running Cessna family of light cabin monoplanes is probably the most successful series of light aircraft ever produced. This Canadian-registered floatplane illustrates the fact that Cessna light aircraft are just at home on water as on land (Photo: John Batchelor).

wing cabin monoplane, and in the subsequent years Cessna's expanding line of such types for private buyers literally 'took-off.' Developments included the tricycle undercarriage two-seat Model 150 series, which commenced production in the late 1950s. Well over twenty-three thousand were built of this series. It was joined in production by the famous Model 170 series, which has literally been a world-beater with well over thirty thousand being built in many different versions and sub-types. Some additional manufacture has also taken place at Reims Aviation in France, and the choice of different models

and sub-types, engine types, equipment levels and other possibilities from the parent company has been truly breathtaking. Currently-available models include the Model 172R Skyhawk. In addition, Cessna has produced and continues to market a successful line of twin-engined light and corporate aircraft additional to its world-famous family of Citation business jets. Other highlights from a truly remarkable company include the single-engined O-1 Bird Dog, which gained its own fame in U.S. Air Force service as a forward air control air strike and artillery spotter during the Vietnam War.

Specifications – Cessna Model 150

Wingspan	32 ft 8.5 in
Length	23 ft 9 in
Maximum speed	122 mph at sea level
Maximum take-off weight	1,600 lb
Range	565 miles
Service ceiling	12,650 ft
Engine	One Continental O-200-A inline piston engine, of 100 hp
Accommodation	Two (two pilots, or one pilot and one passenger)

Boeing 737

The Boeing 737 family is the world's most successful jet airliner. It has been developed in three distinct phases, and is currently one of the most important airliners in production. The type was launched by an order from the German airline Lufthansa, the initial example making its maiden flight on 9 April 1967. The German carrier took the 737-100 into service in February 1968, but only 30 were built before production switched to the longer and heavier 130 passenger 737-200 and – from the 280th example – the Advanced 737-200. Freighters were built in –200C (combi) and –200QC (quick change) versions. All early variants used sub-types of the Pratt & Whitney JT8D powerplant. Military versions included the T-43A navigator trainer for the U.S. Air Force and maritime patrol 737 Surveiller for Indonesia. However, the vast majority of the 1,144 first generation 737s built were delivered to airlines across the globe. The first of what Boeing now refers to as the 'Classic' 737 range, the 737-300 flew on 24 February 1984. Able to carry 128 passengers in a longer fuselage than the –200, the -300 introduced a two-pilot 'glass' cockpit (with advanced display screens for the crew) and CFM56-3 powerplants. Southwest Airlines first used the new 737 in service from December 1984.

The lengthened, 150-seat 737-400 made its maiden flight on 23 February 1988. The final 'Classic' version was the short-fuselage 737-500, flying for the first time in June 1989. By the time that production had concentrated on the Next Generation 737s, around 2,000 'Classics' had been built, including 1,113 737-300s. All Next Generation 737s used an enlarged fin, wings of increased area and CFM56-7 powerplants. They are the 108 seat 737-600 (ex –500X), 128 seat 737-700 (ex –300X), 160-seat 737-800 (ex –400X) and 177 seat 737-900. The 737-700 was the first to fly, doing so on 9 February 1997 and entering service with Southwest. Hapag Lloyd was the launch customer for the –800, the first flying in July 1997, while SAS's order for the –600 launched that variant. The long-fuselage 737–900 was launched by an Alaskan Airlines' order in November 1997. In addition to the four Next Generation 737 models, two Boeing Business Jet (BBJ) variants and the military C-40 are also currently in production. The 737-800ERX will fulfil the U.S. Navy's Multi-mission Maritime Aircraft requirement, with 108 planned to replace its current fleet of Lockheed P-3 Orion turboprop-powered patrol air-

Air Florida is typical of the many smaller airlines that have successfully used the Boeing 737 series in service.

*There have been a number of military variants of the Boeing 737 line.
Illustrated is a C-40 transport for the U.S. Navy (Photo: Boeing).*

craft. Orders for the 737-800 alone topped 1,169 in 2004, making it the most widely produced Boeing airliner variant ever. In addition, over 1,200 orders for the other Next Generation variants had been received, and production of this most successful family of airliners continues in large quantities.

*Recent developments of the very successful Boeing 737 family have included
the long-fuselage Boeing 737-900 for civil customers (Photo: Boeing).*

Specifications – Boeing 737-400

Wingspan	94 ft 4 in
Length	119 ft 7 in
Maximum speed	564 mph at 25,000 ft
Maximum take-off weight	138,500 lb
Range	3,105 miles with reserves
Service ceiling	35,000 ft
Engine	Two CFM International CFM56-3C-1 turbofan engines, of 22,000 lb st each
Accommodation	Two crew plus stewards/stewardesses, 146 passengers in standard

Britten-Norman BN-2 Islander Series

The Britten-Norman Islander is a British success story with a distinctive international flavour. Although in production in a number of versions for nearly 40 years, the name of the company building the type has frequently changed. By 2005, around 1,300 Islanders of various marks have been produced in Britain, Belgium, the Philippines and Romania. Designed as a rugged feederliner, the prototype first flew on 13 June 1965 powered by 210 hp Rolls-Royce/Continental IO-360B piston engines. Later, Lycoming O-540 piston engines were installed, together with a modest increase in wingspan. The aircraft flew again after modification on 17 December 1965. In this configuration the Islander entered production, with a total of 23 built as BN-2s before the BN-2A was introduced in mid-1969, of which 890 were built before production ended in 1989. The first of several hundred built by IRMA of Romania flew in August 1969,

the aircraft usually being delivered to Bembridge, Isle of Wight (the base of Britten-Norman in the south of England), for fitting out prior to delivery. The BN-2 Mk.3 Trislander was a lengthened version for 17 passengers, with unusually, a third engine mounted on top of its reinforced vertical tail. Production commenced in 1970/1971, and 81 had been built when deliveries ended in 1984. A further three were built in America as the Tri-Commutair, and several plans have been made since to put the type back into production. Britten-Norman's financial problems resulted in the company's sale to the Fairey Group in August 1972, leading to a third production line being set up at Gosselies in Belgium. Islanders were also built by the Philippines Aircraft Development Corporation. The Belgium line and Britten-Norman (Bembridge) were sold to Pilatus of Switzerland to create Pilatus Britten-Norman (PBN) in September 1979. The improved BN-2B was introduced

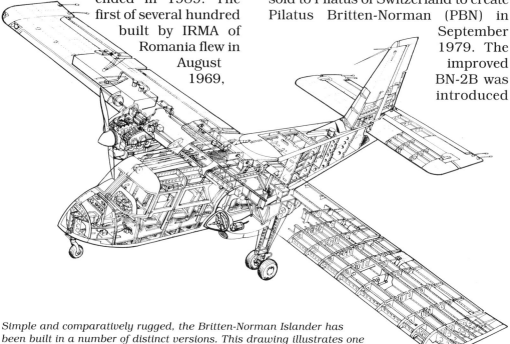

Simple and comparatively rugged, the Britten-Norman Islander has been built in a number of distinct versions. This drawing illustrates one of the more straightforward light transport versions.

around the same time, and built as the BN-2B-20 (with IO-540 engines) and BN-2B-26 (O-540s). In August 1980 the BN-2T powered by 320-hp Allison 250-B17Cs turbo-prop engines made its maiden flight, replacing an earlier Turbo Islander version introduced in 1977. Armed military versions of the BN-2 Islander are known

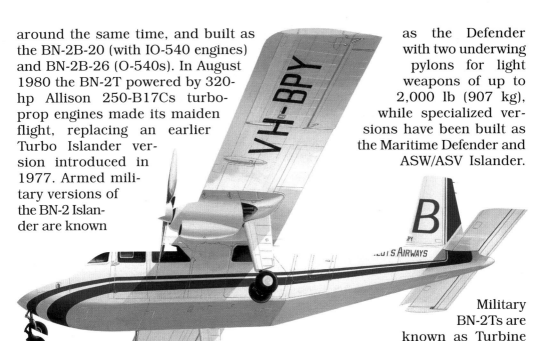

as the Defender with two underwing pylons for light weapons of up to 2,000 lb (907 kg), while specialized versions have been built as the Maritime Defender and ASW/ASV Islander.

The Britten-Norman Islander has achieved sales world-wide. This example was registered in Australia.

Military BN-2Ts are known as Turbine Defenders, with others built as the CASTOR Islander, Internal Security Islander and Multi-Sensor Surveillance Aircraft. On 17 August 1994 the BN-2T-4S Defender 4000 made its maiden flight. It featured a new style nose, increased wingspan, an increased maximum take-off weight, and was powered by two 400 hp Rolls-Royce 250-17F/1s. Ownership of PBN passed to Litchfield Continental in the July 1998, which also acquired the production facilities in Romania. Soon after it became the B-N Group. BN-2B variants, the BN-2T and BN-2T-4S, remain in production in 2005.

Specifications – Britten-Norman BN-2T Turbine Islander

Wingspan	49 ft
Length	35 ft 7.75 in
Maximum speed	196 mph at 10,000 ft
Maximum take-off weight	7,000 lb
Range	679 miles with reserves
Service ceiling	23,000 ft
Engine	Two Allison 250-B17C turboprop engines, of 400 shp each
Accommodation	Two crew, up to ten passengers

Lockheed SR-71 Blackbird

Having designed the Lockheed U-2 spyplane (see pages 198 to 199), Clarence 'Kelly' Johnson knew that surface-to-air missiles would one day be able to shoot down even that high-flying aircraft. The famous Lockheed 'Skunk Works' secret design office therefore started work on a higher-flying, faster replacement, their work receiving funding from the CIA. Under the code name 'Oxcart,' a ground-breaking single-seat Mach 3 recon-naissance aircraft was designed and built as the A-12. The first flight was made on 26 April 1962, and 12 were built, plus one two-seat trainer and a further pair as two-seat M-21s to carry a secret D-21 'Tagboard' drone on a pylon above the M-21. Four test launches of the drone were undertaken, the last ending in disaster when the M-21 and crew was lost. The A-12s were operated by the CIA's 1129th Special Activities Squadron from Groom Dry Lake

(Area 51) in Nevada. The unit deployed aircraft to Kadena, Okinawa, between May 1967 and May 1968 to fly operational missions over Vietnam and North Korea. The last A-12 flight was undertaken on 21 June 1968, the aircraft being put into storage at Palmdale, California, where they had been built. A requirement for an improved interceptor for the U.S.A.F.'s Air Defense Command allowed John-son to put forward a version of the A-12 with an AN/ASG-18 fire control system and Falcon air-to-air missiles, three being built as YF-12As. First flight for the interceptor took place on 8 August 1963. However, the down-grading of ADC made the proposed production F-12B redundant and the three YF-12As were stored, two later entering service with NASA. In a sep-arate development, the U.S. Air Force ordered a two-seat version of the A-12 as the SR-71A Blackbird reconnais-sance aircraft, the first flying in December 1964. A total of 31 were built, including two SR-71B trainers with a raised second cockpit. One SR-71A was loaned to NASA as the YF-12C, while the loss of an SR-71B resulted in the

The Lockheed SR-71 Blackbird was another remarkable aircraft from the United States' aircraft industry. It included the use of titanium in its structure, to better withstand the high temperatures that it underwent at high speed at high altitudes.

The cockpit layout of a Lockheed SR-71 (Photo: N.A.S.A. via John Batchelor).

construction of the one-off hybrid SR-71C from a YF-12A mated to the nose section of a static test airframe. The first SR-71A was delivered to the 4200th (later 9th) Strategic Reconnaissance Wing at Beale Air Force Base, California, in January 1966. Deployments of Blackbirds were maintained at Kadena and at R.A.F. Mildenhall in Britain, the aircraft flying missions around Communist countries and other hot spots until retired in 1990, although two aircraft were briefly returned to service in 1995 until funding was cut. Members of the Blackbird family broke many world records for speed (absolute and point-to-point) and altitude. Over 40 years after the A-12's first flight, no service aircraft can match the performance of the members of the iconic Blackbird family.

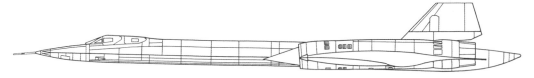

Sleek, powerful and unique, the Lockheed SR-71 Blackbird was in a class of its own.

Specifications – Lockheed SR-71A Blackbird

Wingspan	55 ft 7 in
Length	103 ft 10 in
Maximum speed	2,112 mph at 85,000 ft
Maximum take-off weight	152,000 lb
Range	2,982 miles
Service ceiling	85,000 ft plus
Engine	Two Pratt & Whitney J58-1 (JT11D-20) turbojet engines, of 32,500 lb st each with afterburning
Crew	Two

American Experimental Jets

The need for continuing advancement in aviation technology has led to much research being performed over the years as new concepts and ideas have arisen. As pointed out elsewhere in this book, a considerable amount of research was carried out in the years after World War Two, especially due to the new possibilities brought about by the advent of jet propulsion. In Britain, France, the Soviet Union, and the United States, this research was taken very seriously and much investigative work took place. In the United States in particular, aeronautical research was pursued with much vigour, and eventually this gave the Americans a significant lead in many aspects of aviation. Numerous important research aircraft were created in the United States from the mid-1940s onwards, some under the 'X' experimental series, as shown on other pages in this book. A further important research aircraft, of the immediate post-World War Two era, was the

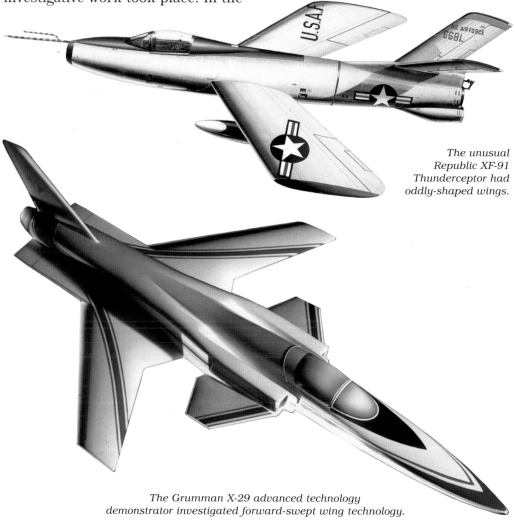

The unusual Republic XF-91 Thunderceptor had oddly-shaped wings.

The Grumman X-29 advanced technology demonstrator investigated forward-swept wing technology.

Although it was intended as a research aircraft, the Douglas D-558-1 Skystreak had an excellent turn of speed, and twice broke the world speed record in August 1947.

Douglas D-558-1 Skystreak series. Developed from 1945 onwards to meet a U.S. Navy and NACA (later NASA) requirement for a high-speed research aircraft able to perform airborne research at speeds and heights that could not be simulated in ground-based wind-tunnel tests, three Douglas D-558 were built. The first flew in May 1947. Although the three aircraft performed useful research, the high performance of the type was particularly commendable. In August 1947 the first Skystreak twice broke the official world speed record, on the second occasion raising the record to almost 651 mph (1,048 km/h). Overall, the Skystreak program provided useful data on high-speed flight. A near-contemporary of the Skystreak was the Republic XF-91 Thunderceptor. This unusual jet-powered interceptor fighter, with auxiliary rocket propulsion and inverse-tapered wings (which were wider at the tips than at the roots), was actually intended as a production supersonic fighter. The first of two XF-91 flew in May 1949 powered by a General Electric J47 turbojet, but the type did not enter production, and instead the two aircraft built were used for research work. The Grumman X-29 program investigated forward-swept wing design layouts, using composite materials for the aircraft's wings. The type successfully flew during the 1980s, and pre-dated the Russian forward-swept wing Sukhoi Su-47 Berkut described on pages 308 to 309.

Specifications – Douglas D-558-1 Skystreak

Wingspan	25 ft
Length	35 ft 8.5 in
Maximum speed	approximately 651 mph at sea level
Maximum take-off weight	10,105 lb
Engine	One Allison J35-A-11 turbojet engine, of 5,000 lb st
Crew	One

Mikoyan-Gurevich MiG-23 and MiG-27

The Mikoyan-Gurevich MiG-23 was one of the Soviet Union's true Cold War warriors, and was built in large numbers in a variety of versions for Soviet forces and for countries that claimed to be friendly towards the Soviet Union around the world. Further development led to a dedicated ground attack derivative, the MiG-27, which was still an important type at the end of the Cold War. Development of what became the MiG-23 began in the early 1960s, MiG's designers even at that stage looking forward to what would ultimately be a successor to the MiG-21 (see pages 196 to 197). The MiG design team decided to employ variable-geometry ('swing-wing') technology for the new aircraft, rather than the delta wing layout of the MiG-21. The swing-wing concept promised good slow speed qualities for landing and take-off on short comparatively unprepared airfield surfaces, while giving the opportunity for high-speed flight with the wings swept back. Two distinct pro-

totypes were built, the swing-wing Ye-23I flying it is believed in April 1967. It made its public debut at Moscow-Domodedovo in July that year. A considerable number of initial evaluation aircraft were built, before the type passed its State acceptance trials and was ordered into production as the MiG-23. It received the NATO reporting name 'Flogger.' The first main production model was the MiG-23M ('Flogger-B'), which set the standard for the type with a powerful nose-mounted radar and infra-red target tracking device for air-to-air missions. There followed a variety of versions, several specifically for export, with different equipment fits. There was also a two-seat MiG-23UB ('Flogger-C') operational and conversion trainer. One of the best export fighter versions was the single-seat MiG-23ML ('Flogger-G'). However, in addition to these fighter models, a separate line of development existed to create a series of attack-configured MiG-23B and MiG-23BN ('Flogger-F')

The Mikoyan-Gurevich MiG-23 was a very important fighter and (in developed form) attack aircraft for the Soviet armed forces. Illustrated is an early fighter-configured example.

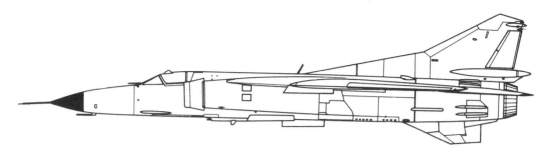

Fighter versions of the MiG-23 have a bulky, radar-nose as shown here, rather than the slimmer nose arrangement of the attack-configured MiG-27 series.

aircraft. These had a noticeably differently shaped nose, which was not the bulky 'radar-nose' of the MiG-23 fighters, but instead featured a laser rangefinder in a redesigned nose/forward fuselage plus other attack-optimised equipment. These models were developed to complement a specialized attack derivative of the MiG-23 which matured as the MiG-27. The initial prototype/development aircraft reportedly first flew in 1972, and a number of production models of the MiG-27 were built which received the NATO names of 'Flogger-D' and 'Flog-ger-J.' As with the MiG-23, the MiG-27 was widely produced, and both types served extensively with Soviet forces. The MiG-23 was also exported to a variety of export customers, and licence production of the MiG-27 was undertaken in India. However, many of these export aircraft are now out of service or set to be withdrawn, and the 'Flogger' has been completely retired from Russian front-line operations. A production total of approaching 4,500 examples is believed to include both the MiG-23 and the MiG-27 series.

Specifications – Mikoyan-Gurevich MiG-23ML

Wingspan	45 ft 10 in (wings un-swept)
Length	54 ft 9.5 in (including nose probe)
Maximum speed	Mach 2.35 at 36,090 ft
Maximum take-off weight	39,242 lb
Radius of action	715 miles with six air-to-air missiles
Service ceiling	60,696 ft
Armament	One 0.9 in (23 mm) cannon, up to 6,614 lb of external weapons including air-to-air guided missiles
Engine	One Tumansky R-35-300 turbojet engine, of 28,660 lb st with afterburning
Crew	One

Boeing 747

Boeing took a big risk in producing the Model 747 – one that has really paid off. Over the years the 'Jumbo Jet' – as it is almost universally known – has become the standard long-range high capacity aircraft in many airlines fleets. The 747-100 was launched in 1966 after Pan American (Pan Am) had signalled interest in 25 aircraft of this capacity. The prototype made its maiden flight on 9 February 1969, and Pan Am flew the first revenue earning service (between London and New York) on 22 January 1970. Production of 747-100 versions accounted for 205 examples. A longer-range version capable of carrying 440 passengers (although the standard was 276) was built as the 747SP (special performance). It was considerably shorter than the –100 and had a taller vertical tail. Production was launched by an order from Pan Am with the first flying on 4 July 1975, 45 being built. They later proved popular as VIP aircraft, especially for Arab governments. The 747-200 was 10 percent heavier than the –100 and featured an improved payload/range capability. The version first entered service with the Dutch national airline KLM in February 1971. A nose-loading freighter, the 747-200F, was built for Lufthansa from April 1972, while a second freighter variant with a side loading door was built as the 747-200(SCD). Conversions of existing 747-200 and –100 airliners as freighters have been offered by several companies and put into service by specialized cargo-hauling airlines as well as some of the major airlines themselves. For the Japanese market Boeing developed the 747(SR), able to carry 523 passenger over shorter ranges. Japan Airlines was the launch customer. A total of 384 747-200s of all variants were delivered by the time production ended in 1990. The 747-300 was designed as the 747(SUD) with its passenger upper deck lengthened. It first flew on 5 October 1982, and 81 were completed. Military variants included tanker/transports for Iran, U.S. Air Force airborne command posts (E-4A/B) and head of state transports for America (VC-25A) and Japan. Unveiled in September 1984, the 747-400 was a major improvement over previous models, making use of composites in its structure, adding winglets, a reduced flight crew of two and an additional fuel tank. The maid-

The Boeing 747-400 is the latest major production version of the ubiquitous 'Jumbo Jet.' This color cutaway drawing was made at the time of the maiden flight of the -400 in the late 1980s.

A staunch supporter of the Boeing 747 with many in service has been Britain's national airline British Airways (Photo: British Airways).

en flight was made on 29 April 1988 and it was certified with General Electric, Pratt & Whitney and/or Rolls-Royce powerplants. Northwest Airlines was the launch customer. The –400 soon became the standard production variant, taking 747 production to over 1,000 aircraft with production continuing. Freighter, combi (passenger or freight), high-density, and increased maximum take-off weight versions have been built. Boeing has continued to study lengthened versions of the 747, but had not committed to building them by early 2005.

One of the many airlines that have used the Boeing 747 is the American carrier Northwest Airlines.

Specifications – Boeing 747-400

Wingspan	211 ft 5 in
Length	231 ft 10 in
Maximum speed	612 mph at 25,000 ft
Maximum take-off weight	870,000 lb
Range	8,314 miles with 420 passengers
Service ceiling	45,000 ft
Engine	Four General Electric CF6-80C2B1F/C2B1F1/C2B7F, Pratt & Whitney PW4056, PW4060, PW4062, or Rolls-Royce RB211- 524G/H turbofan engines, of between 56,750 and 62,000 lb st each
Accommodation	Two flight crew plus stewards/stewardesses, up to 568 passengers,

Saab 37 Viggen

Sweden maintained strict neutrality during the Cold War, backed up by a large and capable air force equipped with indigenous combat aircraft. Seeking a replacement for its Saab 35 Draken combat aircraft family in the mid-1960s, Saab designed a canard delta aircraft as the Saab 37 Viggen. Powered by a Swedish version of the civil Pratt & Whitney JT8D-22 turbofan equipped with an afterburner and thrust reverser built as the RM8A, the first of seven prototype Viggens flew on 8 February 1967. The initial production variant was the AJ 37 all-weather attack aircraft, 108 of which were delivered, armed with various guided air-to-surface missiles including a locally-built AGM-65 Maverick version. From the basic airframe two reconnaissance versions were also produced, the SF 37 for day and night overland reconnaissance and the SH 37 for sea surveillance with a secondary attack role. Some 28 SF 37s and 28 SH 37s (including one converted from an AJ 37) were produced. These three versions were used as the basis for an upgrade in the 1990s to become multi-role AJS 37, AJSH 37 and AJSF 37 variants, while still retaining their specialized capabilities and sensors. Defence budget cut-

backs and the development of the multi-role Saab JAS 39 Gripen (see pages 294 to 295) reduced this program to around 60 (possibly slightly more) conversions. The seventh prototype Viggen was the first Sk 37 two-seater conversion trainer, the type's second cockpit located above and behind the first. A total of 18 were built (including the prototype), ten being adapted for the electronic warfare role from the late 1990s as Sk 37Es. The final production variant was the JA 37 interceptor, the last of 149 bringing Viggen production to an end when it was delivered in mid-1990. JA 37s were armed with licence-built versions of the Sky Flash and AIM-9L Sidewinder guided air-to-air missiles. The fighter Viggen was later upgraded under the JA 37 Mod D package, adding the ability to use the new AIM-120 AMRAAM medium-range guided air-to-air missile. Some of the upgraded aircraft were further improved as JA 37DIs. Operational Viggens were regularly deployed away from their airfields to road bases, a long-standing Swedish air force means of dispersing its assets during periods of tension. Viggens were often encountered over the Baltic by aircraft

The Saab AJ 37 was the attack version of the Viggen, and was the first mark of this powerful warplane to become operational with the Swedish air force.

Close-up detail of the cockpit area of a Swedish air force Saab AJ 37 Viggen from F7 wing at Satenäs in Sweden (Photo: John Batchelor).

from both Eastern Bloc and Western air forces. Saab actively tried to export the Viggen, but was prevented by Sweden's own neutral stance, and the glut of jet fighter designs extant in the early 1970s, ensuring that the Swedish air force was the sole Viggen operator. The AJ 37 was withdrawn from service during 2000, and the remaining Viggens were intended for retirement in 2004/2005.

Specifications – Saab AJ 37 Viggen

Wingspan	34 ft 9.25 in
Length	53 ft 5.75 in
Maximum speed	1,320 mph at 36,090 ft
Maximum take-off weight	45,194 lb
Radius of action	621 miles
Service ceiling	60,000 ft
Armament	Up to 13,228 lb of ordnance on three lower fuselage and four underwing pylons, including air-to-surface missiles and bombs, one 1.18 in (30 mm) cannon in a lower fuselage gun pack
Engine	One Volvo Flygmotor RM8A turbofan engine, of 14,750 lb st (26,015 lb st with afterburning)
Crew	One

BAC/Aérospatiale Concorde

Few aircraft are as instantly recognisable to the general public as Concorde. Although its grace and beauty were things of wonder, the small number built eventually did not financially pay back the effort and money expended. The British and French governments agreed to combine their efforts to produce a commercial supersonic transport (SST) on 29 November 1962, but the first SST to fly was the Soviet Union's Tupolev Tu-144, making its maiden flight on 31 December 1968. Concorde first flew on 2 March 1969 commanded by French test pilot André Turcat, the French prototype being joined by the British example on 9 April 1969. These two prototypes preceded a pair of pre-production aircraft with a revised nose and altered retractable visor (windscreen cover), somewhat increasing the aircraft's length from

that of the prototypes – indeed, there are several slight differences in fuselage length between production Concordes as well. The first three production aircraft were built as Concorde 100 Series, the first two initially used as production prototypes for airline familiarisation, certification, training, publicity and route-proving. Air France was the first airline to sign for Concorde and was followed by a further 17 potential customers for a total of some 80 aircraft. However, by the time the Concorde had flown only Air France (four aircraft) and BOAC (later British Airways, five) remained definitely interested. This was because by then the American environmental lobby (unfairly preaching doom and calamity caused by sonic booms), rising fuel costs (particularly later, in the early 1970s), and the appearance of wide-body airliners all helped to make

The BAC/Aérospatiale Concorde was operated only by two airlines – British Airways, and Air France. It was an excellent example of Anglo-French co-operation, but was seriously hampered by environmental and other opposition particularly in the United States (Photo: British Airways).

The Concorde was one of the best-known and easily identifiable of all modern aircraft. Its fuselage would temporarily lengthen due to the high temperatures encountered while flying at sustained high speed.

SSTs less attractive to the airlines. The British government tried to cancel the program several times, but the Anglo-French agreement signed in 1962 made this course of action prohibitively expensive. Thus only 13 further production Concordes (Series 101s for Air France, Series 102s for British Airways) were produced, both airlines putting the type into service on 21 January 1976. In addition, the third Series 100 Concorde was later modified as a Series 101 and entered Air France service. Concorde subsequently became the flagship for both of these airlines, as well as becoming a status symbol for the rich and famous and the most prestigious and fastest way to cross the Atlantic. Unfortunately, the beginning of the end for Concorde operations started with the fatal crash of an Air France Concorde departing from Paris Charles de Gaulle airport in July 2000, forcing the grounding of both fleets. Uneconomical operations were restarted briefly after modifications had been made but eventually Airbus Industries withdrew its design authority support for the type. The last fare-paying flights concluded with three British Airways Concordes landing in succession at Heathrow Airport on 24 October 2003. The last flight occurred on 26 November 2003, when an ex-British Airways example was delivered for preservation at Filton, Bristol – the airfield where the final assembly of British production aircraft had been carried out.

Specifications – BAC/Aérospatiale Concorde

Wingspan	83 ft 10 in (some examples possibly different)
Length	203 ft 10 in (some examples different)
Maximum cruising speed	Mach 2.04 at 51,000 ft
Maximum take-off weight	408,000 lb
Range	4,090 miles with reserves
Service ceiling	60,000 ft
Engine	Four Rolls-Royce/SNECMA Olympus 593 Mk.610 turbojets, of 38,050 lb st each with afterburning
Accommodation	Three crew plus stewards/stewardesses, a maximum of 128 passengers, standard 100 (British Airways)

Grumman A-6 Intruder

In 1957 the U.S. Navy selected the Grumman A2F Intruder to fulfil a requirement for a long-range, low-level tactical strike aircraft. The prototype flew on 19 April 1960, the initial production version becoming the A-6A with the introduction of the tri-service designation system in 1962. Equipped with the Digital Integrated Attack Navigation Equipment (DIANE), the A-6 proved to be an accurate weapons delivery aircraft, able to drop bombs onto targets obscured by clouds. A total of 488 A-6As were delivered from February 1963 for both the U.S. Navy and Marine Corps, starting combat operations over Vietnam in March 1965. The EA-6A was developed for a Marine Corps requirement to replace its existing EF-10B Skyknights in the electronic countermeasures (ECM) support and electronic-intelligence gathering roles, 12 being built and others produced by conversion. An improved four-seat ECM version of the Intruder was built as the EA-6B Prowler, and this became the standard electronic warfare aircraft of the U.S. Navy and Marines. Since making their debut in the last days of the Vietnam war, Prowlers have flown

sorties in the majority of subsequent U.S. campaigns. Small numbers of A-6As were converted for surface-to-air missile suppression as A-6Bs or equipped with improved attack sensors as A-6Cs. The carrier-based airborne re-fuelling tanker task was also handed to an Intruder variant when the KA-6D entered service with a hose drum unit installed in the rear fuselage. Each Intruder attack squadron subsequently included a small number of KA-6Ds in their inventory when they were deployed on the fleet's aircraft carriers. On 27 February 1970 the A-6E first flew. With navigation and attack system upgrades it became the second major Intruder production version. Conversions of A-6As to A-6Es amounted to 240 aircraft, adding to 205 new-build examples. In service these aircraft were further upgraded from 1974 with a TRAM laser target designator and forward-looking infrared (FLIR) under-nose turret allowing the Intruder to use precision weapons in poor weather conditions. A-6E Intruders were used in limited operations against Libya in 1986. Continued development of the Intruder exchanged the original J52 powerplants for General Electric F404s,

The Grumman A-6 Intruder was a highly-effective and well-equipped attack aircraft. Its four-seat derivative was the EA-6B Prowler electronic warfare aircraft, with a large fairing on its vertical tail and underwing pods for electronic equipment.

A beautiful in-flight view of a Grumman EA-6B Prowler electronic warfare aircraft (Photo: Grumman History Center).

added digital avionics and a new radar to produce the A-6F Intruder II. The U.S. Navy, however, cancelled development of the A-6F to concentrate funds on the planned replacement for the Intruder, the proposed 'stealthy' General Dynamics/McDonnell Douglas A-12 Avenger II. Grumman offered the A-6G – an F-layout retaining the original J52 engines – when the extent of the A-12 program's mismanagement forced its cancellation, but the Navy elected to decline the offer. All Intruders were concentrated in the U.S. Navy in the early 1990s, but the type was finally retired in February 1997, leaving the Prowler as the sole A-6 variant in service in 2005.

Specifications – Grumman A-6E Intruder

Wingspan	53 ft
Length	54 ft 9 in
Maximum speed	644 mph at sea level
Maximum take-off weight	60,400 lb for runway operation
Range	1,011 miles with maximum weapons
Service ceiling	42,400 ft
Armament	Up to 18,000 lb of weapons on six underwing pylons
Engine	Two Pratt & Whitney J52-P-8B turbofan engines, of 9,300 lb st each
Crew	Two

Vought (LTV) A-7 Corsair II

In 1963 the U.S. Navy issued a requirement for a VAL (light attack aircraft) with around twice the payload of the successful but small Douglas A-4 Skyhawk (see pages 166 to 167). The design that became the Vought A-7 Corsair II was duly selected, and seven development examples and 35 initial production A-7As were eventually ordered. The Corsair II – universally known as the SLUF (short little ugly feller) – was a shorter derivative of the Vought F-8 Crusader variable-incidence wing fighter, with a fixed wing and 11,350 lb st Pratt & Whitney TF30-P-6 jet engine, giving the new aircraft good subsonic performance. The maiden flight was made on 27 September 1965 with production of the A-7A amounting to 199 examples before the more powerful A-7B was

introduced. A total of 196 A-7Bs were followed by 67 A-7Cs, an interim type with improved avionics and a 0.787 in (20 mm) cannon. It was followed by the A-7E powered by the Allison TF41-A-2 (a licence-built British Rolls-Royce Spey engine). This was the major production version for the U.S. Navy, with 535 built. A two-seat conversion trainer was produced by converting surplus A-7Bs and A-7Cs as TA-7Cs. Corsair IIs were heavily utilised in the Vietnam War, but were also later involved in operations over Grenada, Lebanon and Libya in the 1980s, operating from U.S. Navy aircraft carriers. The swansong for the type in naval service was the 1991 Gulf War, the last two operational squadrons disbanding later in 1991, although some specialized

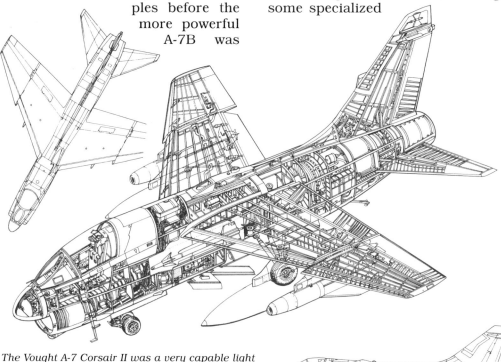

The Vought A-7 Corsair II was a very capable light attack aircraft. Some examples like that shown here mounted a multi-barrel cannon in the lower left-hand fuselage, and carried short-range air-to-air missiles for self-defence (mounted on the fuselage side).

A separate but related line of development to the A-7 created the Vought F-8 Crusader fighter for the U.S. Navy. The F-8 shown here has its unique variable-incidence wing in the raised position.

aircraft (including the EA-7L EW aggressor) remained in service for a little longer. The U.S. Air Force acquired 459 A-7Ds (including prototypes), initially to replace Douglas A-1 Skyraiders in rescue support operations over Vietnam. After the conflict the aircraft were handed over to second-line Air National Guard units, and two-seat A-7Ks were acquired to ease transition for pilots onto the single-seater. The Guard phased out the A-7 – the Air Force never adopting the Corsair II name – in 1993, having cancelled a radical rework known as the A-7F with a Pratt & Whitney F100 afterburning turbofan, lengthened fuselage and upgraded avionics. The first export customer was the Hellenic (Greek) air force, initially taking 60 new-build A-7Hs and five TA-7Hs before acquiring surplus examples from U.S. Navy stocks. From 1981 Portugal received refurbished A-7As as A-7P and TA-7Ps, while the Royal Thai Navy became the last service to introduce the type into service when it acquired surplus U.S. Navy A-7Es from 1996. In 2005 only Thailand still operated the SLUF. Total production of the Corsair II amounted to 1,551 examples including prototypes/ development aircraft.

Specifications – Vought A-7D Corsair II

Wingspan	38 ft 9 in
Length	46 ft 1.5 in
Maximum speed	646 mph at 5,000 ft
Maximum take-off weight	42,000 lb
Radius of action	890 miles
Service ceiling	42,000 ft
Armament	One 0.787 in (20 mm) multi-barrel cannon, up to 20,000 lb of ordnance including unguided bombs of various sizes
Engine	One Allison TF41-A-1 turbofan engine, of 14,250 lb st
Crew	One

Sukhoi Su-17/Su-22 Series

The Soviet Union has sometimes been accused of wringing new life out of an old design, due to the development of the swing-wing Su-17 family from the original 1950s fixed-wing Su-7. As described on pages 134 to 135, the Su-7 was an early jet-powered tactical attack aircraft that for its time had comparatively good performance. The drawbacks of the Su-7, however, included relatively poor qualities for take-off and landing, with long take-off runs in particular. This was not very useful for an aircraft expected to operate from poor-quality airstrips close to the front-line. One way of addressing this problem was found in attaching small rocket boosters to the Su-7's fuselage to give more power for take-off. This helped to shorten take-off runs at high weights, but a more long-term solution was obviously necessary. The Sukhoi designers eventually decided on the integration of 'swing-wing' technology to the established Su-7 layout. This promised good low-speed and short take-off qualities with the wings un-swept, but also allowed high-speed capabilities with the wings

swept back. Design work began in the mid-1960s, and in 1966 a production Su-7BM was modified with a new swing-wing layout to act as the prototype S-22I. It first flew on 2 August 1966, as the Soviet Union's first variable-geometry aircraft. Named 'Fitter-B' by NATO, it was proudly shown-off at the 1967 air demonstration at Moscow-Domodedovo airfield. The S-22I's design layout offered good short-field capabilities and an overall improved performance compared to the Su-7 series, especially for take-off and landing. Designated Su-17, the new type entered production in 1969. The early production examples were named 'Fitter-C' by NATO. Further development led to an increasing number of improved versions which included increasingly more sophisticated equipment and avionics, and increased weapons-carrying capability. The Su-17 was able to carry up to 8,818 lb (4,000 kg) of weapons, well over twice that of a well loaded Su-7. The initial Su-17 production aircraft were soon replaced on

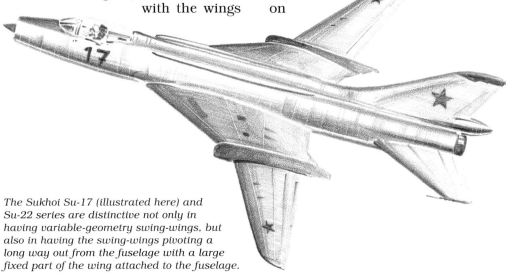

The Sukhoi Su-17 (illustrated here) and Su-22 series are distinctive not only in having variable-geometry swing-wings, but also in having the swing-wings pivoting a long way out from the fuselage with a large fixed part of the wing attached to the fuselage.

The Czech air force was one of many export users of the Sukhoi Su-22, in this case an Su-22M-4 'Fitter-K' (sometimes called Su-22M-4K). All the Czech Republic's Su-22s have now been withdrawn from service (Photo: Malcolm V. Lowe).

the production line by the Su-17M with a Lyulka AL-21F afterburning turbojet, and this and subsequent Su-17 ground attack and reconnaissance versions served widely with Soviet air force and naval aviation units (the latter shore-based). A separate line of two-seat trainers was also developed. From 1974 the Su-17 was exported, initially as the Su-20 and later as the Su-22 in a variety of single-seat and two-seat models. Approximately 17 export customers flew these types, some 1,800 export 'Fitters' being made. The type is now ending its service with some of these customers, while the Su-17 has now completely been replaced in front-line Russian air force units.

Specifications – Sukhoi Su-17M

Wingspan	44 ft 10.5 in (wings un-swept)
Length	55 ft 2 in (including nose pitot)
Maximum speed	Mach 2.1 at 36,090 ft
Maximum take-off weight	40,498 lb
Endurance	2 hours 57 minutes
Service ceiling	51,180 ft
Armament	Two 1.18 in (30 mm) cannons, one in each wing root, up to 8,818 lb of weapons on external pylons including unguided bombs, gun pods, rocket pods, guided air-to-surface missiles
Engine	One Lyulka (Saturn) AL-21F-3 turbojet engine, of 24,691 lb st with afterburning)
Crew	One

Lockheed L-1011 TriStar

In the late-1960s the major American commercial aircraft manufacturers, Boeing, Lockheed and McDonnell Douglas, all started work on so-called 'widebody' airliners. This design work resulted in the Boeing 747, TriStar, and DC-10 respectively. The last two had a similar, three-engined configuration, with the third engine located at the base of the vertical tail. Lockheed started development of the TriStar in response to a requirement for a twin-engined aircraft for American Airlines' Los Angeles – Chicago route. However, the aircraft emerged as a three-engined aircraft launched by orders from Eastern Air Lines and TWA. Development was affected by the company's financial problems and the collapse of the engine supplier, Rolls-Royce – and the RB.211 for the TriStar – was saved by public funds, sparing Lockheed from an extensive redesign. The L-1011-1 TriStar first flew on 16 November 1970, the first service being flown by Eastern in April 1972. It was followed by the L-1011-

500 longer-range version, the L-1011-200 'hot-and-high' version, and the L-1011-500, the Series 500 developed specially for a British Airways requirement. The latter had a shorter fuselage compared to that of the L-1011-1 and –200, and a longer wingspan. When production ended in 1984 a total of 250 TriStars had been built – the type is generally seen as the 'also-ran' in the early widebody market. That it did not achieve greater sales is no reflection on the aircraft itself but indicative of the fierce competition Lockheed experienced against the two giants of American airliner production (Boeing, and McDonnell Douglas) in the 1970s. Lockheed lost over $2.5 billion on the TriStar program. Conversions of existing aircraft produced the L-1011-50, -150 and –250. The 28 L-1011-50s were –1s with an increased maximum take-off weight. The range of the L-1011–1 was increased by about 10 percent to produce the L-1011-150. Delta Air Lines was the driving force in the L-1011-

The Lockheed TriStar has had a comparatively successful career, but has always been overshadowed by the big passenger jets of Boeing and the former McDonnell Douglas.

A publicity photograph showing a Lockheed TriStar in the colors of the major U.S. airline TWA (Photo: Lockheed).

250 program, which centred on increasing the maximum take-off weight of its –1s and re-engining them with more powerful RB211-524 variants. Marshall Aerospace in Britain converted ten British Airways and Pan Am L-1011-500s to four different tanker and transport versions for Britain's Royal Air Force, as Tristar K.Mk.1s, KC.Mk.1s, C.Mk.2s and a sole Mk.2A. Civilian freighter conversions have also been undertaken. The most unusual conversion by Marshall Aerospace was of an Air Canada L-1011-1 to launch the Pegasus rocket-powered satellite launcher for Orbital Sciences. That TriStar made its first post conversion flight in April 1995. In 2005 the TriStar was an increasingly rare aircraft in airline service, although it is still praised for its reliability and performance by its operators.

Specifications – Lockheed L-1011-500 TriStar

Wingspan	164 ft 6 in
Length	164 ft 2.5 in
Maximum speed	595 mph at 25,000 ft
Maximum take-off weight	510,000 lb
Range	7,012 miles
Service ceiling	43,000 ft
Engine	Three Rolls-Royce RB.211-524B4 turbofan engines, of 50,000 lb st each
Accommodation	Three crew plus stewards/stewardesses, maximum of 315 passengers, 280 standard

Tupolev Tu-134 and Tu-154

The Soviet Union gained considerable success with its Tupolev Tu-104 airliner (see pages 118 to 119), which was one of the first-ever jet-powered airliners to enter service. However, the type had essentially been based on the Tupolev Tu-16 bomber design, and for the next generation of airliner Tupolev's designers drew up a new design which was not based on an existing military aircraft layout. In fact the resulting new design was to an extent influenced by the Tu-124 short- to medium-range airliner. There the similarities ended, however, and the resulting Tu-134 design was essentially new. It was a contemporary of France's Aérospatiale Caravelle and Britain's BAC One-Eleven (both covered elsewhere in this book), especially in adopting a rear-fuselage engine location. The prototype first flew in July 1963, and successful trials and performance-proving flights were performed by several early examples. The type entered scheduled airline service in September 1967 with the Soviet Union's State airline Aeroflot. In its standard version the Tu-134 could seat 72 passengers. Further development led to the longer Tu-134A, and the type was exported to several customers outside the Soviet Union. Altogether at least 725 Tu-134 were

built (possibly over 800), and some 199 served with the Soviet air force as navigation trainers or for special test duties in addition to transport tasks. During the mid-1960s Tupolev began the process to find a replacement for the original Tu-104 pioneering jet airliner and other existing medium-range types in Aeroflot service. The purpose was to create a new medium- to long-haul jet airliner, and the resulting Tu-154 has proven to be a successful and widely-used jet airliner. The prototype flew in October 1968, and after the usual considerable development and route-proving work the type entered full Aeroflot service in February 1972. International services began between Moscow and Prague in August 1972. The Tu-154 employed a

The Tupolev Tu-154 airliner was a considerable success for the Soviet Union, and became one of the principal medium-haul airliners of its day. Its three-engined powerplant layout resembled that of the Boeing 727.

The Tupolev Tu-134 proved to be a very successful short-haul medium capacity airliner. This example, registered RA-65566, is an Aeroflot-operated Tu-134A and was photographed in Moscow during the summer of 2001 (Photo: Malcolm V. Lowe).

three-engined layout similar to that of the Boeing 727 (see pages 190 to 191), and could seat up to 167 passengers. The more powerful Tu-154A entered service in 1974/1975, and further development led to the improved Tu-154B. Production ceased after just over 600 examples had been built. However, a further improved Tu-154M was subsequently developed, and production was resumed in 1982. The Tu-154M features different engines (Aviadvigatel D-30KU turbofans) compared to previous versions, and can seat up to 180 passengers. At least 318 were built, but the type's produc-

tion factory at Samara suffered considerable financial problems which undermined this promising design. Some Tu-154 have served with the Russian military but many Russian airline-operated Tu-154s remain available for military operations if the need for increased airlift capacity ever arises – a fact that is also true for airliners and airlines in the West. The Tu-154 has served a variety of export customers outside the Soviet Union, and many continue in service in 2005. The NATO reporting name for the Tu-154 series is 'Careless,' that for the Tu-134 being 'Crusty.'

Specifications – Tupolev Tu-154 (early production)

Wingspan	123 ft 2.5 in
Length	157 ft 1.75 in
Maximum cruising speed	606 mph at 31,168 ft
Maximum take-off weight	198,414 lb
Range	1,740 miles
Service ceiling	36,090 ft plus
Engine	Three Kuznetsov NK-8-2 turbofan engines, of 20,950 lb st each
Accommodation	Three crew plus stewards/stewardesses, up to 167 passengers in high-density seating arrangement

Grumman F-14 Tomcat

The cancellation of the General Dynamics F-111B (see pages 212 to 213) allowed the U.S. Navy to pursue its own program to replace the McDonnell Douglas F-4 Phantom II for the fleet air defence role. Taking the advanced AWG-9 fire control radar system developed for the F-111B, and placing it with the long-range AIM-54 Phoenix air-to-air missile mated to the variable-geometry F-14 Tomcat airframe, eventually produced a formidable fighter able to engage targets at extreme range from an aircraft carrier battle group. A total of 12 YF-14A Tomcats were ordered for development trials, the first flying on 21 December 1970. Deliveries to the Navy started in October 1972, and the first carrier deployment commenced in 1974. Production of the F-14A amounted to 551 aircraft for the U.S. Navy. Early difficulties with the TF30 turbofan were alleviated by the development of the TF30-P-414A, but the cost of the Tomcat also resulted in criticism from several U.S. government bodies and took Grumman close to bankruptcy in the early 1970s. Help came from the Shah of Iran, who put money into Grumman and ordered 80 examples of the Tomcat for the Imperial Iranian

Air Force, bringing down the cost per aircraft for the U.S. Navy. However, the Islamic revolution that overthrew the Shah in 1979 stranded the last Tomcat for Iran in the U.S. and cut off spares to the Iranian-operated aircraft. This did not stop Iranian Tomcats being used to good effect in the eight years of the first Gulf War that was triggered by the Iraqi invasion of Iran in 1980. U.S. Navy Tomcats first saw action downing two Libyan Sukhoi Su-22s on 19 August 1981 over the Mediterranean, also dispatching two Libyan MiG-23s on 4 January 1989. The F-14B designation was initially used by two distinct test variants before being allocated to 38 aircraft built as F-14A+ and 32 upgraded F-14As powered by the General Electric F110-GE-110 turbofan engine, the first flying in September 1986. The F-14B was seen as an interim type before the F-14D entered production that introduced advanced digital avionics, but only 37 of a planned 127 were built before the program was cancelled. By the time of the 1991 Gulf War some Tomcats had been equipped to carry the TARPS reconnaissance pod and others to carry bombs, the aircraft later gaining a

The swing-wing Grumman F-14 Tomcat is a big, complicated fleet fighter that has now been in service for over thirty years.

precision bombing capability. These tasks accounted for many of the sorties flown in combat missions over Afghanistan in 2001 and Iraq in 2003. The days of the Tomcat in U.S service are numbered, as the last squadrons are due to disband in 2006, having been replaced on U.S. aircraft carriers by the F/A-18F Super Hornet.

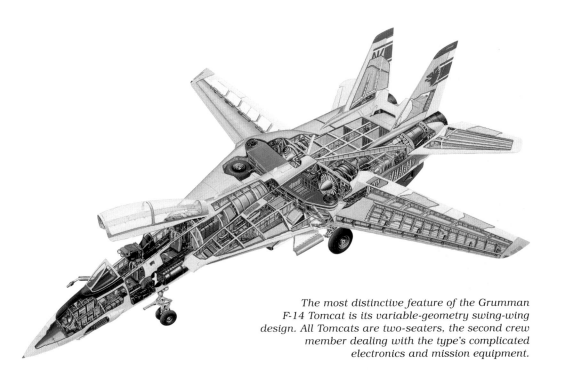

The most distinctive feature of the Grumman F-14 Tomcat is its variable-geometry swing-wing design. All Tomcats are two-seaters, the second crew member dealing with the type's complicated electronics and mission equipment.

Specifications – Grumman F-14A Tomcat

Wingspan	64 ft 1.5 in (wings un-swept)
Length	62 ft 8 in
Maximum speed	1,544 mph at 35,000 ft
Maximum take-off weight	74,349 lb overload take-off weight
Radius of action	766 miles patrol mission
Service ceiling	50,000 ft
Armament	One 0.787 in (20 mm) multi-barrel cannon in the left-hand forward fuselage, four missile stations under the fuselage for AIM-7 Sparrow or AIM-54 Phoenix air-to-air missiles, plus two underwing stores stations for AIM-9 Sidewinders, fuel tanks, Sparrows or Phoenix
Engine	Two Pratt & Whitney TF30-P-412A or -414A turbofan engines, of 21,750 lb st each (34,154 lb st each with afterburning)
Crew	Two

Sukhoi Su-24

Amongst the formidable array of combat aircraft that was ranged against the West by the Soviet Union during the Cold War were a number of highly-capable attack aircraft. One of these was the Sukhoi Su-24, known to NATO as 'Fencer,' which was another successful design from the prolific Sukhoi organisation in the Soviet Union. Still in service today, the Su-24 is a specialized interdiction and strike fighter which had a close Western equivalent in the General Dynamics F-111 (see pages 212 to 213). In a war with NATO – which thankfully never took place – Soviet-operated Su-24s would have been used for fast low-level attacks on NATO surface-to-air missile sites, airfields, communications, and other infrastructure behind the front-line. For this they would have relied on their speed and low-level agility to avoid NATO's extensive air defence system. The Su-24 is capable of precision strikes using advanced avionics and targeting systems, and has so far been used in action over Afghanistan during the Soviet Union's intervention there in the 1980s, and in

the long war against terrorists in Chechnya. Design work on what became the Su-24 started in the early to mid-1960s, to find a successor to existing Ilyushin Il-28 and Yakovlev Yak-28 tactical bombers. Sukhoi was already gaining experience with swing-wing technology for fast low-level flight coupled with short take-off capabilities from poor-quality landing strips, due to work on the Su-17 (see pages 238 to 239). This design concept was also applied to the Su-24. The original swing-wing T.6-2IG prototype flew in the first half of 1970, but considerable development work was required before series production started of the Su-24 some time after. Initial operational capability was achieved in 1974, with the first front-line aircraft entering service probably in late 1974 onwards. These were comparatively simple early 'Fencer' models, but continuing development led to the upgraded and more capable Su-24M 'Fencer-D,' with genuine all-weather capability and the ability to carry a variety of guided air-to-surface missiles. Two further specialized versions of the Su-

The Sukhoi Su-24 uses a swing-wing design layout for fast low-level flight with its wings swept back as illustrated here, coupled to good short take-off capability with its wings un-swept. It is a very capable strike aircraft.

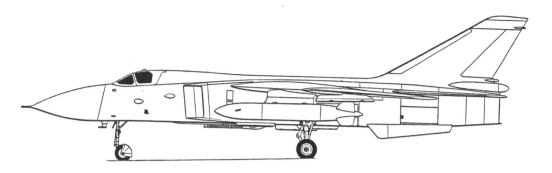

*The Sukhoi Su-24 'Fencer' is a two-seat strike aircraft,
its two crew members sitting side-by-side in its cockpit.*

24 have been developed, the Su-24MR ('Fencer-E') reconnaissance model with various camera and infra-red systems, and the Su-24MP ('Fencer-F') electronic warfare and jamming aircraft. The latter has been built in comparatively small numbers, but in late 2004 some five hundred plus Su-24 of all current versions were thought to be in Russian air force and land-based Russian naval aviation service. The Su-24 has also been exported, the export version of the Su-24M being the Su-24MK. Various countries such as Algeria, Iraq, Iran, Libya, and Syria, have received Su-24s. In addition, the break-up of the old Soviet Union at the end of the 1980s and early 1990s saw a large number of Soviet air force aircraft 'inherited' by newly-independent former Soviet states. In the case of the Su-24, both the Ukraine and Azerbaijan found themselves with Soviet Su-24s on their territory, and have continued to use them since.

Specifications – Sukhoi Su-24M

Wingspan	57 ft 10.5 in (wings un-swept)
Length	80 ft 5.75 m (including nose probe)
Maximum speed	Mach 1.35 at 36,090 ft
Maximum take-off weight	87,236 lb
Radius of action	652 miles with external fuel tanks
Service ceiling	57,415 ft
Armament	One 0.9 in (23 mm) multi-barrel cannon in lower fuselage, wide variety of externally-carried bombs and guided air-to-surface missiles up to 17,857 lb, also including tactical nuclear weapons, and air-to-air guided missiles for self-defence
Engine	Two Lyulka (Saturn) AL-21F-3A turbojet engines, of 24,691 lb st each with afterburning
Crew	Two

Lockheed S-3 Viking

The piston-engined Grumman S2F (S-2) Tracker provided the U.S. Navy with its fixed-wing aircraft carrier-based anti-submarine warfare capability for over 20 years. The threat of a new generation of deep-running, silent Soviet submarines provided the impetus to develop a replacement for the Tracker. The result was the jet-engined Lockheed S-3A Viking. Eight service-test YS-3A were produced, the first making the type's maiden flight on 21 January 1972. They were followed by 179 production S-3A Vikings, with manufacture ending in mid-1978. The type entered U.S. Navy squadron service in the summer of 1974, with the first cruise aboard an aircraft carrier during the following year. A total of twelve front-line U.S. Navy squadrons converted to this initial Viking model. Around 119 of the S-3As were upgraded as S-3Bs with improved mission avionics, acoustic processing, increased radar processing capabilities and provision to carry the highly-capable AGM-84 Harpoon guided anti-ship missile. The first S-3B flew in September 1984, the type reaching the fleet from December 1987. A total of 16 S-3As were extensively modified as ES-3A Shadow carrier-based electronic-intelligence gathering aircraft. The first Shadow with the full avionics suite flew in May 1991. Although a valuable addition to the U.S. Navy's carrier air wings, they were retired prematurely because the cost of upgrading their mission systems was prohibitive. Other versions of the Viking were the US-3A carrier on-board delivery (COD) aircraft, and the sole KS-3A in-flight refuelling tanker. While this dedicated tanker derivative did not serve aboard the U.S. Navy's aircraft carriers, the end of the Cold War saw the Soviet Union's submarine threat diminish virtually overnight, allowing the Viking fleet to concentrate on other tasks, including in-flight refuelling. This role subsequently became an important contribution to the flight hours accumulated by Vikings in support of operations over Iraq in the 1991 Gulf War, but they also sank Iraqi patrol boats and attacked anti-aircraft artillery with unguided bombs. The electronics and sophisticated radar that was incorporated in the B-model upgrade also allowed Vikings to detect and classify enemy radars and radar emissions. Vikings have been integral to all campaigns that have involved American carrier air wings since, including operations over Afghanistan in 2001 and

The Grumman S-3 Viking was a capable anti-submarine aircraft that had to adapt to the new military situation with the end of the Cold War. The example shown here has been upgraded to carry AGM-84 Harpoon anti-ship guided missiles beneath its wings.

A Grumman S-3A Viking is seen here on its 'short finals' making its landing approach to an aircraft carrier, with the deck landing officer's instrumentation panel in the foreground (Photo: John Batchelor).

Operation 'Iraqi Freedom' in 2003. Although it has proven its versatility supporting combat operations, the Viking is a candidate for early retirement from the U.S. Navy, the flight-refuelling role being increasingly taken over by examples of the Boeing Super Hornet as demonstrated by its role in Operation 'Iraqi Freedom.' However, efforts to market surplus examples of the Viking to potential overseas customers continue.

Specifications – Lockheed S-3A Viking

Wingspan	68 ft 8 in
Length	53 ft 4 in
Maximum speed	514 mph at sea level
Maximum take-off weight	52,540 lb
Endurance	7 hours 30 minutes
Service ceiling	40,000 ft
Armament	Up to 7,000 lb of weapons, including 4,000 lb carried internally, comprising torpedoes, bombs, mines, depth charges or rocket pods
Engine	Two General Electric TF34-GE-2 turbofan engines, of 9,275 lb st each
Crew	Four

SEPECAT Jaguar

An excellent example of friendly co-operation between Britain and France that also included such projects as the Concorde supersonic airliner (see pages 232 to 233), the Jaguar was designed and built under the auspices of an Anglo-French body named Société Européenne de Production de l'Avion ECAT (SEPECAT). The ECAT of this name stood for the intended French roles of the aircraft, Ecole de Combat et d'Appui Tactique, or advanced/operational (combat) trainer and tactical support (attack) aircraft. SEPECAT brought together representation from the British Aircraft Corporation, and Breguet Aviation of France (which later merged with the French aviation giant Dassault). Two engine companies (Rolls-Royce and Turboméca) formed a new organisation to work together on the intended aircraft's new engine. In the period leading to the creation of the Jaguar, both Britain's Royal Air Force and the French Armée de l'Air were developing similar needs for this type of attack/operational training aircraft. A joint requirement existed from around 1963, although in the event the Jaguar emerged from the subsequent deliberations as a highly-specialized supersonic low-level attack aircraft, most elements of the original training part of the joint proposals eventually being met by other aircraft types. Several British and French designs were submitted to fulfil the original joint requirements, the successful layout being the Breguet Br.121. From this was developed the Jaguar, and each country devised its own specific versions. The British and French thus had their own slightly different single-seat attack versions (Jaguar A in France, and Jaguar S or GR.Mk.1 in Britain), and two-seat operational trainers (Jaguar E in France, and Jaguar B or T.Mk.2 in Britain). A Jaguar M for the French naval air arm was also planned but later cancelled. The first Jaguar to fly was a French two-seat prototype, on 8 September 1968, and eight prototypes were built in total. Final assembly lines were established in each country for their own respective versions, but manufacture of specific parts was performed in each country (the wings, tail and rear fuselage for all the aircraft, for example, were built in Britain). The

The SEPECAT Jaguar is represented here by an R.A.F. GR.Mk.1, the chisel-shaped nose containing a laser range-finder that is a part of the type's sophisticated precision-attack equipment. British two-seat Jaguar trainers also have combat capability. Jaguars can operate from comparatively short runways and austere landing strips such as roads.

A British single-seat SEPECAT Jaguar. R.A.F. Jaguar GR.Mk.1 strike aircraft have been progressively upgraded over the years, first to GR.Mk.1A standard with more powerful engines and other changes, more recently to GR.Mk.3-series (Photo: John Batchelor).

R.A.F. eventually ordered 203 single- and two-seat versions, many of which have since been upgraded, while France bought 200 single- and two-seaters. Initial R.A.F. deliveries were made in 1973/1974. In addition, the Jaguar International in single- and two-seat form was developed for export, the initial aircraft flying in August 1976. Export orders were received from Ecuador, Oman, Nigeria and India – the latter country also establishing its own production facility at Hindustan Aeronautics. Jaguars have been highly successful in combat, especially with British and French operations in the Gulf War of 1991.

Specifications – SEPECAT Jaguar GR.Mk.1A

Wingspan	28 ft 6 in
Length	55 ft 2.5 in (including nose probe)
Maximum speed	Mach 1.6 at 36,000 ft
Maximum take-off weight	34,612 lb
Radius of action	875 miles with external fuel tanks
Service ceiling	45,930 ft
Armament	Two lower fuselage-mounted 1.18 in (30 mm) cannons, up to 10,000 lb of external stores on five underside pylons including unguided bombs and rockets, guided air-to-surface and air-to-air missiles
Engine	Two Rolls-Royce/Turboméca Adour Mk.104 turbofan engines, of 5,320 lb st each (8,040 lb st each with afterburning).
Crew	One

Boeing (McDonnell Douglas) F-15 Eagle

Combat experience in the Vietnam War highlighted to the U.S. Air Force the need for a dedicated air superiority fighter. A strong body of opinion developed in the Air Force for an overwhelmingly superior fighter, and this was championed in the FX requirement that produced the McDonnell Douglas F-15 Eagle. The first F-15A flew on 27 July 1972, followed by a two-seat TF-15A (later F-15B) conversion trainer on 7 July 1973. With its excellent thrust-to-weight ratio of greater than 1:1, good manoeuvrability, advanced 'look-down/shoot-down' radar and heavy load of air-to-air missiles, the Eagle has set the standard for fighters from the 1970s onwards. From 1976 360 production F-15As and 58 F-15Bs were delivered to the U.S. Air Force. Uprated F100 engines and provision for conformal close-fitting fuel tanks (CFT) were introduced on the F-15C – first flown on 26 February 1979 – and the two-seat F-15D. A total of 408 F-15Cs and 62 F-15Ds were

built for the U.S. Air Force. U.S. Eagles were later upgraded under a Multi-Stage Improvement Program (MSIP), replacing the APG-63 radar with the APG-70 and allowing the F-15A/Bs to use CFTs. Air superiority Eagles were exported to Israel (F-15A/B/C/D) and Saudi Arabia (F-15C/D), while Mitsubishi built the majority of the F-15J/DJs for the Japan Air Self Defence Force. Israel was the first nation to take its Eagles to war, achieving air dominance over the Bekaa Valley in Lebanon during 1979. U.S. Eagles acquitted themselves well in combat sorties during Operation 'Desert Storm' over Iraq in 1991, shooting down 36 Iraqi aircraft, while Saudi Arabian Eagles accounted for a further two. McDonnell Douglas was keen to promote a two-seat ground attack version of the aircraft as the Strike Eagle for the

The Mach 2-capable Boeing (McDonnell Douglas) F-15 Eagle is one of the most important combat aircraft in service today. Illustrated is the F-15E Strike Eagle configuration.

U.S. Air Force, resulting in a production order for the F-15E, known to its crews as the 'Beagle' (bomber eagle). The first production aircraft made its maiden flight in December 1986 and deliveries commenced in 1989. Variants were exported to Israel (F-15I) and Saudi Arabia (F-15S). The latest customer is South Korea, the first of 40 F-15Ks flying in March 2005. Strike Eagles were heavily tasked during 'Desert Storm,' even downing a hovering Iraqi helicopter with a laser-guided bomb. Since 1991, Eagles and Strike Eagles have participated in operations over the former Yugoslavia, Afghanistan and Iraq. Eagles also flew defensive patrols over American cities following the 11 September 2001 terrorist attacks on New York. During the period of the production of the F-15, the famous McDonnell Douglas company was absorbed by Boeing, making the Eagle now one of Boeing's many military programs.

The F-15 Eagle has gained great fame in its successful combat operations while in service with the U.S. Air Force and Israel. As can be seen here it is a big, twin-engined fighter.

Specifications – McDonnell Douglas F-15C Eagle

Wingspan	42 ft 9.75 in
Length	63 ft 9 in
Maximum speed	1,650 mph at 36,000 ft
Maximum take-off weight	68,000 lb with CFTs
Radius of action	1,222 miles interception mission
Service ceiling	100,000 ft absolute
Armament	One 0.787 in (20 mm) cannon in the left-hand wing root, up to 16,000 lb of weapons, primarily AIM-7M Sparrow and AIM-9M Sidewinder guided air-to-air missiles initially, but later AIM-120 AMRAAM
Engine	Two Pratt & Whitney F100-P-220 turbofan engines, of 14,670 lb st each (23,830 lb st each with afterburning)
Crew	One

Panavia Tornado

The Multi-Role Combat Aircraft (MRCA) that grew into the highly-successful Tornado was conceived from a European requirement for an interdiction, close-air support, maritime attack and point interception aircraft for the British, German and Italian air forces. It evolved into one of the most successful international projects, creating the swing-wing Tornado. Two main versions were built, the Tornado IDS (interdictor/strike), and the ADV (air defence variant). The first of nine prototypes and six pre-production aircraft flew on 14 August 1974. On 10 July 1979 the first of a planned 640 production aircraft flew, although a further batch of 57 was later added to this figure. Deliveries to the first unit, the Tri-national Tornado Training Establishment (TTTE) at R.A.F. Cottesmore, started in July 1980. The R.A.F. acquired 164 Tornado GR.Mk.1s, 50 GR.Mk.1(T) dual-control trainers and 14 GR.Mk.1A reconnaissance aircraft, although a further 16 Mk.1s were later modified for

the reconnaissance role and some aircraft were configured for the maritime strike role to replace Buccaneers (see pages 168 to 169) as Tornado GR.Mk.1Bs. The R.A.F.'s peak of eleven operational Tornado strike squadrons was achieved in 1990. The Tornado gained its baptism of fire during the 1991 Gulf War when it suffered seven losses (including six R.A.F. aircraft), mainly because the low-level tactics employed took it to within easy reach of Iraqi anti-aircraft artillery. After the war a mid-life upgrade of 142 Tornadoes was initiated, allowing the aircraft to operate effectively at medium altitude. This upgrade created the current Tornado GR.Mk.4 strike and GR.Mk.4A reconnaissance aircraft fleets. The West German Luftwaffe acquired 212 Tornado IDS, including two refurbished pre-production aircraft and 55 dual control, plus 37 Tornado ECRs (including two prototype conversions) equipped for reconnaissance and suppression of enemy air defences. In addition, 112 IDSs (including 12 two-seaters) were delivered to the West German naval air arm to replace its Lockheed Starfighters. A total of 100 Tornado IDSs, including a refur-

The Panavia Tornado's most obvious feature is its swing-wing design. All Tornadoes regardless of their roles are two-seat aircraft.

bished pre-production aircraft and a dozen dual-control aircraft, were ordered by Italy. The Tornado ADV was developed by British Aerospace as a long-range interceptor for the R.A.F. The first of three prototypes flew in October 1979 and was followed by 18 Tornado F.Mk.2s. These were interim aircraft with RB 199 Mk.103 engines and – at least initially – concrete ballast in the nosecone because development of the intended Foxhunter radar was delayed. The definitive production model was the Tornado F.Mk.3, the first flying on 20 November 1985. A total of 144 F.Mk.3s were built for the R.A.F., with another 24 exported to Saudi Arabia. Saudi Arabia was also the only export recipient of the Tornado IDS. Italy became the third ADV operator when it recently leased 24 R.A.F. aircraft to boost its air defences. Some of the remaining R.A.F. ADV Tornadoes might be converted into defence-suppression attack aircraft.

Specifications – Panavia Tornado GR.Mk.1

Wingspan	45 ft 7.5 in (wings unswept)
Length	54 ft 10.25 in
Maximum speed	1,453 mph at 36,000 ft
Maximum take-off weight	61,620 lb
Radius of action	864 miles strike mission
Service ceiling	50,000 ft plus
Armament	Two 1.06 in (27 mm) cannons in the forward lower fuselage, some 10,000 lb of external weapons, including conventional and nuclear bombs, and precision-guided weapons
Engine	Two Turbo-Union RB.199-34R Mk.101 turbofan engines, of 8,475 lb st each (14,840 lb st each with afterburning) (Mk.103 in later production aircraft)
Crew	Two

Mil Mi-24

If open warfare had ever broken out between the Soviet Union and the West during the stand-off of the Cold War, one of the Soviet Union and Eastern Bloc's most important tactical combat machines would have been the Mil Mi-24 attack/assault helicopter. Principally an anti-tank helicopter, the Mi-24 is in a class of its own in also being able to carry up to eight fully-armed troops, and land them where required on the battlefield. Produced in large numbers and eventually in service in many countries, the Mi-24 was named 'Hind' by NATO. Design began in the latter half of the 1960s, but a change of emphasis during the design phase resulted in the helicopter being both an assault and an attack helicopter. The prototype (called V-24) first flew on 19 September 1969, two prototypes being followed by ten pre-pro-duction/development helicopters (sometimes called 'Hind-B'). The design drew on aspects of the existing Mil Mi-8 and Mi-14 helicopters, and the first production version was the Mi-24A ('Hind-A'), followed by the Mi-24F with its tail rotor changed from the right to the left-hand side of the tail, and the Mi-24U dual-control trainer ('Hind-C'). Some 240 of these early versions were built, followed by the highly-important but interim Mi-24D ('Hind-D') with many refinements including a completely re-designed forward fuselage and altered armament. The Mi-24D entered production in 1973 and some 350 were built, but continuing refinement of the 'Hind's excellent design led to the Mi-24V ('Hind-E'). This more powerful and up-armed version was delivered to Soviet forces from March 1976, approximately one thousand

The Mil Mi-24 is a very powerful, armoured and heavily-armed attack and assault helicopter. Its two crew members sit in tandem in the forward fuselage, and some of the helicopter's armament is carried by the stub wings projecting from the fuselage.

The Mil Mi-24 is used extensively by many air arms around the world. This example is a Mi-24V ('Hind-E') of the Czech Air Force, the Czech Republic being a former Warsaw Pact country that nowadays belongs to NATO (Photo: Malcolm V. Lowe).

being built up to 1986. Some 620 slightly different Mi-24P ('Hind-F') and Mi-24G were built to 1989, with the chin-turret of earlier versions being replaced by two fixed forward-firing 1.18 in (30 mm) cannons. Further versions have included the Mi-24R series ('Hind-G1') and Mi-24K ('Hind-G2') armed reconnaissance or fire-spotting models, plus a wide range of upgrades and associated versions. Export examples include the related Mi-25 and Mi-35 versions, and continuing development has led to further Mi-35-related designs. Several companies are currently engaged on upgrade work on existing examples, to fit the most modern equipment and cockpit instrumentation that is available. Production has reached some 5,200 examples of all 'Hinds' manufactured, serving in approximately 45 countries. Mi-24s have seen combat all over the world, from Afghanistan during the 1980s with Soviet forces, to the conflicts in Chechnya, to the Iran-Iraq War, and to more recent use in the Sierra Leone civil war.

Specifications – Mil Mi-24V ('Hind-E')

Main Rotor Diameter	56 ft 9 in
Fuselage Length	57 ft 5.25 in
Maximum speed	199 mph at sea level
Maximum take-off weight	26,455 lb
Range	280 miles
Service ceiling	14,764 ft
Armament	One four-barrel 0.5 in (12.7 mm) machine gun in chin-turret, up to eight 9M114 (AT-6 'Spiral') anti-tank guided missiles, various rocket pods for unguided air-to-ground rockets, R-60 (AA-8 'Aphid') air-to-air missiles on some examples
Engine	Two Klimov (Isotov) TV3-117V turboshaft engines, of 2,190 eshp each
Crew	Two crew, eight seated troops (more if standing)

Aero L-39 Albatros Series

After its creation in the period at the end of World War One, Czechoslovakia quickly established its own important aircraft industry – parts of which continue to exist today. The Soviet Union exercised control over Czechoslovakia from the late 1940s onwards, and the Czechs built a number of Russian aircraft types such as the MiG-15 (see pages 58 to 59). When this Russian oppression was ended in 1989, the Czechoslovak aircraft industry subsequently continued to make several important aircraft types. In 1993 the Czech Republic was created, and one of its most important companies is Aero Vodochody which has specialized for many years in designing and building jet trainer and light strike aircraft. One of the world's most successful and numerous jet trainer and light attack aircraft is the Aero L-39 Albatros, which was developed as a logical successor to the Aero L-29 Delfin (Dolphin) of the 1960s, but able to fulfil a wider range of training requirements than the L-29 and with a genuine light strike capability. The first L-39 flew in November 1968, and the initial production pilot training model was the L-39C. This entered service with the Czechoslovak air force in 1974 after some re-design of the original L-39 layout. The L-39 duly went on to serve in large numbers with the Soviet Union's air force (2,080 examples) and various other Soviet-aligned countries in the Warsaw Pact and elsewhere in the world. Continued development led to the L-39V target-towing aircraft, the L-39ZO armed trainer, and the L-39ZA ground attack and reconnaissance version in the mid-1970s. The latter has a detachable gun pod that can be fitted beneath the fuselage. Further refinement in the post-Communist era after 1989 led to the updated and more powerful L-39MS, and thence to the new-generation L-59 that was developed from it. This version

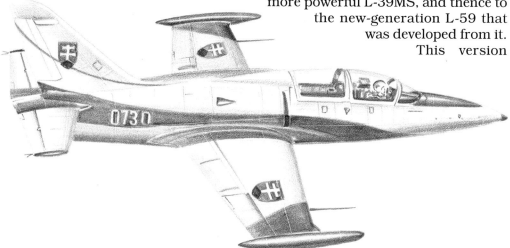

The Aero L-39 Albatros has been exported widely to many countries. This Slovakian-operated example is in the colors of the Slovak air force's aerobatic demonstration team the 'Biele Albatrosy,' and is in fact an L-39V former target-tower although the team mainly uses standard trainer L-39 models. The L-39's excellent manoeuvrability makes it ideal as an aerobatic display aircraft.

Two classic Czech jet trainers fly together. Nearest to the camera is an Aero L-39ZA Albatros wearing Czech markings. In the background is the L-39's distinguished forerunner, the Aero L-29 Delfin (Dolphin) wearing special Czech air force 'tiger squadron' colors (Photo: Aero Vodochody).

first flew in September 1986 and the first L-59 production delivery was in 1993 to Egypt. Continuing development led to the dedicated light strike L-159, a completely Westernised derivative with an American Allied-Signal (Honeywell) F124 turbofan engine and Western avionics. Total production of the L-39 was at least 2,854 L-39s, plus five L-39MS and 60 L-59. So far 72 L-159 have been built for the Czech air force, the first series production example flying in October 1999, and the type is currently available for export.

Specifications – Aero L-39ZA Albatros

Wingspan	31 ft 0.5 in
Length	39 ft 9.5 in
Maximum speed	469 mph at 16,405 ft
Maximum take-off weight	12,500 lb
Range	approximately 621 miles
Service ceiling	36,090 ft
Armament	One underfuselage centreline pod with twin-barrel 0.9 in (23 mm) cannon, four underwing weapons pylons (two per wing) for up to 2,205 lb of Western or Soviet-origin weapons, including bombs, rocket launchers, or air-to-air guided missiles
Engine	One Progress (Ivchenko) AI-25 TL turbofan engine, of 3,792 lb st
Crew	Two

Ilyushin Il-76

Although the majority of the Soviet Union's military transport aircraft were created by the Antonov organisation, a notable exception was the heavy-lift four-engined Ilyushin Il-76. Development of this very powerful transport was initiated to create a long-range aircraft capable of carrying large cargoes including military vehicles into semi-prepared airfields near to the front-line in any war situation. It was intended as a replacement for the four-turboprop Antonov An-12 long-range transport, although in reality the An-12 has itself persisted in service alongside the Il-76. Design work on what became the Il-76 began in the mid- to late-1960s, and the first of three prototypes made its maiden flight in March 1971. Initial deliveries were made to the Soviet air force in 1974, but full combat capability was only achieved some time after that. The Il-76 was given the reporting name 'Candid' by NATO, the first Il-76 production examples being called 'Candid-A.' The main versions in Soviet service have been the Il-76M and its longer-range counterpart the Il-76MD, both called 'Candid-B' by NATO and many were fitted with a cannon-armed tail turret for self-defence. Most of these aircraft are now not armed, instead chaff and flare dispensers have

been fitted to many aircraft to deflect surface-to-air missiles although some examples are believed to be able to carry bombs beneath their wings. Civil equivalents are the Il-76T and the longer-range Il-76TD ('Candid-A'). Approximately 950 of all types have been built, and the Il-76M/MD remain highly-important long-range transports in the current Russian air force inventory. Recent procurement plans have included the re-designed Il-76MF, with a lengthened fuselage and more powerful Aviadvigatel PS-90AN turbofan engines. Budgetary restraints have, however, considerably delayed this program. The basic Il-76 has been exported to several countries including China and India, but not in large quantities, and a number of civil-operated examples have existed including some operated by Syrianair and some by Cubana in Cuba. The recently-independ-

The Ilyushin Il-76 is a big, powerful cargo transport aircraft, that has been very successful in service for the Russian military and Aeroflot in addition to foreign operators.

Aeroflot is Russia's State airline, and this Ilyushin Il-76TD is wearing full Aeroflot colors – although some military-operated examples also carry civil Aeroflot titles. It was photographed at Moscow's Sheremetyevo Airport in the summer of 2001 (Photo: Malcolm V. Lowe).

ent Ukraine flies many military ex-Soviet examples. The United Nations has also employed a number of Russian-operated Il-76s. There have additionally been several special versions of the Il-76, for diverse roles such as fire-fighting as a water-bomber, airborne command post, and Cosmonaut trainer. However, many unfinished Il-76 remain at the production factory in Uzbekistan where all but the initial prototypes were built. A separate but related derivative is the Il-78/Il-78M flight refuelling tanker aircraft known to NATO as 'Midas' with three 'probe and drogue' refuelling pods, used by Russia and recently ordered by India. The A-50 'Mainstay' airborne warning and control system (AWACS) aircraft was developed by the Russian company Beriev using the Il-76 as a basis but with a large radar-equipped rotodome fitted above the fuselage. With a fifteen-man crew, the A-50 entered service in 1984 and is currently a very important type in the Russian inventory.

Specifications – Ilyushin Il-76MD

Wingspan	165 ft 8 in
Length	152 ft 10.25 in
Maximum speed	528 mph at 16,405 ft
Maximum take-off weight	418,874 lb
Range	4,536 miles plus
Service ceiling	approximately 50,853 ft
Armament	Two 0.9 in (23 mm) cannons rearward-firing in tail turret (not fitted to many examples)
Engine	Four Aviadvigatel D-30KP or KP-2 turbofan engines, of 26,455 lb st each
Crew	Seven crew, up to 225 troops or 126 paratroops (or various vehicles)

Boeing H-47 Chinook

The CH-47 Chinook is the standard heavy-lift helicopter of several countries, its distinctive layout and sound making it one of the most recognisable of helicopters. It started life as the Vertol Model 114, a larger development of the existing production Model 107, five prototypes for the U.S. Army being ordered as YCH-1Bs. First flying on 21 September 1961, the YCH-1Bs became YCH-47As in 1962. From 1961 350 CH-47As were delivered, powered by 2,200 shp T55-L-5 or –7 engines. Examples of the CH-47A were sent to South Vietnam and Thailand, while four were modified as ACH-47A gunships for use by American forces in the Vietnam War, where the basic cargo-hauling Chinook soon became a common sight. In October 1966 the YCH-47B made its maiden flight powered by 2,850 shp T55-L-7Cs with modified rotor blades and upgraded avionics. The U.S Army acquired 108 as CH-47Bs. Strengthened rotor components, 3,750 shp T55-L-11C powerplants and more fuel were features of the CH-47C. It was capable of lifting a load equal to the CH-47A's maximum take-off weight of 46,000 lb (20,866 kg). While Boeing delivered 270 to the U.S. Army it also acquired a further 11 built under licence in Italy and originally destined for Iran. CH-47Cs were later built in Italy for Egypt, Greece, Iran, Italy, Libya and Morocco, while Boeing sold examples to Argentina, Australia, Canada, Iran, Spain, and Britain, where they are known as Chinook HC.Mk.1s. Small numbers of the civil Boeing 234 were also produced for specialist commercial operators. In May 1979 the first CH-47D made its maiden flight. The U.S. Army put its surviving Chinook airframes through an upgrade that replaced existing engines with T5-L-712 turboshafts, added fibreglass rotor blades and other

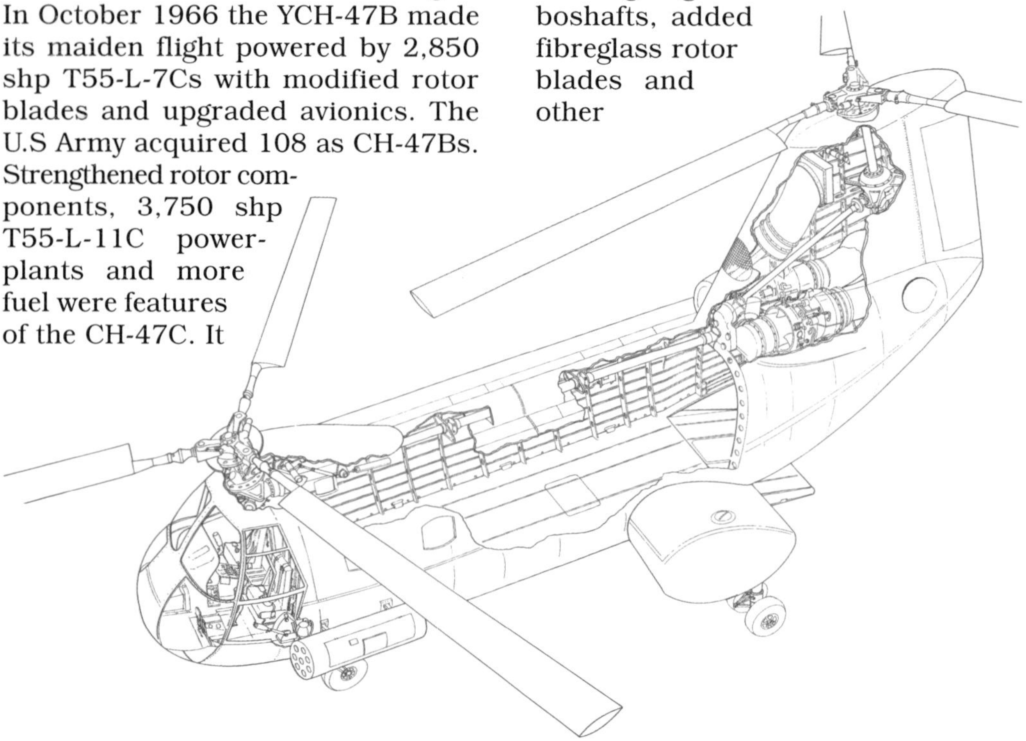

Often wrongly identified as a Chinook, the Boeing-Vertol H-46 Sea Knight illustrated here is similar in overall configuration, but is smaller and significantly different in many respects. Like the Chinook, it serves in important numbers with the U.S. military, specifically the U.S. Marine Corps.

improvements to reduce maintenance costs and increase reliability. Around 400 were created for the U.S. Army while others were produced for Australia, Greece, the Netherlands, South Korea, Spain, Thailand and Britain (as Chinook HC.Mk.2/2As). A licence-built version of the CH-47D was manufactured by Kawasaki in Japan as CH-47Js and CH-47JAs with larger saddle fuel tanks along the fuselage sides. Saddle tanks were a feature of the MH-47E special operations aircraft for the U.S. Army, developed from the MH-47D, and the R.A.F.'s Chinook HC.Mk.3. The latest versions of the Chinook are the CH-47F Improved Cargo Helicopter (and MH-47G special operations aircraft), around 300 of which are expected to be purchased by the U.S. Army to form the backbone of its heavy-lift capability until 2040. Since its debut in Vietnam, the Chinook has been involved in numerous conflicts across the world, including operations over Afghanistan, Iran, Iraq, the states of the former Yugoslavia and in the 1982 Falklands Islands conflict.

Specifications – Boeing CH-47D Chinook

Rotor diameter (each)	60 ft
Fuselage Length	51 ft
Maximum speed	185 mph at sea level
Maximum take-off weight	50,000 lb
Radius of action	348 miles
Service ceiling	22,100 ft
Armament	Usually none, although door-mounted machine guns sometimes carried
Engine	Two Avco (Textron) Lycoming T55-L-712 turboshaft engines, of 3,750 shp each
Crew	Two or three crew, up to 44 troops

Airbus Airliners

The fortunes of the European airliner industry have changed radically in the last 20 years. The catalyst for this change was the establishing of Airbus Industrie, a multi-national European organisation that is today a separate entity with shares held by the European aerospace giant EADS and by BAE Systems of Britain. Airbus has successfully established distinctive families of airliners that have successfully taken on the traditional dominance of the airliner market by American industry. Airbus Industrie was formed in December 1970 to produce the A300 'widebody' airliner. The type first flew in A300B1 form on 28 October 1972. This initial model was soon replaced by the B2 and, in 1974, by the A300B4. These were superseded by the A300-600. Production of the A300 continued in early 2005, by which point over 535 had been delivered, recently mostly as –600F freighters. A shorter version – the A310 – first flew on 3 April 1982 with 255 produced when production was suspended in 1998. To compete with the Boeing 737 and later DC-9 variants, Airbus launched the A320 in 1981, incorporating an advanced fly-by-wire control system. British Caledonian Airways of Britain placed the first order in 1984, the prototype making its maiden flight on 22 February 1984. Only 21 130/140-seat A320-100s were manufactured before production concentrated on the 150/160-seat A320-200. The A320 has proven to be remarkably popular, with over 1,765 ordered by October 2004. A lengthened version entered production at Hamburg, Germany, as the A321-100 and – with an increased take-off weight – the A321-200. On 25 August 1995 the A319 first flew. It is a shorter version of the A320 for 148 passengers, while the even shorter A318 seats up to 100. Orders for the A318, A319 and A321 stood at 82, 994 and 415 respectively by October 2004. Development of a pair of long-range airliners – the two-engine A330 and four-engine A340 – started with

One of the important customers of Airbus Industrie over the years has been the national airline of Greece, Olympic Airways. It is one of many European airlines that flies Airbus airliners.

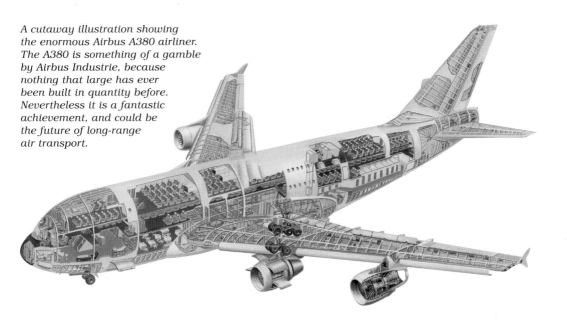

A cutaway illustration showing the enormous Airbus A380 airliner. The A380 is something of a gamble by Airbus Industrie, because nothing that large has ever been built in quantity before. Nevertheless it is a fantastic achievement, and could be the future of long-range air transport.

the launch of the latter in June 1987. Two versions were offered, the 375-seat A340-300 and 263-seat A340–200. These were later followed by the longer 313-seat A340-500 and 380-seat –600. First flying on 25 October 1991, a total of 352 A340s had been ordered by October 2004, compared to 478 A330s. The A330 is offered in –200 and –300 versions, the first being a long-range variant with a shorter fuselage. An updated A330

was launched as the A350 in late-2004. In December 2000 Airbus began a new era in civil transport with the launch of the 550-seat Airbus A380-800, and the related A380–800 Freighter. Rolled out in January 2005, the A380 will be the second largest aircraft in the world at the time of its first flight (after the Antonov An-225 – see pages 282 to 283), with a length of 238 ft 6 in (72.7 m) and a wingspan of 261 ft 10 in (79.8 m).

Specifications – Airbus A320-200

Wingspan	111 ft 3 in
Length	123 ft 3 in
Maximum speed	561 mph at 28,000 ft
Maximum take-off weight	169,765 lb with CFM56 engines
Range	3,222 miles with reserves and standard load
Service ceiling	40,000 ft
Engine	Two IAE V2525-A5 turbofan engines, of 25,000 lb st each, or two CFM International CFM56-5B4 turbofan engines, of 26,500 lb st each
Accommodation	Two crew plus stewards/stewardesses, maximum of 180 passengers, although standard layout is usually for 150

Fairchild A-10 Thunderbolt II

The A-10A Thunderbolt II is one of the relatively few aircraft designed from the outset for close air support to the troops on the battlefield. Specially armoured to survive hits from ground-fired small arms, the A-10 emerged from an 'A-X' close-support requirement drawn up using experience gained during the Vietnam War. Both Fairchild and Northrop built two prototypes, comprising the YA-10A and YA-9A respectively for a competitive fly-off, the YA-10A first flying on 5 April 1972. It was declared the winner of the A-X requirement in January 1973. Six pre-production aircraft were followed by 707 production examples, all for the U.S. Air Force. Primary armament consisted of the huge GAU-8/A Avenger nose-mounted cannon, firing depleted uranium shells capable of penetrating the armour of a main battle tank (MBT). Although a large range of ordnance could be carried, it was the AGM-65 Maverick air-to-surface guided missile that supplanted the Avenger as the aircraft's primary weapon as it allowed the A-10 a greater and therefore safer 'stand-off' range from its targets. The A-10A entered service in March 1976, subsequent-

ly re-equipping U.S.A.F. operational units in the Continental United States, Pacific and Europe. In service, questions were raised about the aircraft's survivability, and plans were drawn up to replace it with General Dynamics F-16s configured for the ground attack role. Surplus A-10As were reconfigured for the forward air control fire-spotting role as OA-10As, but the only difference between the two variants was that the OA-10As were armed with rocket pods to mark targets and carried AIM-9 Sidewinder air-to-air missiles for self defence. The effectiveness of the A-10A was at last demonstrated during Operation 'Desert Storm' over Iraq in 1991, two A-10 pilots destroying a record 23 tanks by themselves on 25 February while another A-10 had shot down a helicopter ten days earlier. Three A-10s were lost during the war, but the A-10 community emerged with a renewed sense of respect. Plans to

The Fairchild A-10A Thunderbolt II can be armed with an impressive array of weaponry in addition to its nose-mounted cannon, and is a very useful close-support aircraft over the battlefield.

The Fairchild A-10A is armed with one of the most powerful and destructive guns ever mounted in an aircraft, the nose-mounted GAU-8/A Avenger rotary cannon. The A-10A is very effective at attacking tanks with this weapon, but can use it against any targets that present themselves (Photo: Fairchild Republic).

retire the type were postponed and several upgrades were put into effect. A-10As have since flown combat missions over Yugoslavia, Afghanistan and again over Iraq in 2003. On 20 January 2005 the A-10C made its maiden flight. The C model is an A-10A with a precision engagement capability to allow it to carry up to six guided missiles. The improvements are expected to be implemented amongst the surviving A-10 fleet, although further plans to re-engine the aircraft have come to nothing.

Sometimes called the 'Warthog,' the A-10A Thunderbolt II has its two engines mounted high up and shielded by its big wing to avoid their being hit by small arms fire or heat-seeking missiles fired from the ground.

Specifications – Fairchild A-10A Thunderbolt II

Wingspan	57 ft 6 in
Length	53 ft 4 in
Maximum speed	439 mph clean at sea level
Maximum take-off weight	50,000 lb
Radius of action	290 miles including additional loiter time over target
Service ceiling	34,700 ft
Armament	One 1.18 in (30 mm) nose-mounted seven-barrel cannon, up to 16,000 lb of weapons on 11 pylons (three under the fuselage, eight under the wings), including AGM-65 Maverick air-to-surface guided missiles
Engine	Two General Electric TF34-GE-100 turbofan engines, of 9,065 lb each
Crew	One

BAE Systems (BAe/Hawker Siddeley) Hawk

When the SEPECAT Jaguar (see pages 250 to 251) became too complicated for one of its intended roles, that of advanced training, Britain's R.A.F. wrote a requirement for a completely new trainer. The result was a low-wing single-engined trainer design by Hawker Siddeley called the HS.1182, with a stepped tandem-seating cockpit. Named Hawk, the initial example (no prototype as such was built) first flew on 21 August 1974. The R.A.F. took delivery of 175 as Hawk T.Mk.1s, the type entering service in April 1976 when the first examples arrived at R.A.F. Valley for use by No.4 Flying Training School. Although Valley continues to be the base for the majority of the R.A.F.'s Hawks today, in the 1980s a pair of Tactical Weapons Units also used Hawks before they disbanded. A total of 88 R.A.F. Hawks were upgraded as T.Mk.1As able to carry a pair of Sidewinder short-range air-to-air missiles as limited air defence aircraft.

R.A.F. Hawks have also been subject to a fuselage replacement program or/and wing replacement program. The most famous operator of the Hawk is the R.A.F.'s aerobatic display team the 'Red Arrows,' whose precision aerobatics have been watched in many countries, helping to promote both the R.A.F. and the aircraft itself. Indeed, the Hawk is one of the best selling British military jet aircraft. The first export customer was Finland in 1977, initially ordering 50 Mk.51s of which Valmet assembled 46 in Finland. Series 50 Hawks were also purchased by Kenya and Indonesia before the Series 60 was introduced. It featured an uprated Adour engine, together with various other revisions. Sales were made to Rhodesia (now Zimbabwe), Dubai, Abu Dhabi, Kuwait, Saudi Arabia, Switzerland and South Korea. The Hawk 100 Series was developed as a dual-role weapons system trainer and ground attack aircraft

The BAe Hawk is world-famous for its aerobatic displays with the R.A.F.'s Red Arrows' display team.

with a longer wingspan, elongated nose and advanced avionics. Sales were made to Abu Dhabi, Oman, Malaysia, Saudi Arabia, Indonesia and the NATO Flying Training establishment in Canada. A single-seat light fighter version with an APG-66 radar was also built as the Series 200, sales being made to some existing Hawk operators. The most recent purchases have been for the Lead-In Fighter version of the Series 100, a two-seater with advanced avionics similar to those of front-line combat aircraft. By early 2005 they were flown by Australia and South Africa had also ordered the type, with Bahrain and India due to receive them in the near future. In addition, the R.A.F. ordered a batch of 'glass cockpit' Hawks in 2004 with advanced cockpit displays to supplement its existing Mk.1s. The Hawk Series 60 also forms the basis of the Boeing (McDonnell Douglas) T-45 Goshawk trainer for the U.S. Navy, with a stronger undercarriage for aircraft carrier deck landing practice amongst other differences. Production of the T-45A was superseded by the 'glass cockpit' equipped T-45C. By mid-2004 over 900 Hawks were in service or on order with 19 customers.

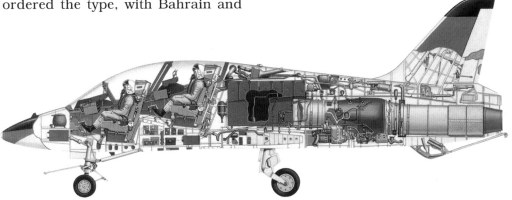

A cutaway drawing of the fuselage of a T-45A Goshawk trainer of the U.S. Navy.
Note in particular the tandem seating arrangement for the two crew members, with the flying instructor seated in the rear seat. Also visible is the arrester hook beneath the rear fuselage for landings aboard aircraft carriers.

Specifications – BAe (Hawker Siddeley) Hawk T.Mk.1

Wingspan	30 ft 9.75 in
Length	36 ft 7.75 in
Maximum speed	645 mph at 11,000 ft
Maximum take-off weight	12,566 lb
Range	1,509 miles
Service ceiling	50,000 ft
Armament	Up to 1,500 lb of weapons on two underwing pylons in R.A.F. service, although 6,800 lb is theoretically possible
Engine	One Rolls-Royce/Turboméca Adour Mk.151-01 turbofan engine, of 5,200 lb st
Crew	Two

Lockheed Martin (General Dynamics) F-16 Fighting Falcon

The F-16 Fighting Falcon is the most widely used post-World War Two jet-powered combat aircraft from the Western World. Initially designed as a Light Weight Fighter (LWF) for America's allies, the aircraft was later selected by the U.S. Air Force to supplement the McDonnell Douglas F-15 Eagle (see pages 252 to 253). The General Dynamics YF-16A prototype first flew on 20 January 1974, beating the competing Northrop YF-17A in the subsequent LWF competition. With its spectacular manoeuvrability derived from its fly-by-wire control system and side-stick control for the pilot (instead of a conventional centrally-mounted control column), the F-16 was selected to re-equip the Belgian, Danish, Dutch and Norwegian air forces in mid-1975, subsequent production being undertaken

in Europe. Many of these were later upgraded. Other F-16A and two-seat F-16Bs were purchased by Egypt, Indonesia, Israel, Jordan, Pakistan, Portugal, Singapore, Taiwan, Thailand and Venezuela. While designed as a fighter, the majority of F-16A/Bs serve in the fighter-bomber role, although some have been converted as interceptors for the second-line U.S. Air National Guard. The later F-16C has improved avionics including a more advanced radar, and first flew in June 1984. From the Block 30 production run, a specially-configured engine bay was offered, able to accommodate either the General Electric F110-GE-100 (Block 30/40/50) or Pratt & Whitney F100-PW-220 (Block 32/42/52) turbofan engine. A version of the Block 30 known as the F-16N and TF-16N was supplied to the U.S. Navy as an 'aggressor' trainer for special air combat training. F-16C/D Block 40/42s intro-

The Lockheed Martin (formerly General Dynamics) F-16 can carry a formidable array of weaponry, in addition to being a very agile fighter and fighter-bomber.

duced a night attack capability using the purpose-designed night-capable LANTIRN detachable equipment pod, while the Block 50/52 had further avionics improvements. Around 100 U.S. Air Force F-16C/D Block 50/52s were modified to give them a defence suppression role against enemy radars. Export customers for the F-16C/D include Bahrain, Greece and Israel, while TAI of Turkey built examples for its own and Egypt's air force. Samsung Aerospace built them for South Korean service. Further development resulted in the F-16I for Israel with conformal fuel tanks, while Advanced Block 50 and 60 variants are still being marketed. In 2005 Poland and Oman were due to receive F-16s. Israel first took the F-16 into combat, newly delivered F-16As successfully attacking the Iraqi nuclear reactor in June 1981. Pakistani F-16s claimed some victories during the Soviet intervention in Afghanistan. Although hundreds of its F-16s participated in the 1991 Gulf War, it was only in December 1992 that a U.S. Air Force F-16 scored an air-to-air victo-

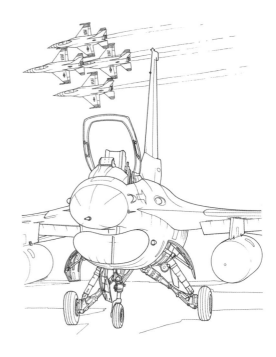

Showing its agility, the F-16 has been the mount of the world-famous 'Thunderbirds' aerobatic display team of the U.S. Air Force for a number of years.

ry, claiming an Iraqi MiG-25. Further enemy aircraft were downed during operations over the former Yugoslavia.

Specifications – Lockheed Martin F-16C Block 50 Fighting Falcon

Wingspan	32 ft 9.75 in (including wing-tip missiles)
Length	49 ft 4 in
Maximum speed	1,432 mph at 40,000 ft
Maximum take-off weight	42,300 lb
Radius of action	over 340 miles as fighter-bomber
Service ceiling	50,000 ft plus
Armament	One 0.787 in (20 mm) cannon in right-hand fuselage, up to 15,200 lb of weapons including AIM-9 Sidewinder and AIM-120 AMRAAM air-to-air missiles, AGM-88 HARM anti-radar missiles, laser-guided or unguided bombs
Engine	One General Electric F110-GE-129 turbofan engine, of some 29,000 lb st with afterburning
Crew	One

Rockwell B-1 Lancer

The cancellation of the North American B-70 Valkyrie program (see pages 194 to 195) left the U.S. Air Force with the Boeing B-52 Stratofortress as its main long-range bomber for many years longer than originally anticipated. The end of the XB-70 Mach 3 bomber plan resulted in a requirement being drawn up instead for an Advanced Manned Strategic Aircraft. North American Rockwell (later Rockwell International, now a part of Boeing) devised a Mach 2.3 variable-geometry swing-wing aircraft with an internal bomb bay and four General Electric F101 turbofan engines, with an extensive electronic warfare system to cope with the increasingly difficult task of penetrating Soviet airspace at medium-level to deliver thermonu-

clear weapons on selected targets. Four were ordered as B-1A prototype/development aircraft, the first flying on 23 December 1974. Difficulties perfecting the type's electronic systems, the great costs involved and the promise of a stealthy Advanced Technology Bomber (ATB) – that finally crystallised as the B-2 Spirit (see pages 296 to 297) – resulted in American President Carter cancelling the B-1 program in 1977. This would have been the end of the B-1 had not Ronald Reagan been elected President in 1979. He re-opened the program in 1981 with an order for 100 improved B-1B Lancers. The B-1B used the same engines as before but with fixed air inlet geometry, reducing complexity but limiting top speed to just above Mach 1.25. Some effort was also made to reduce the radar cross section of the B-1B, although it was in no way a 'stealth' bomber design. The first production example flew on 18 October 1984 and

The Rockwell B-1B uses variable-geometry swing-wings to give it good low-speed characteristics plus a fast low-level 'dash' speed en route to its target, although many missions are nowadays flown at higher altitudes. A direct Russian equivalent is the swing-wing Tupolev Tu-160 bomber.

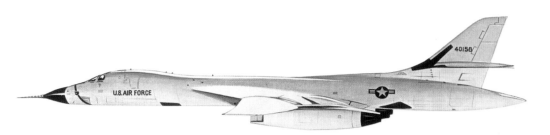

This gleaming, clean B-1 serial number 74-158 is actually the first of the four original B-1A aircraft, which in effect acted as prototypes for the B-1 program and were firstly known as YB-1A aircraft.

the U.S.A.F.'s Strategic Air Command achieved its initial operating capability in mid-1986. The first half of the B-1B's service career was spent perfecting the type's troublesome electronic 'black boxes' – at one point it was commonly referred to as the 'self-jamming bomber' – and the fleet was frequently grounded and often surrounded by controversy. While the B-52 Stratofortress (see pages 176 to 177) could carry conventional weapons, the B-1B was used solely for nuclear deterrence during the last years of the Cold War and into the post-Cold War world. A multi-stage conventional mission/munitions upgrade program (CMUP) was then initiated, and this allowed the B-1B to take part in combat missions over Iraq in 1998, the Balkans, Afghanistan and Operation 'Iraqi Freedom.' However, the planned retirement of 32 of the fleet in order to pay for upgrades to the 60 survivors did not save a defensive systems upgrade program from being cancelled in 2002. Nevertheless, impressive results gained from recent operations over Afghanistan and Iraq have demonstrated that the B-1B has a useful future as a 'bomb truck.' Indeed, the B-1B will operate alongside the B-52H and B-2A in the U.S.A.F. Air Combat Command's long-range strike force for some time to come.

Specifications – Rockwell B-1B Lancer

Wingspan	136 ft 8.5 in (wings un-swept)
Length	147 ft
Maximum speed	823 mph at 8,000 ft
Maximum take-off weight	477,000 lb
Range	7,455 miles
Service ceiling	50,000 ft plus
Armament	Up to 75,000 lb of conventional or nuclear munitions carried internally, plus a further 59,000 lb of conventional weapons carried externally
Engine	Four General Electric F101-GE-102 turbofan engines, of 30,780 lb st each with afterburning
Crew	Four

Dassault Mirage 2000

The Dassault Mirage III family of delta-wing fighters and attack aircraft was highly successful, as shown on pages 182 to 183. However, some disadvantages of the delta wing configuration can be a lack of manoeuvrability coupled with high landing speeds and the need for long runways. This is why some of the re-built and developed versions of the Mirage III family, such as the Atlas/Denel Cheetah and the IAI Kfir, attempted to address these problems with the addition of small canard foreplanes on their air intake side walls to give more lift and better control. Dassault was aware of these difficulties, but the eventual development of 'fly-by-wire' advanced control systems, and the introduction of computerisation to allow otherwise unstable aircraft to fly with ease, gave a potential new lease of life to the delta wing formula. In 1975 Dassault was successful in having a new generation delta-wing Mirage design, employing these new technologies, selected as France's next generation fighter. The first of five prototypes of the new Mirage 2000 flew on 10 March 1978. Successful testing led to the first production version for the French air force, the Mirage 2000C, the first of which flew on 20 November 1982.

Deliveries to the French air force began the following year, with full operational capability reached in 1984, and 124 Mirage 2000C were built for French service. From the 38th aircraft the definitive engine mark and sophisticated radar were introduced. A slightly-lengthened Mirage 2000B two-seat operational and conversion trainer series was also built. Continuing development has led to a second generation version, the single-seat Mirage 2000-5, which first flew in October 1990. This has upgraded radar, better cockpit displays for the pilot, and other more advanced features. Further improvement has created increased upgrades as the Mirage 2000s basic capabilities as a multi-role fighter are further exploited. There has also been considerable export success for the Mirage 2000, the first export customer being Egypt in early 1982. Since then Greece, India, Peru, Qatar, Taiwan, and Abu Dhabi have also signed for the Mirage 2000, each customer having slightly different standards with the latter's aircraft probably the most sophisti-

A drawing of an early development Mirage 2000 with four dummy (orange-colored) missiles beneath its wings. The Mirage 2000 has an excellent weapons-carrying capability, primarily for air-to-air missions but additionally for air-to-ground combat.

A French air force (Armée de l'Air) Mirage 2000C shows off its weapons-carrying capabilities.
It has two Matra Magic 2 guided short-range air-to-air missiles near its wing-tips, and two
large Matra Armat long-range air-to-surface anti-radar missiles (Photo: SIRPA-Air/Matra).

cated. Some of these export aircraft have subsequently been upgraded, and the Mirage 2000 remains available for sale to other buyers. A separate line of development has led to a very different career for the Mirage 2000. In 1979 Dassault was successful in tendering for a replacement for the large Dassault Mirage IV delta nuclear bomber, resulting in the Mirage 2000P. Later called 2000N (for nuclear bomber), this model is a two-seat version with a strengthened airframe for high-subsonic low-level penetration attack with terrain-following radar and related sophisticated targeting avionics. A conventionally-armed bomber model was also developed as the Mirage 2000D. Both the 2000N and the 2000D were designed for French service, but the latter has also been exported to Abu Dhabi. So far, 614 Mirage 2000 of all types including prototypes have been built or ordered.

Specifications – Dassault Mirage 2000C (late production)

Wingspan	29 ft 11.5 in
Length	47 ft 1.5 in
Maximum speed	Mach 2.2 at 36,000 ft
Maximum take-off weight	37,478 lb
Range	1,151 miles
Service ceiling	54,003 ft
Armament	Two 1.18 in (30 mm) cannons in lower forward fuselage, up to 13,669 lb of external munitions including two medium-range and two short-range guided air-to-air missiles
Engine	One SNECMA M53-P2 turbofan engine, of 21,385 lb st with afterburning
Crew	One

Boeing E-3 Sentry

Development of an Overland Downlook Radar (ODR) allowed the U.S. Air Force to replace its ageing fleet of Lockheed EC-121 Constellation early warning and control aircraft with a system that was able to detect enemy aircraft at longer ranges, over land and sea. Mounted in a saucer rotodome above a Boeing 707-320 airframe, the Westinghouse AN/APY-1 (later –2) ODR was mated with an extensive array of other electrical systems to produce the Boeing E-3 Airborne Warning and Control System (AWACS). The first of two EC-137D prototypes made its maiden flight on 5 February 1972, and they were followed by 32 production E-3As. Full-scale development of the AWACS system was completed in 1976, with deliveries commencing to the 552nd AC&CW at Tinker AFB, Oklahoma, in March 1977. They assumed the U.S. Continental air defence role in January 1978. Since then E-3s have supported nearly every campaign American forces have been involved in, providing early warning to friendly fighters as well as managing the whole air battle scenario. Improved electronics were incorporated in 24 E-3As (including the EC-137Ds) to produce E-3Bs, the first being re-delivered in July 1984. Five additional electronic consoles for a slightly larger crew were added to ten E-3As as E-3Cs. Using funds from the majority of the NATO countries, a total of 18 E-3As were purchased and operated in a multi-national force as the NATO Airborne Early Warning Force, based in Germany. Saudi Arabia ordered five E-3As plus eight KE-3A tankers without the rotodome or electronic systems, one of the latter becoming the sole RE-3A. The British government decided to upgrade its own AEW force using surplus Nimrod maritime patrol aircraft, but when the Nimrod AEW.Mk.3 program ran into huge problems and was cancelled, it opted to order seven E-3D Sentry AEW.Mk.1s instead. They are based at R.A.F. Waddington, Lincolnshire, with Nos.7 and 23 Squadrons, Royal Air Force, and have several differences from other E-3 variants, including a flight refuelling probe and CFM56-2A-3 turbofans in place of the usual TF33s. The CFM56 was also used by the Saudi aircraft and four E-3Fs purchased for

The Boeing E-3 Sentry AWACS aircraft are derived from the Boeing Model 707 airliner series and their military derivatives. This is a NATO-operated example (Photo: EADS).

A Boeing E-3D Sentry of the Royal Air Force, which operates seven of these aircraft as Sentry AEW.Mk.1 aircraft.

the French air force. In service, E-3s have continued to be upgraded. One U.S. Air Force E-3C was loaned to Boeing as the JE-3C to develop the AN/AYR-1 electronic support measures system located in canoe-like blisters on the front fuselage. The AN/AYR-1 has since been integrated on both U.S. and NATO E-3s. As production of the basic Boeing Model 707 (see pages 132 to 133) wound down with the last R.A.F. E-3D, Boeing designated the Boeing 767 airliner airframe as its future AWACS platform. Examples have since been sold to Japan as the E-767, and the U.S. replacement for its E-3s is expected to be the 767-based E-10A.

Specifications – Boeing E-3A Sentry

Wingspan	145 ft 9 in
Length	152 ft 11 in
Maximum speed	530 mph at 29,000 ft
Maximum take-off weight	325,000 lb
Endurance	over 11 hours
Service ceiling	40,100 ft
Armament	None usually, although some aircraft had provision for one underwing pylon on each wing capable of carrying an AIM-9 Sidewinder air-to-air missile for protection
Engine	Four Pratt & Whitney TF33-P-100/100A turbofan engines, of 21,000 lb st each
Crew	Four flight crew, 13 or more mission specialists

Mikoyan-Gurevich MiG-29

The past three or so decades have seen many changes. These not only include developments in warplane design and technology, but also in the world in general. In particular, the ending of the arms race of the Cold War has left some of the warplanes of the Cold War era struggling to find a new role. One of the aircraft types that has found the transition to be difficult from the Cold War period into the present-day situation of much greater co-operation between East and West, is the Mikoyan-Gurevich MiG-29. Indeed, the MiG-29's creator, the famous Mikoyan-Gurevich design bureau, has itself gone through many changes due to the altering and scaled-down priorities of the Russian military, and is today a very much smaller organisation compared to Russia's premier warplane designer, Sukhoi. The MiG-29 was originally created in response to a 1971 Soviet operational requirement for a tactical

fighter to eventually replace the MiG-21, MiG-23, Sukhoi Su-15, and Su-17 (some of these types were only themselves then being developed or entering production). Long-running design work on the new type resulted in the first aircraft flying on 6 October 1977. It was given the NATO reporting name 'Ram-L,' later 'Fulcrum.' Major design changes were needed, and these resulted in State trials not being concluded until the early 1980s. The production of the initial MiG-29 9.12 ('Fulcrum-A') did not commence until 1982, and the first deliveries were made to the Soviet air force in 1983. The MiG-29 is basically a multi-role fighter, able to perform air-to-air missions with its radar and infra-red tracking device to detect airborne targets, but also tasked with air-to-ground attack as well when required. The type additionally had a tactical nuclear weapon-carrying role in the early stages of its service. A number

A Mikoyan-Gurevich MiG-29 in flight. Although a capable fighter, it has not made a particularly successful impact in the conflicts that it has been involved in so far.

The MiG-29 caused quite a stir and generated a lot of interest when it started to be shown off in the West in the closing stages of the Cold War. This example was photographed at the 1992 Farnborough international aviation trade show in England (Photo: Malcolm V. Lowe).

of versions were subsequently developed, including the two-seat MiG-29UB ('Fulcrum-B') operational and conversion trainer, and various upgraded marks and specific export versions. The type has been exported comparatively widely, with important overseas operators including Cuba, India, Malaysia, and the Ukraine. However, the end of the Cold War hit the MiG-29 program hard, and several projected developments including a navalised derivative were scaled-down due to defence budget cuts. In addition, MiG-29s have not fared particularly well in combat. Serbian-operated aircraft were not successful against U.S. fighters over the former Yugoslavia during the 1990s, and Eritrean-operated examples were shot down by Ethiopian Sukhoi Su-27s in the conflict between those two countries in 1998/1999. The exact number of MiG-29s built is open to conjecture, but 840 of the early production models were thought to have been built by 1991, and 1,257 by 1997. Today the MiG organisation itself is a shadow of its former self, and development of the MiG-29 has all but ended.

Specifications – Mikoyan-Gurevich MiG-29 (early production)

Wingspan	37 ft 3.25 in
Length	56 ft 10 in (including nose probe)
Maximum speed	Mach 2.3 at 36,090 ft
Maximum take-off weight	40,785 lb
Range	932 miles
Service ceiling	55,774 ft
Armament	One 1.18 in (30 mm) cannon in left-hand wing root, six guided air-to-air missiles, various combinations of air-to-air missiles and air-to-ground weapons including bombs and unguided rockets up to 4,850 lb
Engine	Two Klimov RD-33 turbofan engines, of up to 18,298 lb st each with afterburning
Crew	One

Sikorsky S-70 Black Hawk/Seahawk

Developed for the U.S. Army's Utility Tactical Transport Aircraft System as a replacement for the Bell UH-1 Huey (see pages 180 to 181), the Sikorsky UH-60 defeated the Boeing UH-61 to become the U.S. Army's standard utility helicopter. The YUH-60A first flew on 17 October 1974, and the UH-60A entered service with the 101st Airborne Division in June 1979. As equipment was added to the helicopter its power margin diminished, so uprated T700-GE-701C turboshafts were added to produce the UH-60L. The UH-60L first flew in March 1988, superseding the A-model on the production line for the Army. Continued development produced the UH-60M with improved structure, powerplant, dynamic components and avionics. While the initial plan was to remanufacture 1,217 existing Black Hawks and acquire 300 new examples, the Army was considering an all-new construction program by early 2005. In addition to the utility Black Hawks, the

U.S. Army has acquired several special operations versions. The EH-60A carries the 'Quick Fix' target location system, while aeromedical variants are known as UH-60Qs and HH-60Ls. The U.S. Air Force operates HH-60G and MH-60G 'Pave Hawks,' the majority for the combat rescue role. The S-70A Black Hawk has been widely exported, with examples having been built in Australia (S-70A-9), Japan (UH-60J) and South Korea (UH-60P). Countries operating them include Austria, Bahrain, Brunei, Columbia, Egypt, Hong Kong, Israel, Mexico, Morocco, Saudi Arabia and Turkey. As part of the Light Airborne Multi-Purpose System III (LAMPS III) Sikorsky adopted the Black Hawk as the S-70B for 'over-the-horizon' search and strike role in the maritime environment. Designed to operate from frigates and destroyers, the first YSH-60B Seahawk flew on 12 December 1979 and was followed by the first production example in February 1983. A version without the LAMPS III system to operate from aircraft carriers was built as the SH-60F Ocean Hawk. Carrier air wings also include HH-60H Rescue Hawks, while a SAR version for the Coast Guard was produced as the HH-60J Jayhawk.

Plans to

The Sikorsky Seahawk has folding main rotor blades and rear fuselage, so that it can be stowed when not in use in the confined space available aboard warships.

For a number of years Westland Helicopters in Britain had a connection with the Black Hawk, and the example shown here carrying a light combat vehicle actually wore a British military serial number,
but the type has not served operationally with the British armed services *(Photo: Westland Helicopters).*

rebuild the U.S. Navy's Seahawk and Ocean Hawk fleets into a single SH-60R standard were replaced by a program to build new MH-60Rs. Vertical replenishment of ships at sea is undertaken by the MH-60S Knight Hawk, while the type is also due to take on the mine countermeasures role from the existing Sikorsky MH-53E Sea Dragon. Naval exports include examples to Australia, Greece and Spain, while Mitsubishi built SH-60Js for Japan. The U.S. Marine Corps also uses a version of the H-60 family – the VH-60N – tasked with Presidential and VIP transport. Civil versions of the H-60 are generally known as S-70Cs. S-70s used in the fire suppression firefighting role are called Fire Hawks.

Specifications – Sikorsky UH-60A Black Hawk

Main Rotor Diameter	53 ft 8 in
Fuselage Length	50 ft 0.75 in
Maximum speed	167 mph at 4,000 ft
Maximum take-off weight	20,250 lb
Range	345 miles
Service ceiling	19,000 ft
Armament	None usually, but door-mounted machine guns can be carried
Engine	Two General Electric T700-GE-700 turboshaft engines, of 1,560 shp each
Crew	Three crew, up to 11 troops

Antonov An-225

If you have ever wondered what is the largest aircraft in the world at the moment, then here is the answer. It is the huge, impressive Antonov An-225 from the Ukraine. This enormous six-engined aircraft can carry massive loads within its huge fuselage, but it is also configured to carry large external loads on top of its upper fuselage. The Ukrainian Antonov company has a long and well-established tradition of producing transport and cargo-carrying aircraft. The Antonov An-24/An-26 series of transports (see pages 174 to 175) has had a long and significant history, but the company has also designed a variety of other transport and cargo aircraft including some very large turboprop and jet-powered aircraft. One of the latter is the An-124 Ruslan, which first flew in December 1982. Over fifty of these heavy-lift four jet-engined cargo aircraft have been built so far, and the general design layout and configuration of the An-124 provided the basis the An-225 when Antonov was tasked to produce an even larger heavy-lift aircraft. That was in the days of the former Soviet Union, and the motivation for the creation of the An-225 came from the need to carry from one location to another some ultra-large outsize loads, including parts for rockets of Russia's Space program, and machinery for civil engineering projects. It had already become commonplace in the Soviet Union by the mid-1980s for very large components of space rockets to be carried in the air externally 'piggy-back' fashion. Originally used for the role of carrying such huge external loads above its fuselage was a specially-configured jet-powered Myasishchev VM-T Atlant (based on a bomber design), but a new aircraft to continue this difficult task was eventually required. Design work on what became the An-225 began in 1984/1985, and the first aircraft made its initial flight on 21 December 1988. This huge aircraft subsequently set no less than 106 records for weight and payload-carrying within specific classifications during a flight in March 1989. In May 1989 it flew for the first time with a Buran space shuttle vehicle (the Russian equivalent of the American Space Shuttle) above its fuselage.

Two photographs of the Antonov An-225 at an air show.
The aircraft can carry loads 'piggy-back' style on its upper fuselage in addition to its huge cargo hold within the fuselage (Photos: John Batchelor).

*With six powerful engines, seven sets of main wheels and a length of 275 ft 7 in (84 m),
the impressive Antonov An-225 is currently the world's largest aircraft. Only one example
exists at the moment.*

Unfortunately the Russian Space program ran into large financial difficulties after the end of the Cold War when its funding was cut back, and the Buran is no longer being developed. Nevertheless this has not ended the usefulness of the An-225, which has many other large loads to carry. In fact, the An-225 can transport loads up to 551,150 lb (250,000 kg) within its fuselage, loaded through the nose which opens upwards to accomplish this, and large loads on its back are carried on special external attachments. So far only one An-225 has been built, despite persistent reports that a second example is going to be completed. In fact the original aircraft was out of service for several years, but it is now fully airworthy again. It can operate world-wide to carry outsize cargoes, and is operated by the Antonov company itself. The NATO reporting name 'Cossack' was given to the An-225, which is also often called Mriya (Dream).

Specifications – Antonov An-225

Wingspan	290 ft 0.25 in
Length	275 ft 7 in
Cruising speed	at least 497 mph at 29,528 ft
Maximum take-off weight	approximately 1,322,760 lb
Range	2,485 miles with 440,920 lb cargo
Cruising altitude	29,528 ft
Engine	Six ZMKB Progress D-18T turbofan engines, of 51,590 lb st each
Crew	Six

Boeing (McDonnell Douglas) F/A-18 Hornet

While losing out to the General Dynamics F-16 (see pages 270 to 271) in the Lightweight Fighter competition, the Northrop YF-17A was used as a basis for the U.S. Navy's Air Combat Fighter program to replace its McDonnell Douglas F-4 Phantom IIs and LTV A-7 Corsair IIs (both covered elsewhere in this book) on its aircraft carriers. McDonnell Douglas took over the development of the aircraft as the F-18 Hornet, while Northrop remained in charge of a land-based export version – the F-18L. However, all exports were made by McDonnell Douglas, a source of friction between the partners for some years. The first YF-18A flew on 18 November 1978. Initially fighter (F-18) and attack (A-18) versions were planned, but both roles were combined into one airframe as the F/A-18. The two-seat TF-18A became the F/A-18B. When it entered service in 1983 the Hornet was seen as a quantum leap in capability over the aircraft it replaced. It was a true multi-role aircraft that could exceed in both of its primary missions. Production of the F/A-18A amounted to 371 aircraft for both the U.S. Navy and Marines. Export customers of first generation Hornets were Australia, Canada (CF-18) and Spain. With

an expanded weapons capability and an avionics upgrade, the F/A-18C replaced the A-model on the production line. Finland, Kuwait and Switzerland acquired F/A-18C models along with the U.S. Navy and Marine Corps. The Marines ordered a two-seat attack version of the Hornet as the F/A-18D to replace its Grumman A-6 Intruders, the majority of the aircraft being delivered with the capability to attack targets at night, a capability that was built into the F/A-18C from the 138th example. F/A-18Ds were exported to Malaysia. One of the criticisms levelled at the Hornet was its limited range and load-carrying capability. Work was undertaken on a larger variant and, after the A-12 Avenger II was cancelled, single-seat and two-seat versions were ordered as F/A-18E and F/A-18F Super Hornets for the U.S. Navy, powered by General Electric F414-GE-400 turbofans. The F/A-18E was destined to replace earlier Hornets and the Grumman F-14 Tomcat. Super Hornets first entered service with the U.S. Navy during 1999. A total of 222 Super Hornets are on

The Boeing (McDonnell Douglas) F/A-18 Hornet is a vitally important aircraft to the present-day U.S. Navy aviation elements. This example carries an AGM-84 Harpoon guided anti-ship missile beneath its right-hand wing.

Two photographs of F/A-18 Hornets aboard a U.S. Navy aircraft carrier (Photos: John Batchelor).

order, although the U.S. Navy wants over 500. A version of the F/A-18F for the electronic warfare role, the EA-18G, was under development in 2005 to replace the Grumman EA-6B Prowler. Hornets were first involved in combat operations when they used against targets in Libya in 1986. They were heavily utilised during Operation 'Desert Storm' over Iraq in 1991, the Balkans and Iraq in the 1990s, Afghanistan in 2001 and Iraq again during 2003.

Specifications – Boeing F/A-18C Hornet

Wingspan	40 ft 5 in (including wing-tip missiles)
Length	56 ft
Maximum speed	1,190 mph at 20,000 ft
Maximum take-off weight	56,000 lb
Radius of action	662 miles attack mission
Service ceiling	50,000 ft
Armament	One 0.787 in (20 mm) cannon, up to 15,500 lb of weapons, including air-to-air guided missiles, conventional unguided bombs, cluster bombs, AGM-84 Harpoon anti-ship missiles, tactical nuclear bombs, or AGM-88 HARM anti-radar missiles
Engine	Two General Electric F404-GE-402 turbofan engines, of 17,700 lb st each with afterburning
Crew	One

Sukhoi Su-27

The Cold War between East and West resulted in a continuing arms race in which the Soviet Union and the West countered each other's weapons developments with new projects of their own. In the late 1960s, design work began on a new air superiority fighter for the Soviet air force, partly to counter the American FX fighter requirement that led to the McDonnell Douglas F-15 Eagle (see pages 252 to 253). The result was one of the world's great contemporary fighters, the agile, very powerful and capable Sukhoi Su-27. Initial design studies firstly led to the T-10 prototype, which made its maiden flight on 20 May 1977. Concepts behind the new aircraft were good manoeuvrability, long range, and the ability to carry a wide range of weapons with advanced avionics. The development of this excellent aircraft took a considerable time, and it was not until 20 April 1981 that a production-like prototype took to the air. This aircraft was effectively the first of the original Su-27 first pre-production/production series, there also being a considerable number of prototype/development aircraft in addition to the prototypes themselves. The type was named 'Flanker' by NATO, the initial production aircraft being called 'Flanker-B.' Successful State trials resulted in the T-10 being placed into full production as the Su-27, and it was destined to become another of Sukhoi's successful front-line combat aircraft for the Russian armed forces. Initial operational status of the original single-seat Su-27 'Flanker-B' long-range interceptor/air superiority fighter was achieved in 1985. It is a formidable fighter, with very long range even without in-flight refuelling, increasingly sophisticated avionics and equipment for detecting and tracking enemy aircraft, and is able to carry up to ten air-to-air missiles. The aircraft's fly-by-wire control system and onboard computers give it excellent manoeuvrability. Two major production variants now operate with Russian air force units, the Su-27S and the Su-27P (the latter has special communications equipment to integrate with the Russian air defence network). The Su-27K (Su-33 'Flanker-D') is a naval fighter derivative for the Russian naval air arm. A two-seat trainer development of the Su-27, the Su-27UB ('Flanker-C') also exists. A considerable amount of additional development has resulted in a whole family

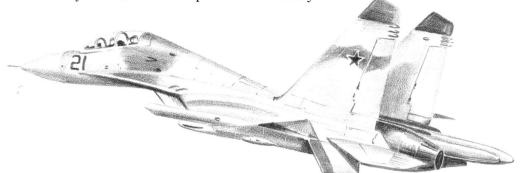

The Sukhoi Su-27 is a uniquely-powerful and capable fighter. It is famous for its 'Cobra' manoeuvre, in which it is literally stood still, vertically, at the top of a climb – useful for dogfighting, and impressing air show audiences.

The Sukhoi Su-27 is as good if not better than any fighters that the West has so far produced. One of its many advanced features is a helmet-mounted weapons sight for its pilot.

of related fighters, fighter-bombers, and long-range bomber/strike aircraft. Most of these are two-seat derivatives, including the Su-30 two-seat long-range fighter, and the two-seat Su-34/Su-32FN long-range bomber/strike aircraft. In addition, the Su-27 series and derivatives has gained export suc-cesses from such countries as Viet-nam, Malaysia, Ethiopia, India, the Ukraine, and Communist China, and the latter country has agreed terms to licence-build the Su-27. By late 1999, some 567 of all types were in service, and low-rate production continues in 2005.

Specifications – Sukhoi Su-27 (early production)

Wingspan	48 ft 2.75 in
Length	71 ft 11.75 in (excluding nose probe)
Maximum speed	Mach 2.35 at 36,090 ft
Maximum take-off weight	72,752 lb
Range	2,287 miles on internal fuel
Service ceiling	59,055 ft
Armament	One 1.18 in (30 mm) cannon in right-hand wing root, up to ten guided air-to-air missiles, or up to eight 1,102 lb bombs
Engine	Two Lyulka (Saturn) AL-31F turbofan engines, of 27,557 lb st each with afterburning
Crew	One

Rockwell STS Space Shuttle Orbiter

The Space Shuttle Orbiters were built as a part of America's Space Transportation System (STS) program, as reusable launch vehicles designed to reduce the cost of access to space and increase the frequency of launches. Having tested and rejected lifting bodies, America's National Aeronautics and Space Administration (NASA) decided to use a winged design with a 59 ft (17.98 m) long cargo bay behind the cockpit as its shuttle, covered in ceramic tiles to survive the intense heat of re-entry into the Earth's atmosphere. For launch the Orbiter is strapped to a large external fuel tank containing liquid oxygen and hydrogen with a pair of Thiokol solid-propellant rocket boosters (SRB) attached each side of the tank. The SRBs provide 1,300 tonnes of thrust during launch, that when added to the 168 tonnes of thrust produced by each of the three Space Shuttle Main Engines allow the Orbiter to achieve sufficient velocity to escape the Earth's atmosphere and enter space. The SRBs and external tank are jettisoned after launch and parachute into the sea to be recovered. The Orbiter

itself lands on a runway at the end of each mission. The first Orbiter was named 'Enterprise'; it was rolled out in September 1976 but was never sent into space. Instead, during 1977 it made the first flights carried aloft on top of a modified Boeing 747. Three captive flights were followed by five flights during which Enterprise was released to glide to a landing. The first of four test launches occurred on 12 April 1981 from Cape Canaveral, Florida, using the second Orbiter, 'Columbia,' commanded by John Young and flown by Robert Crippen. Retro-rockets were fired 53 hours 5 minutes after launch to begin a decent that ended with a successful landing at Edwards Air Force Base, California. On 12 November 1981 during flight number STS-2, commander Joe Engle and pilot Richard Truly took 'Columbia' into Space again, proving the viability of the reusable concept. 'Challenger' made its first flight on 4 April 1983, and

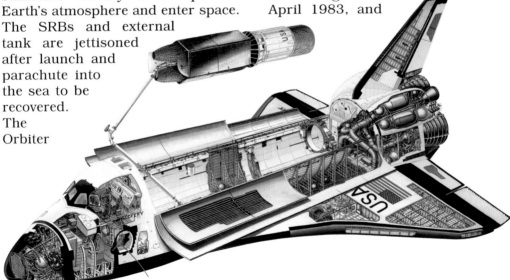

The Space Shuttle is an excellent achievement, but sadly the whole program has suffered two fatal and very highly-publicised crashes.

An amazing sight, as the Space Shuttle 'Enterprise' takes a ride on the back of NASA's specially-converted Boeing 747 (Photo: Rockwell International).

'Discovery' joined the launch program on 30 August 1984, while 'Atlantis' was the last of the five original Orbiters ordered. They were later joined by a sixth example, 'Endeavour.' Disaster struck the program on 28 January 1986 during the 25th launch when 'Challenger' exploded, killing all on board. The Orbiters were grounded for some 33 months while NASA conduced a safety review that resulted in improvements being made to the SRBs, the cause of the disaster. Returned to flight status, the four surviving Orbiters continued to fly until 'Columbia' broke-up over the United States during re-entry on 1 February 2003, killing all seven on board. It was the 113th Shuttle mission and 'Columbia's 28th flight. Again the fleet was grounded, and remained so in early 2005.

Specifications – Rockwell STS Space Shuttle Orbiter

Wingspan	78 ft 0.7 in
Length	122 ft 2 in minus external tank
Orbital speed	17,321 mph
Maximum take-off weight	4,500,000 lb including the fully loaded main tank and two solid rocket boosters
Service ceiling	590 miles
Engine	Three Rocketdyne main propulsion engines, of 375,000 lb st each, and two Thiokol solid-propellant rocket boosters (jettisoned after launch) of 2,900,000 lb st each. In orbit, two Aerojet orbit manoeuvring engines, 38 reaction control engines and six Marquardt-built Vernier thrusters are used, all using liquid bi-propellant rocket motors
Crew	Two pilots, plus mission specialists

Boeing (McDonnell Douglas/Hughes) AH-64 Apache

While the Bell AH-1G HueyCobra had been ordered into production as the U.S. Army's interim helicopter gunship, it was only expected to remain in service until the Lockheed AH-56A Cheyenne could replace it. However, the cancellation of the complex Cheyenne in August 1972 opened the way for a new Advanced Attack Helicopter (AHA) competition for a less sophisticated and less costly aircraft that was still able to undertake day and night anti-armour missions. Bell produced two YAH-63As and Hughes two YAH-64As for the AHA requirement. Both were powered by twin T700 turboshaft engines, could carry up to 16 TOW or Hellfire anti-tank guided missiles and had a 30 mm cannon mounted under the nose. The YAH-64A first flew on 30 September 1975. Following a competitive fly-off, the YAH-64A was announced as the winner. While the prototypes had a 'T' tail, the three pre-production aircraft that followed adopted the production-standard low tailplane. They also had a nose-mounted Target Acquisition and Designation Sight/Pilot's

Night-Vision Sensor (TADS/PNVS) in a gimballed turret. Development of the AH-64A Apache was complicated, and it was not until eight years to the day after the first flight that the first example for the U.S. Army was rolled out. The first unit to convert to the Apache was the 7th Battalion, 17th Cavalry Brigade at Fort Hood in April 1986. The last of 821 AH-64As (excluding prototypes) for the U.S. Army was delivered in April 1996. The first combat use of the Apache was in Panama in December 1989. Apaches opened Operation 'Desert Storm' in 1991 by destroying key radar sites in Iraq to allow aircraft to penetrate Iraqi airspace unseen. Plans to upgrade the Apache fleet as AH-64Bs were replaced by a more comprehensive program to produce AH-64Cs and AH-64D Longbow Apaches, the latter adding T700-GE-701C engines and Longbow millimetre-wave detection

The Boeing (McDonnell Douglas) AH-64 Apache is a very important anti-tank helicopter type, that has already seen much combat service.

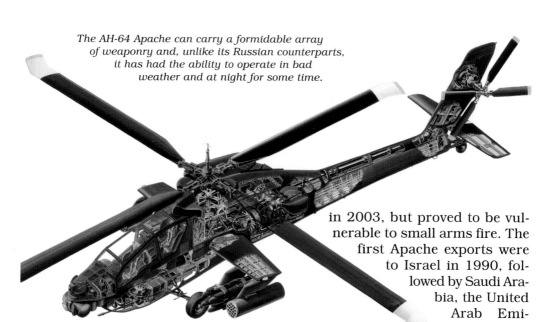

The AH-64 Apache can carry a formidable array of weaponry and, unlike its Russian counterparts, it has had the ability to operate in bad weather and at night for some time.

radar to the C-model's improved avionics. Ultimately all surviving Apaches were intended to receive the new powerplant, and the AH-64C designation was duly abandoned in 1993. The first AH-64D Longbow Apache flew on 15 April 1992 and over 500 AH-64As had been converted to the new standard by early 2005. AH-64Ds flew combat missions in Afghanistan in 2001 and Iraq in 2003, but proved to be vulnerable to small arms fire. The first Apache exports were to Israel in 1990, followed by Saudi Arabia, the United Arab Emirates, Egypt, Greece and the Netherlands. Britain's Army Air Corps ordered the Westland WAH-64 Apache AH.Mk.1, 67 of which were subsequently delivered – with assembly being accomplished by GKN Westland (now AgustaWestland) in Britain. Japan and Singapore have also ordered the helicopter.

Specifications – McDonnell Douglas AH-64A Apache

Main Rotor Diameter	48 ft
Fuselage Length	49 ft 1.5 in
Maximum speed	182 mph at 5,000 ft
Maximum take-off weight	21,000 lb
Range	300 miles on internal fuel
Service ceiling	21,000 ft
Armament	One trainable 1.18 in (30 mm) cannon beneath the forward fuselage, up to 16 AGM-114 Hellfire long-range anti-tank guided missiles on the stub wings, or 19-round 2.75 in (70 mm) Hydra 70 rocket pods, and AIM-9 Sidewinder, AIM-92 Stinger or Mistral air-to-air guided missiles
Engine	Two General Electric T700-GE-701 turboshaft engines, of 1,695 shp (de-rated) each
Crew	Two

Lockheed F-117 Nighthawk

Attempts to reduce the radar cross section of combat aircraft started with the Lockheed U-2 in the early 1960s, the Lockheed A-12/SR-71 aircraft subsequently using radar absorbent material in their construction. Continued studies into low observable technologies resulted in the Experimental Survivable Test-bed (XST) program, contracts being issued to Lockheed and Northrop under the code name 'Have Blue.' Lockheed's fabled 'Skunk Works' got to work on the design of a suitable aircraft using all this new technology and knowledge. Mathematical equations were developed to predict the radar returns from surfaces, allowing an aircraft with a very small radar cross section to be constructed. However, the resulting designs were aerodynamically unstable, needing a fly-by-wire control system to allow the pilot to fly the aircraft. Eventually the Lockheed design was selected to be built, and first of two 'Have Blue' aircraft flew on 1 December 1977. 'Have Blue' was a special

design with a 72.5° swept wing and two fins cantered inwards to cover the exhaust ports. Although both 'Have Blues' suffered crashes, they did demonstrate an extremely low radar cross section. A production version of the 'Have Blue' for precision attack was ordered under the 'Senior Trend' code name, the first flight of the new design being on 18 June 1981 under the strict conditions of secrecy that surrounded the whole stealth program. Designated F-117A and later named the Nighthawk, the aircraft differed from the test-beds by having a wing sweep of 67.5°, outward canted fins and two weapons bays. Total production amounted to 60 aircraft (of which one was lost before delivery and never assigned a serial) plus five development aircraft. Service use from the Tonopah Test Range airfield, Nevada, started in 1982 and the aircraft was eventually revealed to the public in November 1988 as the world's first operational 'stealth' aircraft. The F-117A was first used in action over

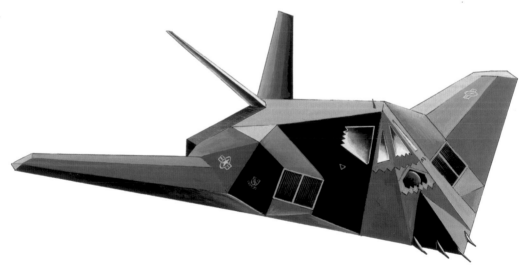

The Lockheed F-117A Nighthawk is a remarkable aircraft, and has been combat-proven. Its shape is like nothing else in the skies today.

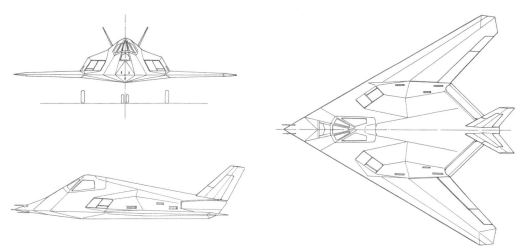

Three views showing the distinctive shape of the Lockheed F-117A Nighthawk.

Panama on 19/20 December 1989, but it was in Operation 'Desert Storm' in 1991 over Iraq that the aircraft justified its existence. Entering the most heavily defended airspace in the world, the F-117A's first attacks took out command and control bunkers in Baghdad. During the war they emerged without a scratch from many combat sorties. From May 1992 the F-117As moved to Holloman Air Force Base, New Mexico, and the fleet was put through an Offensive Capability Improvement Program. Combat operations over Kosovo were spoilt by the first combat loss, in the early morning of 28 March 1999, but further combat sorties were flown safely over Iraq again in 2003. While the possibility of further production was raised several times, the U.S. Air Force declined to purchase any more F-117As in order to protect other procurement programs. Two naval variants – the F-117N and A/F-117X – were briefly promoted but rejected by the U.S. Navy.

Specifications – Lockheed F-117A Nighthawk

Wingspan	43 ft 4 in
Length	65 ft 11 in
Maximum speed	646 mph at 10,000 ft
Maximum take-off weight	52,500 lb
Range	690 miles with 5,000 lb bomb load
Service ceiling	not revealed
Armament	Up to 5,000 lb of weapons carried internally, usually laser-guided bombs
Engine	Two General Electric F404-GE-F1D2 turbofan engines, of some 10,800 lb st each
Crew	One

Saab JAS 39 Gripen

Sweden has successfully maintained a neutral stance for many years, its geographic position in Scandinavia giving it the opportunity to remain neutral between the Soviet Bloc and the West during the Cold War. As explained on pages 230 to 231, part of Sweden's success in remaining neutral has been the possession of a strong military establishment, created with the help of indigenous manufacture of some major weapons systems. The Saab 37 Viggen was a highly-successful combat aircraft during its years of Swedish air force service, but in 1980 Sweden began the search for an eventual successor. Under the defence system designation JAS 39, a new, fourth-generation multi-role fighter was developed. This has now matured as the Saab JAS 39 Gripen (Griffin). Design work on this advanced aircraft was a comparatively long process, particularly in perfecting the type's complicated avionics and fly-by-wire control system. Five prototypes were ordered, the first of these flying on 9 December 1988. The complexities of designing and bringing to production such a complicated aircraft are shown by the fact that the first production aircraft did not fly until September 1992, and two early examples were lost in crashes. Finally the Gripen became

operational with the Swedish air force in the autumn of 1997. The single-seat front-line Gripen is the JAS 39A, and there is also a two-seat combat-capable JAS 39B trainer. Production plans have been subject to various defence cuts and re-assessed defence priorities, especially due to the end of the Cold War, but 204 Gripens are at present planned for Swedish procurement. Later production aircraft are of the more advanced single-seat JAS 39C and two-seat JAS 39D standard. These include in-flight refuelling capability as standard, improved cockpit displays and upgraded on-board avionics and computer capabilities. Saab teamed with British Aerospace (now BAE Systems) of Britain in the mid-1990s to market the Gripen for export, and in 1998 this teaming was successful when South Africa signed for an eventual 28 Gripens as a part of a huge defence order. In early 2003 Hungary signed a ten-year lease deal for 14 'second-hand' Gripens (including two two-seaters), with the intention for these to be fully in service in 2007. A very long-running procurement process for a new-generation fighter for the Czech Republic at last resulted in the definite selection of the Gripen in 2004 for lease, comprising

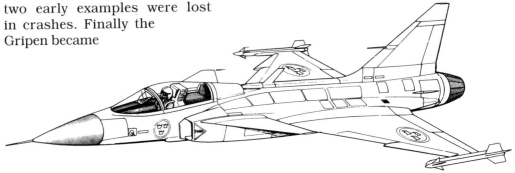

This drawing depicts the general Saab Gripen layout as revealed during the late 1980s.

Two detail photographs showing the front undercarriage and rear fuselage of a Swedish air force JAS 39 Gripen (Photos: John Batchelor).

twelve single-seaters and two two-seaters. The first example flew in 2004, with initial deliveries planned for 2005. The Hungarian and Czech Gripens will be of the JAS 39C and JAS 39D advanced variants.

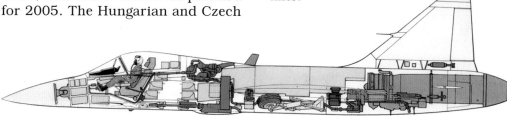

A sectional drawing showing some of the important components within a Saab JAS 39A Gripen's fuselage, including very obviously the powerful turbofan engine in the rear fuselage.

Specifications – Saab JAS 39A Gripen

Wingspan	27 ft 6.75 in
Length	46 ft 3 in
Maximum speed	Mach 1.8 at 36,090 ft
Maximum take-off weight	27,557 lb
Radius of action	approximately 497 miles
Service ceiling	65,617 ft
Armament	One 1.06 in (27 mm) cannon in lower front fuselage, two AIM-9L (Rb74) air-to-air guided missiles on wing-tip rails, up to 14,330 lb of air-to-air and air-to-surface guidedmissiles and bombs
Engine	One General Electric/Volvo Flygmotor RM12 (F404-GE-400) turbofan engine, of 18,100 lb st with afterburning
Crew	One

Northrop Grumman B-2 Spirit

The Northrop (Northrop Grumman from 1994) B-2 Spirit is unique as an operational flying wing 'stealth' bomber. It is the culmination of Northrop's work on flying wings – see pages 98 to 99. It is also the world's most expensive combat aircraft, each reputed to cost more than its weight in gold. The possibility of a bomber that could evade radar detection and thus be able to penetrate Soviet airspace successfully was one of the prizes that the development of low-observable technologies ('stealth') research in the late 1970s offered. Advances in computing power allowed the complex calculations needed to produce a second-generation stealthy compound curved shape (as opposed to the angular shape used on the Lockheed F-117 Nighthawk – see pages 292 to 293) to be produced. Starting as a secret program known as the Advanced Technology Bomber (ATB), Lockheed and Northrop worked on preliminary designs for the new aircraft after pro-

gram go-ahead was given in 1979 by the government of President Carter. Lockheed's 'Senior Peg' design was beaten by Northrop's 'Senior Ice,' and the ATB contract went to the latter company in October 1981 – gaining the code name 'Senior CJ.' At that time 132 ATBs were required to renew the U.S. Air Force's bomber fleet alongside 100 Rockwell B-1Bs. The ATB was to have been used after a Soviet first strike to destroy mobile Soviet intercontinental ballistic missile launchers. For this role a high degree of autonomy and protection against radiation were required. Effective all-aspect stealth was needed too for this role and Northrop's flying wing configuration potentially provided this. The first example was rolled out at Palmdale, California, in November 1988. It first flew on 17 July 1989. By then the cost of the program had escalated while the number to be built had plummeted, first to 75 and finally to 21 when the end of the Cold War eliminated the need for the B-2's primary role. The B-2A aircraft (as the ATB was designated) were delivered in three different standards, Block 10, 20 and 30. Block 10 was

The Northrop Grumman B-2A Spirit 'stealth bomber' is now well-established in service. Although this brightly-painted example looks pretty, in reality in-service B-2s have a drab grey color scheme.

The B-2 Spirit has one of the most unusual shapes of any warplane. Not only is it a flying wing, it also has specially blended curves and a radical zig-zag wing trailing edge due to its 'stealthy' design.

the basic aircraft with limited capability. Block 20 introduced precision weapons, and Block 30 increased the selection of weapons available, introduced improved radar absorbing materials and allowed safe operations down to 200 ft (61 m). All aircraft delivered in earlier configurations were destined to be upgraded to Block 30 standard. B-2As were delivered to the 509th Bomb Wing from December 1993, being integrated into the Single Integrated Operation Plan (the Pentagon's nuclear war fighting strategy) on 1 January 1997. Much effort since has been expended to give the B-2A a conventional strike role, and the results of this effort were first used during attacks on targets in the former Yugoslavia in March 1999. Since then B-2s have flown missions over Afghanistan and Iraq.

Specifications – Northrop Grumman B-2A Spirit

Wingspan	172 ft
Length	69 ft
Maximum speed	over 470 mph at 36,000 ft
Maximum take-off weight	375,000 lb
Range	7,250 miles
Service ceiling	50,000 ft plus
Armament	Up to some 40,000 lb of conventional unguided, or GPS satellite system guided weapons, or nuclear weapons
Engine	Four General Electric F118-GE-110 turbofan engines, of 19,000 lb st each
Crew	Two

EH Industries EH 101

An important current multi-role medium-lift military helicopter is the EH Industries EH 101. This helicopter is an international collaboration between Agusta of Italy and Westland Helicopters (GKN Westland) of Britain, and has been produced for both of these countries in addition to several export customers. Both the Agusta and Westland companies have a long history of designing and manufacturing helicopters, Westland having produced several important helicopter types such as the Sea King (see pages 186 to 187). In the late 1970s Britain began the process to find a replacement for the successful Westland Sea King helicopter then in service. At the same time the Italians were formulating a similar requirement, and in 1980 these two processes were brought together to create a common helicopter design. Westland and Agusta formed a new company named EH Industries to create the new helicopter, and a very long development phase was started. The initial prototype EH 101 first flew on 9 October 1987, and nine development/pre-production development EH 101 were built. The decision was made by EH Industries to develop the EH 101 into several distinct versions, using a common EH 101 airframe. These versions include two main military layouts, the naval (ship-based) derivative (so far the most successful EH 101 version), a land-based military model, and a civil transport airliner-type layout named the Heliliner. It was hoped that the civil transport model would be purchased by companies flying men and supplies to oil and gas rigs in the North Sea, but so far only one civil EH 101 has been sold – to the Tokyo Police in Japan. The naval air arms of Britain and Italy have purchased the naval derivatives of the EH 101, the first production example for Britain's Royal Navy flying in December 1995. The type entered service as the Merlin HM.Mk.1 in 2000/2001, and 44 have been supplied for anti-submarine war-

The EH Industries EH 101 has been successfully marketed in its naval derivatives. This example is a Merlin HM.Mk.1 of Britain's Fleet Air Arm, fitted with radar in the lower forward fuselage, and capable of carrying torpedoes and depth charges for anti-submarine work.

A development/trials EH 101 is seen here in flight above the factory of Westland Helicopters (now AgustaWestland) in Yeovil, Somerset, in southern England. In this famous aviation site during World War Two, the Westland Lysander army co-operation and agent-dropping aircraft was built (Photo: AgustaWestland).

fare (ASW), based principally aboard Royal Navy frigates. The Italian naval air arm contracted for 20 examples. Britain's R.A.F. operates the Merlin HC.Mk.3, 22 having been purchased. They can carry troops, or underslung cargo beneath the fuselage, and each has a rear-loading ramp. Although usually unarmed, they can be armed if necessary with flexible-mounted weapons. Important export orders have been achieved from Canada (as the CH-149 Cormorant, for Search and Rescue [SAR] duties), Portugal, and Denmark. Total EH 101 orders in 2004 stood at 128.

Specifications – EH Industries Merlin HC.Mk.3

Main Rotor Diameter	61 ft
Fuselage Length	64 ft 1 in
Maximum speed	173 mph at sea level
Maximum take-off weight	32,188 lb
Range	702 miles plus
Service ceiling	15,000 ft
Armament	normally unarmed, but provision for flexible-mounted machine guns in doorways and rear-loading ramp area, or a chin-mounted machine gun
Engine	Three Rolls-Royce/Turboméca RTM 322-02/8 turboshaft engines, of 2,240 shp each
Crew	Three or four crew, 24 seated troops (more if standing)

Boeing (McDonnell Douglas) C-17 Globemaster III

In the early-1970s the U.S. Air Force evaluated two prototypes each of the Boeing YC-14A and McDonnell Douglas YC-15A as contenders for the Advanced Medium STOL Transport (AMST) program, seeking a future replacement for the famous Lockheed C-130 Hercules. Although not ordered, the U.S. Air Force retained its interest in a possible future jet 'widebody' transport able to carry main battle tanks to rough airfields near the front-lines. A C-X requirement for such an aircraft was therefore eventually raised. McDonnell Douglas won the C-X in August 1981, but a shortage of funds resulted in a slow development for the new aircraft which was designated C-17. While resembling the YC-15A, the C-17 was a new design with a two-man cockpit, wingtip fins, F117 turbofan engines developed from the civil PW2040, and the

traditional rear-loading ramp all combined with a widebody fuselage able to carry all but the largest piece of Army equipment. While the AMST was seen as a Hercules replacement the C-17 – named Globemaster III after the Douglas C-74 and C-124 transports of the past – was envisaged as a replacement for the Lockheed C-141 Starlifter jet-powered transport. The first C-17A (acting as a prototype) made its maiden flight on 15 September 1991. It was followed by the first production example in May 1992. Deliveries commenced in June 1993, with the 17th Airlift Squadron at Charleston AFB, South Carolina, becoming the first service unit. Production of 40 aircraft was ordered, but this figure was raised by a further 80 examples. While the U.S. Air Force was pleased with its new airlifter, the cost of the aircraft forced several air-

The Boeing C-17 Globemaster III is a formidable heavy-lift transport, able to fly from comparatively short runways and carry a large payload. It is shown here making a low-level parachute-retarded drop of an armoured vehicle fitted onto a pallet.

The Boeing C-17A Globemaster III will be an important transport aircraft for the U.S. Air Force (Painting by John Batchelor, reproduced by courtesy of The Boeing Company).

lift studies to be undertaken before the military was allowed to proceed with buying extra examples. Overseas interest in the C-17 was generated by the aircraft's unique abilities, and resulted in four aircraft being leased for an initial seven years by Britain's Royal Air Force to fulfil its Short Term Strategic Airlift requirement. No.99 Squadron re-formed at R.A.F. Brize Norton, Oxfordshire, in May 2001 to fly the aircraft. The R.A.F. expects to purchase them at the end of the lease. In 2002 the U.S. Air Force raised its order to 180. It has so far employed its fleet of C-17s to support combat operations in Yugoslavia and Afghanistan and, in 2003, Iraq. McDonnell Douglas promoted a civil freighter version of the aircraft, known as the MD-17, but failed to sell any. After the company was taken over by Boeing a second (also unsuccessful) attempt was made to sell civil C-17s (as BC-17Xs) to cargo airlines, but with a clause inserted into any contract to allow the aircraft to be used on Air Force missions during times of need.

Specifications – Boeing (McDonnell Douglas) C-17A Globemaster III

Wingspan	169 ft 10 in including winglets
Length	174 ft
Cruising speed	403 mph at 5,000 ft
Maximum take-off weight	580,000 lb
Range	5,412 miles ferry range unloaded
Service ceiling	45,000 ft
Engine	Four Pratt & Whitney F117-PW-100 turbofan engines, of 40,700 lb st each
Crew	Three crew, up to 75 troops or 102 paratroops

Dassault Rafale

One of the most important combat aircraft of the early years of the 21st Century, France's Dassault Rafale has both land-based and aircraft carrier-based roles for the French air force (Armée de l'Air) and French naval air arm (Aéronavale) respectively. The Rafale is the latest military front-line product of France's aircraft industry, which can boast so many excellent combat aircraft from previous decades. Indeed, the Rafale is unusual amongst current production fighters in being a purely national project – many other countries nowadays preferring to collaborate and share the huge costs of modern combat aircraft design and manufacture. Nevertheless, the Rafale also demonstrates the often extremely long period that can be involved in this process. Designed as a successor to several front-line French aircraft types, the Rafale began life as the Rafale A demonstrator in the 1980s.

This single aircraft first flew on 4 July 1986. Originally powered by the American General Electric F404 turbofan engine type, it was later re-engined with French SNECMA M88 turbofans which also power the current production Rafales. Attempts were made to attract international participation in the late 1980s and early 1990s, but when no overseas partners were found France went it alone with the program. A production launch for the Rafale was announced in 1992, and there were at first ambitious plans for large numbers of Rafales to be built. However, the cost of developing and series manufacturing the Rafale proved to be very high, and in late 1995 the whole program was suspended. Fortunately this decision was reversed shortly after, following alterations to the Rafale's planned equipment and costing, and by the early years of the 21st Century the program was progressing very well. The Rafale has now been developed into one of the most sophisticated current warplanes. It has an advanced Thales RBE2 multi-mode look-down/shoot-down radar able to track up to eight airborne targets at the same time together with other state-of-the-art avionics to allow air-to-

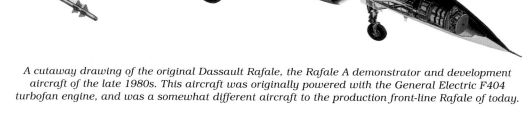

A cutaway drawing of the original Dassault Rafale, the Rafale A demonstrator and development aircraft of the late 1980s. This aircraft was originally powered with the General Electric F404 turbofan engine, and was a somewhat different aircraft to the production front-line Rafale of today.

The Dassault Rafale is currently entering service with the French armed forces. This example is the first production Rafale M for the French naval air arm the Aéronavale (Photo: Dassault Aviation).

ground as well as fighter combat, and an advanced flying helmet ('bone dome') for the pilot with helmet sight and displays. In addition to the basic single-seat Rafale C for the French air force, there is a single-seat Rafale M version for the French navy (35 planned) with a strengthened undercarriage and other modifications to allow for operations from aircraft carriers. There will also be combat-capable two-seat derivatives for the French air force (Rafale B, the first production example of which was delivered in 2004), and for the French navy (Rafale N, 25 planned). The first production single-seat Rafale M for the French navy was delivered to this customer in 2000, and the first operational French naval unit (Flotille 12F) gained its initial operational status in 2002. The first operational French air force unit was intended to be combat-capable in approximately 2006, and the total French requirement is currently for 294 Rafales. There are also planned export derivatives, but so far no foreign customers have been announced.

Specifications – Dassault Rafale C

Wingspan	35 ft 5.25 in (including wing-tip missiles)
Length	50 ft 1.25 in
Maximum speed	Mach 1.8 at 36,090 ft
Maximum take-off weight	49,604 lb
Radius of action	655 miles armed penetration attack
Service ceiling	55,003 ft
Armament	One 1.18 in (30 mm) cannon in right-hand air intake, normal weapons load of 13,228 lb on up to 14 external stores attachments (pylons) for air-to-air, air-to ground and anti-ship guided missiles
Engine	Two SNECMA M88-2 turbofan engines, of 10,950 lb st each (16,400 lb st each with afterburning)
Crew	One

Lockheed Martin/Boeing F/A-22 Raptor

During the high-spending years of President Reagan's government, the U.S. Air Force outlined a requirement for an Advanced Tactical Fighter (ATF) to replace the McDonnell Douglas F-15 Eagle. When the ATF directors were briefed about low observable ('stealth') technology they realised that it could provide a fighter with many advantages, allowing a 'first look, first launch, first kill' capability. The ability to supercruise (cruise supersonically without having to resort to afterburners) with a useful un-refuelled range, to be easier to maintain than the Eagle, and to outfight the latest generation of Soviet fighters, were all factors that were mandated to two teams to produce demonstrators. They were allowed to determine how 'stealthy' to make their aircraft. Two prototypes each were constructed of the Lockheed/Boeing/General Dynamics YF-22A and the Northrop Grumman/McDonnell Douglas YF-23A for a demonstration/validation (dem/val) competition, the winner being selected to develop the U.S. Air Force's next fighter. One of each com-petitor's dem/val aircraft was powered by Pratt & Whitney YF119-PW-100s, the other by General Electric YF120-GE-100s. On 29 September 1990 was the first flight of the YF120-powered YF-22A, the YF119-powered aircraft flying four days later. While both teams fulfilled the test criteria, the Lockheed-led team went beyond the test program (including firing missiles) and was also judged able to better handle a production program. In April 1991 the YF-22A airframe and the F119-PW-100 powerplant was selected as the winner. Lockheed's team was awarded a contract for 9 F-22A (and two later cancelled F-22B two-seat) engineering and manufacturing development (EMD) aircraft. In March 1994 Lockheed acquired General Dynamics, increasing its share in the F-22 project to 67.5%, Boeing having the other 32.5%. The first EMD F-22A Raptor flew on 7 September 1997. Development of the aircraft was slowed by software development problems, the slow delivery of EMD aircraft, spiralling costs and funding difficulties. The number of F-22s to be acquired has steadily fallen over the years, from 750, to 648, to 442, to around 331, to possibly as few as 180, although the U.S. Air Force says it needs 380. In order to protect the program the Air Force decided to do

This unique cutaway illustration of the F/A-22 Raptor was drawn by Artist John Batchelor with the full co-operation of the manufacturer, fully respecting the type's highly secret nature.

The official roll-out of the original YF-22 was accomplished with considerable ceremony. The type is set to become a highly important warplane in the future, despite budgetary cutbacks to the whole F/A-22 program (Photo: Lockheed Martin).

a 'u-turn' and emphasise the F-22's suit-ability as an attack plat-form, resulting in the designation F/A-22 being adopted. By early 2005 27 F/A-22As have been delivered to the Air Warfare center at Nellis Air Force Base, Nevada, to an initial training unit, to the first operational unit at Langley AFB, Virginia (the 1st Fighter Wing), and to the relevant test organ-isation at Edwards AFB, California.

Specifications – Lockheed Martin F/A-22A Raptor
(some data provisional and Classified)

Wingspan	44 ft 6 in
Length	62 ft 1 in
Maximum speed	1,189 mph estimated at 30,000 ft
Maximum take-off weight	55,000 lb
Range	1,997 miles estimated
Service ceiling	50,000 ft plus
Armament	One 0.787 in (20 mm) six-barrel rotary cannon, fuselage bays for various air-to-air guided missiles or GPS satellite system guided weapons, plus optional wing pylons for up to 5,000 lb of weapons or fuel tanks.
Engine	Two Pratt & Whitney F119-PW-100 turbofan engines, of 35,000 lb each with afterburning
Crew	One

Eurofighter Typhoon

Building on the success of the Panavia Tornado project (see pages 254 to 255), the Eurofighter consortium was created by Britain, Germany and Italy in June 1986 to produce a new agile fighter aircraft, the European Fighter Aircraft (EFA). Spain also soon joined the consortium. France had earlier participated in studies before backing Dassault to go it alone with the Rafale described on pages 302 to 303. Much groundwork on the new fighter was undertaken using the British Aerospace Experimental Aircraft program demonstrator aircraft. This aircraft was a canard test-bed, and it flew between May 1986 and May 1991. However, EFA itself was soon mired in political and budgetary problems, and the end of the Cold War reduced the aircraft on the list of governmental priorities. In order to stop Germany pulling out of the program the EF 2000 was proposed as a cheaper EFA. Procurement was reduced from 765 aircraft to less than 600, expected deliveries comprising of 232 for Britain, 180 for Germany, 121 for Italy and 87 for Spain. Each nation was

intended to assemble its own aircraft on its own production line. The number of prototypes was cut from eight to seven, the first flying on 27 March 1994 from Manching, Germany. Two prototypes were built in Britain (including one two-seater), Germany and Italy, while the seventh (a two-seater) was constructed in Spain. The first of five instrumented production aircraft flew on 5 April 2002, followed by a second example three days later. In February 2002 the first production aircraft – a two-seater for the Luftwaffe – made its maiden flight. The name Typhoon was adopted in July 2002, R.A.F. two-seaters becoming Typhoon T.Mk.1s and its single-seaters F.Mk.2s. Under a unique arrangement for the R.A.F., the first aircraft were delivered to an operational evaluation unit (OEU) based at Warton, Lancashire, where BAE Systems assembles the aircraft. The OEU was later assigned the unit identity of No.17 Squadron. Operational R.A.F. Typhoons will be based at the airfields of Coningsby, Leeming and Leuchars. In Spain the first unit is 111 Escuadron

One of the main customers for the Eurofighter Typhoon is Britain's Royal Air Force. British-operated Typhoons are unlikely to look like this rather fanciful camouflaged representation, instead wearing a neat overall scheme of grey paint.

This two-seat Eurofighter is one of the British prototype/development aircraft, photographed during a test sortie (Photo: BAE Systems).

of Ala 11 based at Moron, while Jagdgeschwader 73 at Laage became the first German unit and the 4° Stormo was the first Italian unit. The Eurofighter organisation announced in 2000 the first export customer for the Eurofighter. This was Greece, but the country failed to sign for the 60 aircraft it wanted, instead using the money to pay for the 2004 Olympic Games. Austria signed for 18 (reduced from 24) Typhoons in the summer of 2003, and expects to become the first export operator in mid-2007.

Specifications – Eurofighter Typhoon (single-seat)

Wingspan	35 ft 11 in including wing-tip pods
Length	52 ft 4.25 in
Maximum speed	1,321 mph clean at 36,090 ft
Maximum take-off weight	51,808 lb
Radius of action	864 miles air defence mission
Service ceiling	55,000 ft plus
Armament	One 1.06 in (27 mm) cannon, up to 14,300 lb of weapons on 13 pylons, five (four of which are semi-recessed for air-to-air missiles) under the fuselage and four under each wing
Engine	Two Eurojet EJ200 turbofan engines, of 13,500 lb st each (20,000 lb st each with afterburning)
Crew	One

Sukhoi S-37/Su-47 Berkut

Jet-powered combat aircraft design has come a long way since the late 1940s and early 1950s. The advent of very powerful engines, fly-by-wire control systems that allow even unstable design layouts to fly safely, and the increasing use of composite materials rather than metal, all make today's front-line military aircraft very different to early post-World War Two jet aircraft. Just what future fighter aircraft will look like is an interesting point to contemplate, as aircraft designers look to produce new generations of combat aircraft in the future. In Russia, much thought has gone into the design of future fighter aircraft, either for a long-standing 'heavy fighter' requirement, or for a future light combat aircraft. The innovative and highly-successful Sukhoi organisation, which has already designed the excellent Su-27 family of combat aircraft (see pages 286 to 287), has recently incorporated several extreme design concepts into a concept aircraft called the S-37 Berkut. This impressive prototype is especially remarkable in having a forward-swept wing, in addition to an advanced fly-by-wire control system and very powerful engines. The aircraft's unusual wing layout

is a part of the type's overall advanced aerodynamic configuration which also includes all-moving forward canards, some blended shapes and curves to reduce radar cross-section, and radar-absorbing paint. The forward-swept wing has a number of advantages for future warplanes, including allowing greater manoeuvrability by its efficient use of airflow over its surfaces. Sukhoi designed this wing to be made from composite materials, which are better able to absorb the huge stresses that forward-swept wings would have to endure in a turning dog-fight. Design work on what became the S-37 began in around 1983, but the one and only S-37 experimental prototype did not fly until September 1997. Its name, Berkut, stands for Golden Eagle or Royal Eagle. It is a remarkable aircraft and has apparently been very successful in its flight testing so far. However, many aspects of this aircraft, even its true dimensions, remain secret. Its great rival in Russia has been the MiG 1.42/1.44 prototype/fighter demonstrator, and it is not thought likely that the S-37 will be the basis of a future fighter design. However, recently the S-37 (S = experimental) was re-designated Su-47, the latter being more in line with a produc-

The Sukhoi Su-47 Berkut is in a class of its own, its unconventional swept-forward wing layout and apparently excellent all-round performance perhaps being a pointer to how future combat aircraft might look.

Although there are two Su-47s drawn in this illustration, only one example of this radical aircraft has in fact been built, and there are no plans at present for the type to be put into full-scale production.

tion designation. There has also been speculation that some of the S-37's design layout might be incorporated in a planned Russian multi-role fighter program provisionally named the Sukhoi T-50 PAKFA, that was launched with Sukhoi as the main contractor in 2002.

Specifications – Sukhoi Su-47 Berkut (some data provisional)

Wingspan	54 ft 9.5 in
Length	74 ft (possibly slightly more)
Maximum speed	Mach 1.6 (possibly M 2.1) at 36,090 ft
Maximum take-off weight	74,956 lb
Range	2,050 miles
Service ceiling	59,055 ft
Engine	Two Aviadvigatel D-30F6M turbofan engines, of 20,930 lb st each (34,392 lb st each with afterburning)
Crew	One

Scaled Composites GlobalFlyer

Burt Rutan's Scaled Composites is a specialist manufacturer of unusual – usually one-off – aircraft. Based at Mojave, California, the company has built prototypes for military programs such as the Northrop Grumman X-47A Pegasus, the White Knight and SpaceShipOne prototypes of commercial Space launch systems and long-distance record breaking aircraft such as the Voyager, the first aircraft to fly unrefuelled around the globe in 1986. Arguably the last great record in aviation was to fly around the world in an aircraft solo, the Voyager flight having in fact been undertaken by a crew of two comprising of Dick Rutan and Jeana Yeager. Dick Rutan put the idea of a solo flight into the mind of adventurer Steve Fossett,

while Dick's brother Burt was working on an aircraft that could possibly achieve the flight. Fossett had already claimed records on land, sea and air, including the first flight around the world alone in a balloon in 2002. Sponsorship for the aircraft was provided by Sir Richard Branson's airline Virgin Atlantic. The GlobalFlyer is of unusual configuration, with a long sailplane-like wing with a center fuselage containing a flush cockpit with an FJ44 turbofan engine mounted above it. A turbofan was chosen to allow the aircraft to climb above bad weather, its operating height being around 45,000 ft (13,716 m). Two booms either side of the fuselage contain the undercarriage and fuel. When fully loaded the fuel consists of 83% of the

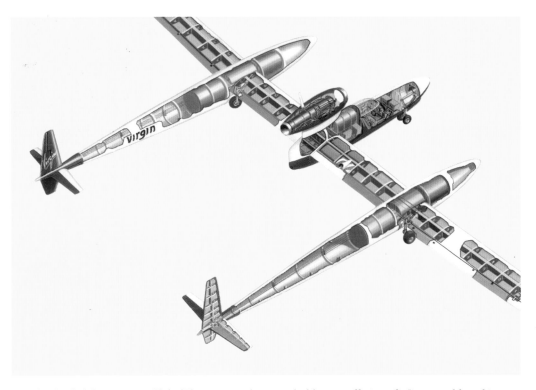

The Scaled Composites GlobalFlyer is a truly remarkable one-off aircraft. Its record-breaking round-the-world flight in March 2005 was one of aviation's great achievements.

total weight, the aircraft's empty weight being only 3,350 lb (1,520 kg). In order to decrease speed for landing it is equipped with small drogue parachutes that are released on descent. GlobalFlyer first flew on 5 March 2004 on a still day at Mojave. Because of the danger posed by rough weather, the start of the record flight was delayed many times, but on Tuesday 1 March 2005 Fossett took off from Salina Municipal Airport, Kansas. Fuel consumption was noted as being higher than expected, requiring more effective fuel management techniques to be adopted during the flight, but passing Hawaii on the Wednesday Fossett elected to continue. Tail winds helped push the aircraft along faster than expected and also conserved fuel. The landing took place back at Salina Municipal Airport on Thursday 3 March 2005. The flight had taken 67 hours, 2 minutes and 38 seconds. It also broke a distance record that had been established as far back as 1962 by a Boeing B-52 Stratofohrtress. During the flight Fossett had slept less than one hour. One of aviation's last great adventures had been successfully accomplished.

The GlobalFlyer over the Atlas Mountains
(Photo: Courtesy of Virgin Atlantic).

Specifications – Scaled Composites GlobalFlyer

Wingspan	114 ft
Length	44 ft 1 in
Maximum speed	285 mph at 45,000 ft
Maximum take-off weight	22,000 lb
Range	21,862 miles
Service ceiling	52,000 ft
Engine	One Williams FJ44-3 ATW turbofan engine, of some 3,000 lb st
Crew	One

Lockheed Martin F-35 Joint Strike Fighter

We look very much to the future of this new aircraft type. The Joint Strike Fighter program grew out of several U.S. projects started in the late 1980s to investigate new technologies for combat aircraft. These included the ASTOVL (Advanced Short Take-Off and Vertical Landing) and CALF (Common Affordable Lightweight Fighter), which later became part of JAST (Joint Advanced Strike Technology). JAST was started in the early 1990s, but quickly grew from initial technology demonstrations and studies to a family of similar combat aircraft to replace many existing U.S. Marine Corps, U.S. Navy, and U.S. Air Force combat aircraft. A request for proposals for JAST was issued in 1996. JAST was retitled the Joint Strike Fighter (JSF) program soon after. Boeing and Lockheed Martin were selected in November 1996, each being contracted to build two Concept Demonstration Aircraft (CDA). The aims were to demonstrate that the basic requirements of the three services could be met with a common airframe – a very demanding specification. Boeing was allocated the designation X-32 to produce the X-32A for conventional and aircraft carrier landing, and X-32B to demonstrate STOVL (Short Take-Off and Vertical Landing). Lockheed Martin used X-35A for its conventional take-off and landing demonstrator, X-35B as its STOVL demonstrator, and X-35C for its aircraft carrier version. The X-35A made its maiden flight on 24 October 2000, and the X-35C on 16 December 2000. After completing its test program the X-35A was transported to Palmdale, California, and converted as the X-35B for its STOVL trials at Naval Air Station Patuxent River, Maryland. The X-32A first flew on 18 September 2000, the X-32B flying in early 2001. By the time of the first flights the JSF program had gone international. It was quickly realised that the winner of the JSF program would be in a unique position as a supplier of combat aircraft not just for American but for export customers as well – JSF is therefore seen as the biggest fighter program ever. A method for countries to participate in the development program at different levels was provided, development money buying access to the program and a share in the production of components. The only top level participant is Britain, its interest having gone back to the ATOVL program when the search for a Hawker

The Lockheed Martin JSF is the world's most up-to-date and biggest combat aircraft program.

Siddeley Harrier/Sea Harrier replacement was first contemplated, but many other countries have joined at lower levels. Lockheed Martin, teamed with Northrop Grumman and BAE Systems was announced as the winner of the JSF competition in October 2001, and the X-35 will be developed into three operational F-35 variants related to the CDAs. JSF is worth around $200 billion to the winning team. Current requirements stand at around 3,000 examples for the U.S. and Britain, with the export market expected to account for between 2,000 to 3,000 more.

Specifications – Lockheed Martin X-35A Joint Strike Fighter

(some data provisional and Classified)

Wingspan	33 ft
Length	50 ft 9 in
Maximum speed	1,056 mph at 30,000 ft estimated
Maximum take-off weight	50,000 lb estimated
Range	1,100 miles estimated
Service ceiling	approximately 40,000 ft planned for test program
Armament	Internal 0.787 in (20 mm) cannon planned for U.S.A.F. production versions, and internal bays for up to 4,000 lb of ordnance plus an external load of up to 15,430 lb
Engine	One Pratt & Whitney JSF119-PW-611 (now F135) turbofan engine, of approximately 32,000 lb st
Crew	One

Index

Index

Index

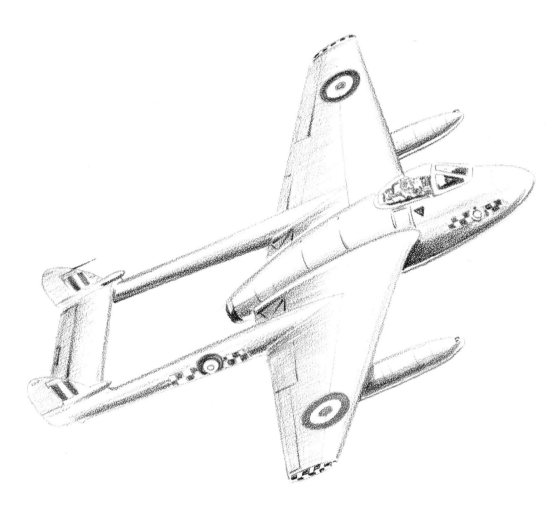